PRACTICING LEADERSHIP

Principles and Applications

PRACTICING LEADERSHIP

Principles and Applications

ARTHUR SHRIBERG
Xavier University

CAROL LLOYD
Lloyd & Associates

DAVID L. SHRIBERG
Northwestern University

MARY LYNN WILLIAMSON
Arkansas State University

JOHN WILEY & SONS, INC.
New York • Chichester • Brisbane
Toronto • Singapore • Weinheim

Acquisitions Editor	Ellen Ford
Marketing Manager	Karen Allman
Production Editor	Edward Winkleman
Designer	Laura Nicholls
Manufacturing Operations Director	Susan Stetzer
Illustration Coordinator	Anna Melhorn

Cover photo by Bill Binzen / The Stock Market

This book was set in 10/12 New Caledonia by University Graphics York and printed and bound by Courier/Westford. The cover was painted by Phoenix Color.

Library of Congress Cataloging-in-Publication Data
Practicing leadership : principles and applications / Arthur Shriberg . . . [et al.].
    p.   cm.
   Includes bibliographical references.
   ISBN 0-471-11374-3 (pbk. : alk. paper)
   1. Leadership.   I. Shriberg, Arthur.
HD57.7.P7   1997
658.4'092–dc20

96-36096
CIP

Printed in the United States of America

10 9 8 7 6 5 4 3 2 1

OUR METHODS FOR TEACHING LEADERSHIP

Our approach mirrors our belief about learning: As Baxter Magolda (1992) writes, learning is "constructing meaning collaboratively with others" (p.xviii). Just as we see no universally accepted theory of leadership, just as the information age has cast doubt on the image of leader as omnipotent hero, we do not pretend to have all the answers about leadership. Students of leadership are experts in their own right. Readers bring with them unique backgrounds, experiences, and perceptions that are important to the discussion of leadership. We see learning about leadership as melding the ideas and experiences of our readers with our ideas as authors of this text, as well as with the ideas of the scholars whose works we present. In this way, learning becomes a relational activity, a dialogue, or, in the words of Parker Palmer, a "communal act" (1987, p.5). We seek to engage readers in examining the material, their own perspectives, and those of current leaders to make sense of this phenomenon called leadership.

We have included several pedagogical features in the text that underscore our belief that knowledge is socially constructed. We use a journey as a metaphor for how we have come to understand leadership over the centuries. This journey through the paradigms of leadership is graphically depicted by a map at the beginning of each chapter that indicates, "You are here." We will give you frequent reminders of where you are on the journey, where common roadblocks can be found, and much commentary about the passing scene. Be prepared for delays in your journey, however; a large part of the trip is under construction.

Some other guidelines for the trip:

- We have attempted to integrate the implications of diversity and internationalism throughout the text rather than relegating it to a separate chapter. Isolating differences in today's world is an anachronistic way to study such an inclusive concept as leadership.

- Along with a variety of lenses with which to view the scenery, we don't hesitate to pose questions—questions without one clear answer. We want to engage you in the process.

- And speaking of process, the way in which we developed this text illustrates the notion of practicing leadership. The authors are a mix of managers, administrators, and professors from several disciplines and practitioners in a variety of settings.

- We use the technique of a parable, which weaves throughout the text, to demonstrate how fictional college students might experience growth in their understanding of leadership as we progress through each phase of the journey.

- The text does not necessarily have to be read sequentially. Different instructors may want to highlight different aspects, depending on the backgrounds of students and their own teaching strengths.

- You will learn about current leaders as we recount parts of their history. Their stories are intended to bring to life how one's closely held assumptions about leadership directly shape the behavior of leaders.

- We offer exercises and cases to strengthen the link between theory and practice. In the *Instructor's Manual,* additional ideas are offered for teaching and supporting each chapter. Each paradigm suggests certain skills, attitudes and approaches as important for effective leadership. Experiential activities help readers explore some of those skills and attitudes.

- Finally, in the closing chapter, we encourage readers to refine their own theories about leadership as well as their action plans for practicing leadership. Leaders and collaborators in the twenty-first century must be able to reflect on what they believe and why, make sense of situations from multiple perspectives, and form sound conclusions about what actions to take based on those interpretations.

A PREVIEW OF THE JOURNEY

The first chapter highlights the broad array of views about leadership and explains why this text is different from other leadership textbooks. In chapter 2, we consider today's popular "take" on leadership with a review of other books on leadership. Chapter 3 chronicles the most prominent stories of leadership that have been told in Western history, beginning with the ancient Greeks. Each of these stories has added to our collective image of leadership. Each has its own prescription for the skills, behaviors and attitudes needed to be an effective leader. Our objective is to engage you in examining these stories of leadership and in recognizing which of them have been the most influential in shaping your own assumptions about and practice of leadership.

The journey continues with stops at the various disciplines that have contributed significantly to the study of leadership: psychology and communication in chapter 4 and management, quality, political science, and military science in chapters 5 and 6. Chapter 7 considers the theories and models that have comprised leadership study up to this point. In chapter 8, a new model of leadership, the Hero's Journey, is depicted as a compelling way to view the necessary courage and commitment required by postindustrial leaders and collaborators as they work to bring about change. We visit the transitional approaches that will help advance the postindustrial views of leadership in chapter 9. Chapter 10 concludes this part of the journey with some thoughts on being a leadership theorist and practitioner throughout life.

ACKNOWLEDGMENTS

This text has evolved over several years due to the dedication of a number of people. Carol Lloyd has been involved in all aspects of the publication and has applied her considerable skills as a professional writer to giving the text continuity. She also created the parables that introduce most chapters. David Shriberg wrote the chapter summarizing the works of current well-known authors, contributed to several chapters, and developed most of the questions and critical incidents that follow each chapter. Mary Lynn Williamson's creative exercises and activities are found in most chapters. She and Judy Rogers also helped in the initial development of the conceptual plan for the text. Judy Rogers, Gordon Barnhart, Tim Kloppenborg, and Paul Colella are each experts in their fields and their chapters add special depth to the project.

I am grateful to John Pepper, the CEO of Procter & Gamble and the well-known leadership authorities Steven Covey, James Kouzes, and Barry Posner, for their original contributions to this text.

Researchers for this publication include Katia Zhostkova, Gwen Homan, and Svetlana Belousov. We appreciate the typing and technical support provided by Shirlee James, Cyrina Wolf, and Greta Davis. Valuable input was given by Sara Wagner, Brett Palmer, Jennifer Nill, and Sarah Leupen. It has been a great pleasure working with the staff at Wiley, especially Ellen Ford. I appreciate the permission given to us by many publications to use their charts and tables.

Invaluable advice was given by Dennis Slevin, University of Pittsburgh; Bill Bolton, Washington University; Richard Boyatsis, Case Western Reserve University; Paula Hill, Southern Methodist University; William Howe, University of Richmond; Dan Costly, New Mexico State University; Dayle Smith, University of San Francisco; Charles Sterrett, Frostburg State University; Joseph Koppel, University of San Francisco; Jeffrey Miles, University of Illinois at Urbana-Champaign; Michael Whitty, Santa Clara University; Bill Greenwood, Shepherd College. Carol and I received both practical and emotional support from our families—Margie, Michael, and Steven Shriberg, and Al, Chris, and Ben Lloyd. It has been a wonderful experience.

Art Shriberg

TABLE OF CONTENTS

CHAPTER 3   PRE-INDUSTRIAL PARADIGMS OF LEADERSHIP
E. Paul Colella

CHAPTER 4   THE DISCIPLINARY ROOTS OF LEADERSHIP: PART I
Arthur Shriberg, Carol Lloyd, David Shriberg

Practicing Leadership:
A New Approach

The Leadership Journey:
A map of the terrain
Chapter 1

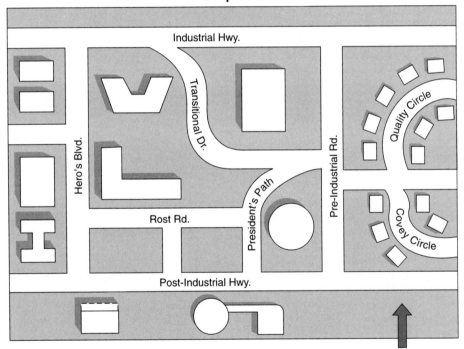

Industrial Hwy.

Transitional Dr.

Hero's Blvd.

Pre-Industrial Rd.

Quality Circle

President's Path

Rost Rd.

Covey Circle

Post-Industrial Hwy.

You are here

1

Terri, Mike, Ray, and Juanita hear their names read as one of the randomly selected groups assigned to a project in Leadership 101. Never having met before, they look uncertainly at each other as they move toward the rear of the classroom.

"I hate these project things," Juanita announces. "The professor only does this to avoid doing her own work."

"Yeah," laughs Ray. "I'm tired of it, too. Like, why can't they just teach us, you know? Not all this other stuff. Just tell me all the facts about leadership, and I'll write them down and memorize them. Then I'll write it all down again on the final. Isn't that the American way?"

"Works for me," Juanita says.

"Well, sometimes this way isn't so bad," Mike says hesitantly. "I mean, look, I kind of learned a lot in the last class we did projects in." The others look at him questioningly. "That's not so unusual, is it—learning something?"

"Depends," says Terri. "A lot depends."

The professor hands them a piece of paper with the following words: "Assignment: Develop a working definition of leadership. Then consider who among your group fits the definition. Why? Report back to the group."

Terri slams her purse to the floor. "That does it. I'm dropping this class. Who needs this show-and-tell routine? I didn't enter college so I could go back to preschool!"

"Wait, don't quit just yet," says Mike, blocking her path. "I mean, what's the big deal? So we talk about it and decide. This will be OK. C'mon."

"Yeah," says Juanita, looking at the assignment. "It's better than having to read some dumb old textbook about leadership. We can sort of make this stuff up."

"OK," says Terri in a challenging tone. "Tell me what a leader is and who here is one."

"Not me," Ray says quickly. "No way."

"I thought you were some big swimmer—captain of your high school team that won some big championship. I read about you in the Daily Rag*," Terri says.*

"Yeah, but I'm only a leader when I'm surrounded by water. That's not the same thing, is it?"

"Depends," Terri says, with a hint of a smile.

"I think a leader is someone who's elected to office," Juanita says. "In my high school, I was sent to the office a lot. Hey, I was in charge of all the money for our band, the Bizarros."

"So what about you?" Juanita says to Mike. "Are you a leader?"

"Of course I am."

"What's that supposed to mean?"

"Well, a leader is someone who gets others to do things. And I got this group to start the assignment, right? And we're all going to ace this class, right? Just because of little ol' me. Am I right?"

"Depends," the others say.

We hope you can relate to something about these students, because we'll listen in on their conversations throughout this "dumb old textbook." Even if their attitudes or expressions are different from yours, you might find some similarities in terms of the process of discovering what it means to practice leadership.

As we race toward the next millennium, everyone is talking, writing, theorizing about—and searching for—leadership. We have only to look at the abundance of literature, popular videos, seminars, and formal courses to see how captivated we are by the notion of leadership. Leadership development is now considered an increasingly important part of a college education, as evidenced by the burgeoning number of graduate and undergraduate leadership courses and the new centers and schools for leadership established at numerous colleges.

Actually, however, our fascination with leadership is nothing new. Long before the psychologists and management scientists of the twentieth century worked at defining and measuring leadership, Plato, Machiavelli, and Shakespeare offered images of leadership cast in the context of their times. And yet there is no common agreement on what leadership means. James McGregor Burns (1979) captured the elusiveness of the concept when he noted that "Leadership is one of the most observed and least understood phenomena on earth."

Whatever it is, we need it, desperately. We yearn for a great leader who, we imagine, can foresee what we must know and do to negotiate the constant change and ambiguity facing us in the next century. We bemoan the absence of great leaders who can give us rock-solid answers in these uncertain times.

Because it is generally agreed that leadership is vital for our survival as a society, we should hasten to prepare people to be leaders. It is in this context—the call for twenty-first-century leadership—that we set about writing this book.

WHY THIS BOOK?

Why add to the already towering pile of books on the subject? We offer a fusion of several different ways to examine leadership in a decidedly unconventional leadership text. Although we include some of the traditional perspectives on the subject, we have tried to build into the text a more comprehensive approach.

It's not simply a collection of theories—intricate diagrams, a review of research. Our review of research and theories, instead, has an eye toward the ones most useful to build a personal approach to practice leadership. Nor is it a skills approach. Don't look to this text as *The Five Minute Leader*. We will certainly incorporate information about the implications of many disciplines for practicing leadership, but it's not a how-to book.

Finally, it is not strictly a modeling approach. We haven't found the "perfect leader" we can all simply study and emulate. We don't think there is such a person. However, we have included "snapshots" of people practicing leadership in a variety of settings and cultural contexts.

What is this thing called leadership? If you look in the popular press, you might think leaders are:

quick-change artists
quarterbacks
referees
trapeze artists

servants

multiple personalities

brown-nosers

nose guards

visionaries

personal trainers

The whole is more than some of its parts, even more than the sum of its parts. Let's look at a few definitions of this seemingly all-encompassing notion. Each of the following contains kernels of truth about leadership, but certainly not the comprehensive picture:

> Leadership is all about getting people to work together to make things happen that might not otherwise occur or prevent things from happening that ordinarily would take place. (Rosenbach & Taylor, 1993)
>
> Leaders are people who perceive what is needed and what is right and know how to mobilize people and resources to accomplish mutual goals. (Cronin, 1993)
>
> To be a leader for the next century, you must be able to bring out the best in people. You must be able to motivate people. . . . You have to have humility. Humility says, "I don't have to act like a big shot, like I've got all the answers. I can ask you what your answers are, what your ideas are. And I can be open." Openness is really important.
>
> So leadership requires a wholeness, and the ability to contain two seemingly contradictory qualities simultaneously: "power" and "humility." (Patricia Aburdene, co-author of *Megatrends 2000* and *Megatrends for Women*)

Leaders are listeners. They know how, as Cronin puts it, "to squint with their ears. . . . If we are to have the leaders we need, we will first have to agree upon priorities. In one sense, if we wish to have leaders to follow, we will often have to show them the way."

According to Du Brin, leadership is the ability to inspire confidence and support among the people who are needed to achieve organizational goals (Du Brin, 1995). Du Brin reviewed five other representational definitions of leadership—after noting that as of 1995, approximately 30,000 research articles, periodical articles, and books had been written on the topic in this century. Those representative definitions include:

- Interpersonal influence directed through communication, toward goal attainment
- The influential increment over and above mechanical compliance with directions and orders
- An act that causes others to act or respond in a shared direction
- The art of influencing people by persuasion or example to follow a line of action
- The principal dynamic force that motivates and coordinates the organization in the accomplishment of its objectives

Most definitions include some aspect of influence, some consideration of the interaction between leader and others, and some notion of direction or goals.

DIFFERENT ASSUMPTIONS

We are convinced that we must begin thinking about leadership in new ways in the twenty-first century. The old prescriptions are not as useful as they used to be. Our approach is built on seven basic premises:

1. *Where we are in our understanding of leadership is a function of where we have been.*

   We must learn from our past attempts to understand leadership. Most texts trace leadership back only to the middle of the twentieth century, but this one returns to Plato and considers the evolution of leadership. Looking at historical approaches to leadership allows us to examine their holds on our perceptions, weigh their merits, and, if necessary, demystify them so we can advance our thinking about what leadership is and is not.

2. *There is no one formula for leadership.*

   This is so even though many bestsellers such as *The Leadership Challenge* by Kouzes and Posner and *Seven Habits of Highly Successful People* by Covey, among a plethora of others, suggest techniques that are helpful. Practicing leadership involves a multidimensional integration of theory, process, and practice.

   What is effective in one situation may not be useful in another. Leadership comes in many shapes and forms.

3. *Leadership is not differentiated by setting.*

   Currently, most leadership texts are written primarily for a specific market such as education, management, the military, and nursing. We assert that "Practicing Leadership" applies in all settings, so this multidisciplinary text speaks to the concept rather than to a particular setting. We draw from many disciplines in both our theoretical discussions and our examples. This book is not written only for those who aspire to organizational or political leadership, but for anyone who wishes to make a difference by exerting leadership for a valued cause.

4. *Our understanding of leadership requires the vantage point of multiple perspectives.*

   During this century, leadership came under intense scrutiny as a subject of study, largely because the Industrial Revolution led to large organizations and large organizations need people to run them. Researchers set about finding out just what kind of leadership was required to make these new enterprises effective.

   The body of research accumulated from this effort over the past ninety years has molded much of what we think about leadership. These perspectives, now labeled the industrial paradigm of leadership, are often presented as the "best way" to perceive and practice leadership.

   We propose, instead, that as valuable as it has been, the industrial paradigm is only one way of viewing leadership. It is definitely not the only way to do so.

Alternative perspectives, particularly several developed in the past twenty-five years, help us understand how to practice leadership for today's world. We will examine leadership through many perspectives or lenses, identifying as we go the various assumptions underlying each perspective.

While we discuss the past and attempt to explain where leadership is today, we also emphasize the future and suggest a paradigm that will be useful for readers as they develop their own working theories of leadership.

5. ***Studying leadership across a range of human differences is the only way to approach the subject in the twenty-first century.***

The study of human differences—those of race, gender, age, ethnicity, religion, and lifestyle, among other factors—affects nearly every discussion about leadership. Adding a chapter on "diversity considerations" at the end of the book would be too much like an afterthought. Leadership in the next millennium is inextricably linked to the spectrum of human differences. Period. Therefore, we have tried to incorporate this knowledge throughout the book. We have tried to make a credible start in this process, but there is much more to do.

6. ***Leadership can be best understood through metaphors and described indirectly through paradigms.***

Since no single, straightforward definition or view of leadership captures all of its essence, our approach to studying leadership gathers from a variety of disciplines. In Rost's groundbreaking book, *Leadership for the Twenty-First Century*, the hundreds of definitions he cites show how difficult an entity leadership is to pin down. We follow his example and find that leadership is better understood when we don't come straight at it.

7. ***Leadership is a verb.***

We are committed to the notion that training to BE a leader is a misguided, though pervasive, focus of leadership development. The view that great men and women are the sole practitioners of leadership—what some have dubbed the "John Wayne" view of leadership—is deeply embedded in Western culture.

The information age has begun to show the difficulties with this image of the leader as the lonely-at-the-top, all-knowing hero. In every context, a flood of information makes it impossible for one person to solo. We need each other's eyes, ears, and insights to better gauge the situation and the necessary actions for exerting leadership.

In the new paradigms of leadership, leaders and *collaborators* (a term we prefer to followers) together "practice leadership." Leadership is the process by which they work together to achieve their mutual goals. We focus, accordingly, on the roles of collaborators as well as on those who practice leadership. Both are vital in twenty-first-century leadership and we must develop the skills to do both well.

A central point of this book is that while each of the disciplines we discuss has made a contribution to our understanding of the concept of leadership, none can stand alone as the defining set of assumptions. By viewing leadership through multiple lenses, we come closer to understanding it and more skilled in practicing it in different contexts.

This point can be illustrated by the Indian tale of the six blind men and the elephant. The first man felt the elephant's trunk and announced that the animal was a snake. The second, feeling a leg, said it was a tree. Grabbing a tusk, the third asserted the animal was a spear; a fourth patted the elephant's side and claimed it was a wall. Holding onto the tail, the fifth man said it was much more like a rope, while the sixth, having seized the elephant's ear, pronounced it closer to a fan.

Although each man's perspective held some truth, we can see that none on its own captured the reality of the elephant. Only by combining these views do we begin to understand this phenomenon called elephant.

The metaphor suggests that each person, depending on his or her position in relation to the "elephant," can contribute some important information to the task of describing an elephant; however, each can only "see" the animal from a narrow vantage point. Each has only a partial perception. These restricted views would lead each person to reach very different conclusions about the nature of an elephant and its possible use in their lives.

Thomas Kuhn (1970) describes the utility of paradigms in much the same way. We use paradigms as tools to make sense of nature, as a means to create knowledge.

"To be accepted as a paradigm, a theory must seem better than its competitors [at describing reality], but it need not, and in fact never does explain all of the facts with which it is confronted" (Kuhn, 1970, pp. 17–18).

A paradigm that is widely accepted becomes a foundation for research and practice; consequently, it shapes what we "see" and also what we study and how we study it.

An example is Louis Pasteur's introduction of the rabies vaccine. The vaccine represented a paradigm shift in medicine. Prior to that time, blood-letting was the favored approach to cleanse the body of its evil invaders. Pasteur's discovery completely reversed this set of assumptions by showing the value of actually introducing a virus into the body to spur the development of immunities.

Yet, as Kuhn tells us, no paradigm can explain all the facts that confront it. We see certain things about the world because of this new perspective, but are unable to perceive others. In this way, competing paradigms coexist and some eventually fade away. Newer ones come onto the scene and more fully describe the reality of the moment.

In the same way, the stories about leadership in this text should be viewed with the understanding that there are no universal truths about leadership. Our purpose in offering multiple stories of leadership for critique and evaluation is to help you become your own leadership theorist. It is vital that you retain the images of leadership that hold the most power for you, for these images shape your behavior and eventually become part of how you "practice leadership." The way you practice leadership is a direct result of how you imagine it.

To help in that process, we have included "snapshots" of leaders in most of the chapters of this textbook. Although the leadership profiles could have been organized in many different ways, we included leaders who illustrated some important aspect discussed in the chapter.

We begin with three leaders for our time: Nelson Mandela; Maureen Kempston Darkes, the first female head of GM Canada; and Miep Gies.

NELSON MANDELA: ENDURING TO TRIUMPH

The saga sounds more like a myth than a historical event: after spending twenty-seven years behind bars for protesting South Africa's oppression of blacks and people of color, Nelson Mandela became the first popularly elected president of South Africa in the nation's first all-race election.

His autobiography, *Long Walk to Freedom*, chronicles his birth to a royal family in the Transkei section of South Africa, his decision to renounce his right to succeed his father as chief of the Tembu in order to study law, and his gradual awakening to the realities of the political situation in his country. Mandela became convinced of the need to join forces with the other people of color—the "coloreds" and the Indians—who were also discriminated against by the government. Deeply influenced by Mahatma Gandhi's teaching and by his example in South Africa, Mandela espoused nonviolence for years, until he determined that armed hostility would be the only way to overcome the oppressor. He set about to help plan armed resistance to the government.

Mandela had complied with countless bans against participating in any meeting or group event. Finally, after the 1960 massacre of thousands of unarmed people protesting the pass laws (limiting travel by blacks and insisting that they submit to checks of their passes), he became a fugitive. He lived underground for eighteen months, donning a variety of disguises to avoid being caught. He was disguised as a chauffeur when he was arrested by security police in 1962. Two years later, Mandela was found guilty of sabotage against the government. He was eventually taken to desolate Robben Island to begin his long imprisonment.

In his trial, Mandela summarized the purpose of his wrongdoings:

> I would say that the whole life of any thinking African in this country drives him continuously to a conflict between his conscience on the one hand and the law on the other. This is not a conflict peculiar to this country. The conflict arises for men of conscience, for men who think and who feel deeply in every country. . . . The law as it is applied, the law as it has been developed over a long period of history, and especially the law as it is written and designed by the Nationalist government is a law which, in our views, is immoral, unjust, and intolerable. Our consciences dictate that we must protest against it, that we must oppose it and that we must attempt to alter it . . . men, I think , are not capable of doing nothing, of saying nothing, of not reacting to injustice, of not protesting against oppression, of not striving for the good society and the good life in the ways they see it.

Never losing hope that both he and the people would eventually be free, Mandela somehow survived his time in prison and continued to communicate with the still-banned African National Congress. When South African President F.W. de Klerk announced to Parliament a series of sweeping reforms that signaled the death knell of apartheid, he also announced that the ANC was no longer banned and that political prisoners would be freed.

On February 11, 1990, Mandela walked out of prison to a tumultuous welcome. He delivered his first remarks after the long silence: "Friends, comrades and fellow South Africans. I greet you all in the name of peace, democracy and freedom for all! I stand here before you not as a prophet but as a humble servant of you, the people. Your tireless and heroic sacrifices have made it possible for me to be here today. I therefore place the remaining years of my life in your hands."

He wrote in his autobiography, "I wanted first of all to tell the people that I was not a messiah, but an ordinary man who had become a leader because of extraordinary circumstances. I wanted immediately to thank the people all over the world who had campaigned for my release. . . . It was vital for me to show my people and the government that I was unbroken and unbowed, and that the struggle was not over for me but beginning anew in a different form. I affirmed that I was 'a loyal and disciplined member of the African National Congress.' I encouraged the people to return to the barricades, to intensify the struggle, and we would walk the last mile together."

In the next few days he reiterated the dream of a nonracial, united and democratic South Africa based on one-person, one-vote rule, expressing no hatred for whites but rather, outrage at the system that turned blacks and whites against each other.

He was under enormous pressure after his release. Knowing that the government wanted nothing more than to see him appear foolish and fallible to the people, Mandela nevertheless had to begin negotiations about the future of the country.

Time and time again, he sought to assure the whites that they were also South Africans and that this was their land, too. "I would not mince words about the horrors of apartheid, but I said, over and over, that we should forget the past and concentrate on building a better future for all."

He set about what he explains is his mission: "One of preaching reconciliation, of binding the wounds of the country, of engendering trust and confidence. . . . At every opportunity I said all South Africans must now unite and join hands and say we are one country, one nation, one people, marching together into the future."

In *Days of Grace*, Arthur Ashe Jr. expressed many people's marvel about Mandela:

> To have spent twenty-seven years in jail for political reasons, to have been deprived of the whole mighty center of one's life, and then to emerge apparently without a trace of bitterness, alert and ready to lead one's country forward, may be the most extraordinary individual human achievement that I have witnessed in my lifetime. I marvel that he could come out of jail free of bitterness and yet uncompromising in his basic political beliefs; I marvel at his ability to combine an impeccable character, to which virtually everyone attests, with the political wisdom of a Solomon. In jail, I am told his white guards came to have such respect for him that in some ways he was their warden and they the prisoners, more prisoners of apartheid.

MAUREEN KEMPSTON DARKES: VALUING DIVERSITY AT GM CANADA

Maureen Kempston Darkes assumed the presidency of GM Canada on July 1, 1994. As the first woman to head Canada's largest industrial company, she has attracted intense media scrutiny. Her young administration boasts several ground-breaking changes in GM Canada's corporate culture.

The former vice president of corporate affairs and general counsel for GM Canada notes that she always enjoyed setting direction and trying to create something of value. From her early days with GM, she's been very interested in ensuring that people could have a voice in the company.

"I was a founding member of the Women's Advisory Council," she says, explaining that the group works to ensure that employees can genuinely participate in the business. "It's a very strong group that provides me with feedback and insight about a number of issues." Kempston Darkes credits the Council with helping her develop new policy, such as the flexible working hours and alternative work schedules recently adopted by the company.

"What's interesting about the flexible working arrangement," she says, "is that we originally looked at it for women. It turns out, however, that it's really been used more by people moving toward retirement age. It helps them transition. Every time we become more flexible we serve more people, and we develop a better product."

Valuing Differences

A leader, says Kempston Darkes, must provide clear vision, motivation, and guidance. "But leadership is also about counseling and mentoring. The end result is creating an environment where people can fully participate.

"People, after all, are our most important resource. Unless we can focus on their unique abilities, we're not fully utilizing our resources," she asserts.

Dealing with diversity is a key component of leadership to her. "To me, the challenge is creating a culture where people can contribute to the company regardless of sex, cultural difference, age, any other kind of difference. When we can create this climate, we can better understand our workforce, the marketplace—the whole environment."

She stresses the connection between diversity in the workforce and the increasingly diverse marketplace. "If I have a very diverse sales force, I can better relate to that market. Or take a look at the college graduates. I want to attract and retain talent. That means recruiting them, but also once they're here, making sure they're respected and considered. So this is not just about managing diversity. It's about valuing diversity. And there's a quantum leap between the two."

She has directed her senior management staff to examine every aspect of GM Canada's corporate culture in an attempt to value diversity. "We're very much in the beginning stages here. Our goal is to have a fully empowered workforce."

Listening

"For me," she says, "real listening begins with understanding the customer base. So any leader should be prepared to be out in the field. I spend a considerable part of my time in the field."

Listening makes good business sense. "Sloan said it best: 'The quickest way to profit is to serve the customer in ways the customer wants to be served.' We do that and then ask ourselves, ' How can we exceed that?'

"If we're pushing up market share, it's because we listen to the customer better and translate what he/she wants into products or services."

One example is twenty-four-hour roadside assistance offered on any new car or truck purchased from GM Canada. "Why do we know that's important to the customers? Because they told us," she says.

Leaders must also listen to the workforce, Kempston Darkes says, and they must be willing to appreciate constructive feedback. "Our business is so competitive, you can't have a huge ego. You have to continually get better, and you can't do that sitting still."

To promote accessibility, she shuns the traditional grand executive office in favor of a smaller, less imposing one with a glass conference room next door. "It's symbolic that I and my senior managers are quite open."

GM Canada has also instituted a less formal dress code, which the employees monitor themselves. Depending on outside contact, the employees don't have to wear shirts and ties. Further, there is no executive dining room, no preferred parking. "It's symbolic, of course," she says, "but we're trying to promote the idea of openness and teamwork."

Insisting that she wants to hear what employees have to say, she adopts what she calls "a no fuss routine." On her frequent stops at dealerships and plants across Canada, she talks to people, asking them questions and giving them the chance to offer their own ideas and suggestions.

"I come back and work on those ideas. Empowered people have so much to contribute. Most people want to be able to contribute. The most frustrating thing in the world is to have an idea but no one willing to listen to it."

Finally, Kempston Darkes asserts that leaders must have a sense of balance. "Home and family are very important. Workaholics get a lot accomplished, true, but they can be too hard on others. You're more able to understand your employees when you search for the balance yourself." She and her husband have recently built a log home an hour north of Toronto, where they try—not always successfully, she admits—to escape for quiet time together.

MIEP GIES: HIDER, HELPER

In the Prologue to *Anne Frank Remembered, The Story of the Woman Who Helped to Hide the Frank Family,* Miep Gies wrote:

> I am not a hero. I stand at the end of the long, long line of good Dutch people who did what I did or more—much more—during those dark and terrible times years ago,

but always like yesterday in the hearts of those who bear witness. Never a day goes by that I do not think of what happened then.

More than twenty thousand Dutch people helped to hide Jews and others in need of hiding during those years. I willingly did what I could to help. My husband did as well. It was not enough.

Just over five feet, this blue-eyed blond was a sickly child in Vienna when WWI began. Sent to the Netherlands in a humanitarian program for hungry Austrian children, Gies was informally adopted by a large and loving Dutch family. Eventually she came to consider herself a Dutch national. In her early adolescence she kept a diary, much like her future friend Anne Frank was to do.

In Amsterdam, Gies started working for Travies and Co., makers of products for the homemaker. She became friends with the president, a shy man named Otto Frank. Gradually she and her fiancé became good friends with the entire Frank family.

Gies was given increasing responsibility in the small company, and eventually she became a trusted advisor to Otto. She and her husband, Jan, were among the very few to know the whereabouts of the Franks and the four others hidden above the business address in Amsterdam. Daily she visited the residents of the "Annex," as Anne called it in her diary. She saw to every detail of their lives, growing exhausted with the strain of trying to feed eight people on stolen ration cards for five, a situation made more frantic by the poor conditions in occupied Holland.

She and Jan also sheltered another Jew in their own house for months at a time, although she never told the Franks of this fact, fearing that it would worry them. Jan also took part in the underground resistance.

Despite their careful efforts, the German Secret Service discovered the secret annex, and on August 4, 1945, Miep watched them take away her friends. She was able to save the diary that became a classic tale of courage. Miep notes that she had to be persuaded to write *Anne Frank Remembered*:

> I had to think of the place that Anne Frank holds in history and what her story has come to mean for the many millions of people who have been touched by it. I'm told that every night when the sun goes down, somewhere in the world the curtain is going up on the stage play made from Anne's diary. . . . Her voice has reached the far edges of the earth.

Gies and her husband hoped for an eventual return of the Franks—in fact, she even went on foot to the Gestapo in a bold attempt to bribe officials for their freedom. She kept the business going despite horrible conditions—no food, no coal, little hope. Many times she bicycled out to the country, evading German guards to beg for food from farmers. She somehow managed to keep the company alive, knowing once again that others depended on her.

After the Germans surrendered, Otto Frank came home from Auschwitz; the rest of the Frank family did not. Miep relinquished the leadership of the business to him. She had been an effective leader in an extremely difficult period, but she knew it was time to step down.

Otto Frank lived with Jan and Miep, coming to consider them family, for seven years until he moved to be near his mother in Switzerland. For long months after the war ended, Mr. Frank, Miep, and Jan waited to hear about Anne and her sister who had been sent to a work camp at Bergen-Belsen. Finally, a letter from the camp nurse confirmed the worst: both girls had died from typhus. Anne had died only a few weeks before the camp was liberated.

It was only then that Miep turned to Anne's diary. Having left it untouched for over a year, she gave the papers to Mr. Frank, saying, "Here is your daughter Anne's legacy to you."

Miep withdrew totally from the business, feeling that taking care of three men at home—Jan, Otto Frank, and another family friend—was her full time job.

She has since turned her attention to keeping Anne's memory alive. Working with the Anne Frank Foundation, Miep Gies has traveled throughout the world, telling the story of a young girl whose humanity could not be silenced. Characteristically, she shrugs off praise for her role in the drama:

> My story is the story of very ordinary people during extraordinarily terrible times. Times the like of which I hope with all my heart will never, never come again. It is for all of us ordinary people all over the world to see to it that they do not.

FOR DISCUSSION AND REVIEW

1. What are some common characteristics ascribed to leaders by the media?
2. When you think of a leader, what images come to mind?
3. What are some more prominent definitions of leadership? Which speak to you most, and why? What are some common denominators of these definitions?
4. What are some advantages of viewing leadership from multiple perspectives?
5. What is the lesson to be learned from the tale of the blind men and the elephant? What are some examples of situations you've been in where people have approached the same problem from different perspectives?
6. What are some situations in which you feel you have demonstrated leadership? What distinguishes these situations in your mind?

CRITICAL INCIDENT

Imagine that you have just been funded to start your own business. One of your strategies for developing that business is to employ a diverse workforce. What steps would you take to promote differing perspectives in your organization? What type of leadership style would you adopt? What are some of your assumptions underlying adopting this approach?

EXERCISES FOR CHAPTER 1

Like Terri, Mike, Ray, and Juanita, our fictional group of students introduced at the beginning of the book, a major assignment of the course will be to develop a personal, working definition of leadership. The following exercises constitute a first attempt at such a definition.

These exercises should help in determining where you currently are in understanding and practicing leadership in your everyday life.

Exercise 1.1

YOU ARE HERE

A	C
In the space below, fill in the blanks about the leader (past or present) with whom you are most impressed:	Circle the adjectives that best describe the leader you have chosen:
Name: Occupation: Gender: Age (approx.): Nationality: Race: Area of influence (politics, religion, etc.): General physical description: Most prominent physical characteristic: Trademark or signature style:	Forceful Organized Attractive Efficient Talented Effective Orator (great speaker) Focused Motivational Dynamic Optimistic Charismatic Passionate Inspirational Noble Tough Intelligent Demanding
B Briefly note this leader's major accomplishments: 1. 2. 3.	Honorable Committed Powerful Persuasive Wealthy Kind Considerate Self-confident Patient Honest

Exercise 1.2   Your leadership assumptions

Most people have stored images of leaders and leadership. Some typical images include:

A. *Lone Ranger/Cowboy:*   Archetype is John Wayne or Charles DeGaulle. They excel at figuring out and solving problems, frequently on their own, with little or no help from others, even against great odds. They have high standards of conduct and morality.

B. *Negotiator:*   Archetype is Jimmy Carter or Boutros Boutros-Ghali. They excel at getting those with differing views and interests to talk/listen to each other. They mediate, bargain and compromise effectively, frequently using their own reputation and credibility as a starting point.

C. *Teacher:*   Archetype is Buddha or Socrates. They excel at sharing their knowledge and wisdom with others in ways that inspire.

D. *General:*   Archetype is George Patton or Ho Chi Minh. They excel at strategy and planning in the "big picture" context. They seem born to command, are decisive, and do not hesitate to confront.

E. *Coach:* Archetype is Dean Smith or Jimmy Johnson. They excel at team building and motivating the team to perform extraordinarily well. They have a depth of knowledge about their particular "game."

Each of these images is based upon certain assumptions about leadership. The self-assessment survey which follows is designed to help identify which assumptions you hold, and what your image of a leader is.

IMAGE ASSESSMENT (Lone Ranger/Cowboys, Negotiators, Teachers, Generals, and Coaches) Circle the number underneath each question which most closely reflects your own opinion.

A. A leader's most important job is to:
   1. Have a clearly defined strategy for success
   2. Be able to help others (followers) understand their roles and responsibilities
   3. Be able to motivate one's self and others
   4. Never lose sight of what's right and wrong
   5. Be able to get those with competing interests to agree

B. How important is it that the leader communicate with others (followers/participants)?
   1. Not very important—what matters is getting the job done or the problem solved.
   2. May be important—but what counts is the leader's ability to see the big picture, not every follower needs to know every detail of the operation.
   3. Somewhat important—it is important that the leader be able to communicate well enough that each follower/participant understands the role they need to play.
   4. Important—the leader needs to be able to explain, guide, and direct each follower/participant.
   5. Very Important—often followers/participants have different ideas, concerns, or issues: a leader must be able to understand everyone and get everyone involved talking to each other.

C. People get to be leaders because:
   1. They can get everyone to agree on what needs to be done.
   2. They are able to get the job done—they solve problems.
   3. They have the knowledge/wisdom/experience so others turn to them.
   4. They are able to effectively build a team.
   5. They are good at establishing objectives, securing resources, and planning activities.

D. Which set of descriptors is most important for a leader?
   1. Motivational, able to compete, collaborate and be practical
   2. Inspirational, able to inform, analyze and articulate
   3. Conversational, able to mediate, compromise and persuade
   4. Sensational, able to be heroic, charismatic, and take action
   5. Confrontational, able to command, prepare, and be decisive

E. A majority of a leader's time is spent on:
   1. Building group unity, providing followers/participants with instruction and feedback to improve performance, and recognizing team members.
   2. Training, planning strategy, giving clear directions and providing a forceful personal example.
   3. Acquiring the knowledge and experience for a particular job, then sharing that expertise with others.
   4. Figuring out what the problem situations are and being willing to commit unselfishly for the greater good, even against tremendous odds.

5. Bargaining with influential others, mediating disputes, acknowledging the competing needs/interests of others and structuring reciprocal relationships.

DRAFT

Image Assessment Key

Question #A 1. G
    2. T
    3. C
    4. LR/C
    5. N

Question #B 1. LR/C
    2. G
    3. C
    4. T
    5. N

Question #C 1. N
    2. LR/C
    3. T
    4. C
    5. G

Question #D 1. C
    2. T
    3. N
    4. LR/C
    5. G

Question #E 1. C
    2. G
    3. T
    4. LR/C
    5. N

Lone Ranger/Cowboy = LR/C
Negotiators = N
Teachers = T
Generals = G
Coaches = C

Directions:
After circling the answer under each question that most closely reflects your own opinion, use the key to determine the corresponding image (teacher, general, etc.).

Follow-up Questions:
1. Was there a pattern to your answers?
2. Which image of a leader is most prevalent in your thinking?
3. What did this exercise teach you about your leadership assumptions?

CHAPTER 2

Leadership by the Book: Contemporary Perspectives

Books on various aspects of leadership have become increasingly popular. The shelves of bookstores, in fact, are overflowing with guides and publications, including 'how-to' books, biographies, and autobiographies. To attempt to do justice to all of these books in one chapter is an impossible task, yet their impact cannot be ignored.

The best books, in our view, explain different paradigms for viewing leadership or new approaches to considering the topic. We have summarized several of these works here. More than a collection of lists, facts, and terms, these summaries emphasize one or two major themes articulated by each author. The chapter thus provides a brief synopsis of many different ideas in the hopes that readers integrate the ideas into their own theories of leadership.

JAMES A. BELASCO AND RALPH C. STAYER, *FLIGHT OF THE BUFFALO*, 1993

Conventional wisdom on management dictates that managers follow the **"command and control" paradigm** in which leaders are responsible for planning, organizing, and coordinating. The underlying premise in this model is that the leader is responsible for other people's performance.

Belasco and Stayer maintain that placing responsibility solely on leaders is a formula for failure, a relic, created and perfected to control a relatively uneducated and untrustworthy work force in an environment of very slow change. Modern leaders, recognizing both the increasing skill and education levels of the work force and the need for organizations to embrace change, adopt what the authors term an **intellectual capitalism paradigm**, whereby it is the leader's job to make employees*
responsible for their *own* performance.

---

*Although the authors of the text prefer the word *followers* rather than *employees,* we frequently use *employee* in deference to the terminology found in the majority of the popular books cited in this chapter.

The authors cite an example of a CEO who sees an employee attempting to rake the grounds with a battered old rake, devoid of most of its combs. When the CEO asks why he does not get a new rake, the worker states that it's not his job. The CEO becomes enraged at the supervisor who has not supplied the employee with a proper rake and then decides that, as a good manager, he should find the rake himself to demonstrate the "hands-on" leadership approach he has been advocating. Thus, at a juncture when the organization is lagging in production in several critical areas, the CEO is now running around chasing rakes.

As long as leaders see themselves as problem-solvers, Belasco and Stayer assert, people will bring them problems to solve. This, in turn, creates a pattern in which the people who know a specific situation best do not see it as their role to solve problems, bringing the problem instead to a central leader who is not as intimately involved with the problem area. The intellectual capitalism paradigm turns this situation on its head by shifting problem-solving responsibility from the leader to the person who reports to the leader. In this way, those who know the situation best are responsible for addressing problems in their area.

Fostering the intellectual paradigm requires leaders to accomplish four tasks. First, transferring ownership for work to those who execute the work helps leaders avoid the problem-solving trap of trying to modify all proposals. Leaders should provide information and support, but ultimately employees must take ownership for finding and implementing solutions.

The second task is creating the ownership environment. This involves decentralizing authority and creating an environment where the smaller units most directly involved with specific areas become responsible for finding solutions and creating incentives for performance in that area.

The third component for leaders is coaching personal competence—that is, helping employees to see not only what they are now, but what they can be. Coaches do not merely pose hypothetical questions; they provide guidance so that employees can find the "right" answers.

The final task for the leader in Belasco and Stayer's paradigm is the ability to learn quickly and to continue to learn. Leaders do not become complacent when they experience success. Pointing out that armies are often quite prepared to fight the previous war rather than the current one, Belasco and Stayer tell of a French army unit that continued to fight in armor even after the English had developed armor-piercing longbows. Although armor had been successful in the past, times had changed, and the French had become slow-moving targets and eventually, losers in battle. The "if it ain't broke, don't fix it" mentality ensures that business remains stuck, when success is predicated on the ability to adapt to the future.

JAMES BELASCO, *TEACHING THE ELEPHANT TO DANCE: THE MANAGER'S GUIDE TO EMPOWERING CHANGE,* 1990

Organizations resistant to change are like shackled elephants, says Belasco: Although both have the *ability* to change, they are conditioned by previously learned behavior to feel powerless.

How can leaders remove the shackles that hinder change? The first step is to identify the problem. Then, create a vision for change, and finally, motivate others to share and commit energy toward that vision. Noting that resistance is a common reaction to those who try to initiate change, Belasco identifies five potentially significant obstacles to change:

1. **Time**   In attempting to change behaviors, particularly behaviors deeply rooted within an organization, one must assess how long this process will take. Often people who share in the overall vision will become impatient if change does not occur rapidly enough, and they may grow frustrated or disinterested.

2. **Exaggerated expectations**   After people become committed to change, there may be inevitable frustration when obstacles begin to emerge and the desired outcome is not achieved smoothly. Belasco suggests that leaders use honesty and empowerment to combat this obstacle.

3. **Carping skeptics**   No matter how skilled a person is in creating and selling a shared vision, there will always be individuals who either are afraid of change or simply do not agree with the vision. Rather than ignoring skeptics, Belasco suggests taking a personal interest in their concerns and incorporating them into the decision-making process.

4. **Procrastination**   Many people would like to see changes, but think that they have a hard enough time completing their basic tasks, let alone adapting to new ones. Belasco urges leaders to address procrastination by breaking down vision-supporting change tasks into manageable pieces and then reinforcing employees for completing them.

5. **Imperfection**   Understanding that mistakes are not only inevitable, but also great learning opportunities, leaders should be supportive and encouraging when setbacks occur.

Producing change involves developing a strategy based on the needs and resources of the organization. Once the strategy is in place, it is important to identify key people in the organization who will be instrumental in providing the funding and expertise needed to support the vision.

Belasco counsels that the vision should meet the following criteria: (1) it should be a short, simple statement; (2) it must address an issue of value to the organization in terms of the marketplace; (3) it must distinguish the organization in a positive manner, and (4) it should provide clear, inspiring criteria for decision-making.

Once the vision has been established, the primary goal of leaders is to empower others to use the vision. This can be accomplished in a number of ways, including, but not limited to: modeling the vision; conducting employee meetings where the vision is discussed and fine-tuned; setting specific, qualitative measures supporting the vision from which performance will be evaluated; and recruiting employees who support the vision. The long-term goal is to change the organizational culture from that of a "shackled elephant" to one that is vision-based and thus conducive to teamwork and positive change.

KENNETH BLANCHARD AND SPENCER JOHNSON, *THE ONE MINUTE MANAGER*, 1981

The central premise in this approach is that good management need not take a lot of time. Blanchard and Johnson stress the greater importance of quality versus quantity of time with employees, and explain that the goal of these interactions should be employees' self-management.

Three management techniques, they say, promote brief and effective management as well as the development of self-leadership. The first technique, **one minute goals,** involves several components. First, the manager and the subordinate must agree about what needs to be done. Second, a brief, understandable statement of each goal must be recorded on paper. Third, there must be a clear line of communication between manager and subordinate regarding performance standards for each goal. Finally, there must be continuous review of each goal, performance related to that goal, and discussion of any discrepancy between the two. The ultimate objective of "one minute goals" is to empower employees to fuel the goal-setting process and to create their own objectives and measuring-sticks of progress.

One minute praising, with its roots in psychology's reinforcement theory, advocates looking for successes to reward rather than for mistakes to censure. Blanchard and Johnson recommend a two-step procedure for applying positive reinforcement: First, make sure that all employees know that they will be given feedback on how they are doing. Second, clearly link the praise to an objectively measured success as soon as possible. Third, allow a moment for your positive message to sink in and encourage the employee to do the same. Finally, use a handshake or another appropriate form of touch during the praising conversation. Again, the primary goal is self-management. If the leader establishes an environment where praise is given and is linked to desirable acts, employees will begin to give themselves praise more often.

Similarly, **one minute reprimands** need not be as negative as they sound. With employees expecting feedback, managers give reprimands as close to the undesired behavior as possible. In this manner, they clearly associate the reprimand with the undesired behavior and not a neutral or positive behavior that has occurred in the interim. In issuing the reprimand, managers should make clear that they are reprimanding the behavior, not the person. The use of touch, this time to communicate support, helps to distinguish between the behavior and the person. Finally, be certain that once the reprimand is over, it's over.

PETER BLOCK, *STEWARDSHIP*, 1993

The traditional leadership model, Block says, is essentially patriarchal and elevates leaders as problem-solvers, both for their own and others' problems. Block proposes that we replace this system of complete leader responsibility with a system emphasizing stewardship. In the proper work culture, he maintains, people are willing to act as stewards of the organization, putting the good of the community over their own self-interests.

A **stewardship model** rejects the traditional "control, consistency, and predictability" model in favor of a model that promotes empowerment. The idea is that people who feel empowered will accept greater responsibility without demanding complete control.

One mechanism for promoting stewardship is establishing a partnership across levels of the organization. Block identifies four primary requirements for this partnership: (1) both parties must define their own purpose within the organization; (2) parties have the right to say no and thus maintain personal responsibility for their work; (3) there is joint accountability for organizational tasks and individual accountability for one's own tasks; and (4) both parties act honestly. Forming partnerships can decentralize power and make organizations more flexible and customer-focused.

Among the other principles Block identifies as central to stewardship are shifting power to the person doing the work directly, ensuring that the work being done has value, creating and maintaining clear and measurable standards for performance, localizing problem-solving, and placing a primary emphasis on services.

Beyond these general parameters, the author does not offer a "cookbook" for creating a system based on stewardship. Not only does conforming to a stewardship model make sense for the organization in terms of leadership development and the financial bottom line, Block says, but this approach is also more consistent with the principles of participative democracy and thus will be more warmly embraced and supported than the traditional, autocratic model.

LEE G. BOLMAN AND TERRENCE E. DEAL, *REFRAMING ORGANIZATIONS: ARTISTRY, CHOICE AND LEADERSHIP,* 1991

When problems arise in an organization, different persons within the organization will necessarily have different values guiding their proposed solution to the problem. Bolman and Deal refer to these differing perspectives as *frames*. Skilled leaders are adept at understanding others' perspectives and at adjusting their own frames in a manner best befitting specific situations.

Bolman and Deal identify four primary frames prevalent in organizations: structural, human resources, political, and symbolic frames. The **structural frame** is taken up by those who, valuing order and rationality, believe that organizations must have clearly defined roles and structures to function efficiently. Their response is to reorganize to eliminate confusion.

People with the **human resources frame** emphasize finding a match between personal and organizational interests. Employees should feel confident in their ability, good about their job, and pleased with the organization.

Persons coming from a **political frame** are most concerned with the power aspects of the organization. They see the organization as a competitive arena where limited resources mean they must develop and maintain power.

Finally, persons adopting the **symbolic frame** tend to emphasize meaning. Because they value the organization's history and tradition and believe in what it has come to represent, their work has acquired symbolic as well as practical importance.

Bolman and Deal show the interconnection of these four frames via a vignette based on a news story in the *Boston Globe* in 1983. The story told of a doctor who worked for a national health service organization who had been reassigned from a small island community in Maine to a desk job in Maryland. The doctor, who had been the sole physician on the island for years, protested the reassignment because he enjoyed living in the community and felt needed there. If he left, who would service the island in an emergency? Likewise, residents of the community protested because the doctor had become a beloved and trusted fixture in the town. Reacting to numerous community members' complaints, a Maine senator requested from the health service corps a more detailed explanation for the transfer. The health service corps maintained that the town had grown large enough to hire a private physician on its own, and thus, the doctor's skills could be better utilized elsewhere.

In this vignette, all four frames are represented. The health service corps adopted the structural frame. The doctor's services were now needed elsewhere, and it was impractical to keep him on the island based on personal factors. Just as soldiers refusing reassignment face recriminations, the health service cannot have its staff dictating their placements for fear of jeopardizing the entire structure. The doctor's human resource perspective acknowledged that while he was capable of handling a desk job, he required more than ability to do the job. He felt the job must also meet personal needs. On the island, he filled an important role both medically and personally. The senator approached the situation from a political frame, needing to solidify community support. Finally, the town residents came from the symbolic perspective. Perhaps they could afford to hire a new physician, but they had grown attached to the current doctor, whose value to the community far exceeded that defined in his job description.

When conflicts arise, leaders must be able to identify participants' frames of reference and adapt their own views to meet the needs and demands of those affected by the proposed resolution.

JAY A. CONGER, *THE CHARISMATIC LEADER*, 1988

Many call themselves leaders, but only a select few can truly be called **charismatic leaders.** History's numerous examples, from Julius Caesar to George Washington to Lee Iacocca, show that charismatic leaders come in all shapes and sizes. Franklin Delano Roosevelt and Adolf Hitler—both charismatic leaders—shared the ability to take risks to promote change while pursuing strikingly different ultimate objectives.

According to Conger, charismatic leaders possess an ability to introduce quantum change in an organization. He says these leaders progress through four stages, beginning with sensing opportunity and formulating a vision. Their strong sense for the needs of consumers and their equally powerful ability to dissect the flaws in the current organizational strategy help them develop a vision that is both exciting and realistic.

The second stage is articulating the vision. Charismatic leaders use their advanced communication skills to portray the vision's core aspects.

The third stage is building trust in the vision. As important as promoting the vision is, it is equally important that charismatic leaders sell themselves so that others see them as skilled and trustworthy. This trust-building is not accomplished by co-ercion, but rather via methods such as personal risk-taking, unconventional exper-tise, and self-sacrifice. Supporters of charismatic leaders not only subscribe to the vision, but they also respect the leaders and trust their ability to accomplish the vi-sion.

The final stage is achieving the vision. Empowerment is instrumental in this stage, since it imbues followers with a sense of self-worth and belief in their com-petence to overcome obstacles. If followers believe in the vision and in their ability to overcome the inevitable obstacles, they stand a far greater chance of achieving success.

Conger also reviews methods for nurturing charismatic leaders, including fo-cusing recruitment efforts to search for and select those with the potential to be-come such leaders. Once recruited, charismatic leaders need the flexibility and free-dom to develop a vision and mobilize resources toward change.

MAX DEPREE, *LEADERSHIP IS AN ART*, 1989, AND *LEADERSHIP JAZZ*, 1992

Max DePree, CEO of Herman Miller, Inc., contemplates the human terms of lead-ership in these two brief texts. In his original work, *Leadership Is an Art*, he states that the primary skill of a leader is an ability to understand and liberate the talents of a diverse work force. He advocates a leadership style that promotes participative management and outlines a number of tasks for leaders, including leaving behind as-sets and a legacy, providing and maintaining momentum, assuming responsibility for effectiveness, and taking an active role in developing, expressing, and defending ci-vility and values.

To achieve these leadership objectives, DePree says one must work to enhance workplace relationships by respecting people, understanding that people's beliefs precede organizational policy and practice, agreeing on the rights of workers, un-derstanding the respective role and relationship of contractual agreements and covenants, and understanding that *relationships* count more than structure. When workplace relationships are developed, employees are able to work as a team, with the whole often greater than the sum of the parts. He asks: "Would you rather work as a part of an outstanding group or be a part of a group of outstanding individuals?" (p. 78)

He uses the analogy of the pitcher–catcher relationship to explain the partner-ship between a creator and an implementer. If a pitcher can throw a ball 100 miles per hour but the catcher cannot catch a pitch that fast, the pitcher must throw more slowly, becoming less effective. To be successful, a partnership is needed. Often-times in organizations, what should be a partnership is translated into "boss" and "subordinate" roles. Thus, a leader may be throwing fastballs when the follower is not yet prepared to catch them. This is why teamwork is needed, so that people can support each other and individuals can maximize their strengths, rather than yield-ing to the demands of their immediate supervisors.

DePree distinguishes between formal leaders and what he terms "roving leaders." Roving leaders, he says, are "those indispensable people in our lives who are there when we need them." For example, when a congregant collapsed in the middle of a church service, a number of official church leaders were present, but the person was ultimately saved by the alert and immediate responses of other congregants, from the person who dialed "911" to medical practitioners who helped prior to the arrival of the ambulance. Roving leaders can exist at any level of an organization, and often they are instrumental in facilitating meaningful responses and changes.

Like many other authors of leadership books, DePree promotes participative management and cites examples demonstrating strong leadership. What distinguishes DePree's work is his emphasis on the importance of human relationships at a level that goes beyond standard organizational topics such as communication and motivation techniques. Chapters with titles such as "Tribal Storytelling" and "Why Should I Weep?" examine why leaders must take a personal interest in the history of the organization and in the lives of the people who make the organization run. He believes there are many ways to balance the market demands of capitalism with organizational values of inclusiveness, and he lists six core values:

1. Being faithful is more important than being successful.
2. Corporations can and should have a redemptive purpose.
3. We need to become vulnerable to each other.
4. Belonging requires us to be willing and ready to risk.
5. Belonging requires intimacy.
6. We need to be learners together.

By practicing participative management within the framework of these core values, leaders can inspire and structure an organization to empower individuals and allow them to exercise their strengths, which, in turn, keep the organization vibrant and adaptive to change.

In *Leadership Jazz*, DePree extends his previous work, maintaining his informal narrative style and tackling such issues as finding one's voice, understanding the importance of delegating, and discussing the ethics of leadership. He summarizes much of his philosophy on leadership in the chapter "The Attributes of Leadership: A Checklist." Here he outlines and defines several key attributes of leadership, including integrity, vulnerability, discernment, awareness of the human spirit, sense of humor, intellectual energy and curiosity, respect for the future, regard for the present, and understanding of the past, predictability, breadth, comfort with ambiguity, and presence.

JOHN W. GARDNER, *ON LEADERSHIP*, 1989

In this text, Gardner examines the role of leadership from a societal perspective. It is not so much the problems organizations face that are so daunting, he says; rather, it is the apparent inability of many organizations to address these problems. Of particular concern is the increasing fragmentation and specialization in organizations and the resulting loss of community these arrangements produce. He views one of leaders' primary challenges as developing a sense of community within an organization based on values shared by leaders and followers.

He differentiates leaders from managers in a number of ways. First, leaders tend to think long-term. Leaders also have a greater sense of the organization as a whole, similar to the systems view advocated by Senge, discussed later. Finally, leaders display an ability to unify and integrate differing levels and units of an organization behind common goals and values.

How does one go about developing a sense of community? First, a leader must have certain skills, including coalition-building skills, strong political skills, and vigorous networking skills. Leaders then set about the task of creating the community environment. Gardner identifies the following as conditions that foster community:

- Wholeness that incorporates diversity
- Shared norms and values
- Good internal communication among community groups
- Attitudes of caring, trust, and teamwork
- Institutional provisions for governance
- Sharing of leadership tasks
- Development of young people
- Permeable boundaries to the outside world

According to Gardner, the primary task of leaders should be to release human energy and talent. Towards this end, leaders must create an empowering climate, based on the eight conditions just listed, where power is decentralized and all members are held accountable for their performance. Leaders must also model community and empowerment values by maintaining and expressing confidence in followers' ability to do their jobs and optimism about the direction the organization is heading.

SALLY HELGESEN, *THE FEMALE ADVANTAGE: WOMEN'S WAYS OF LEADERSHIP*, 1990

Helgesen's book is perhaps the most widely read in an emerging genre of texts devoted to leadership from a feminist perspective. Helgesen notes that as women continue to enter the work force in record numbers, they offer potentially "fresh eyes to see what was no longer working and to identify new solutions." As historical outsiders, female leaders tend to motivate others based on their knowledge of human nature, as opposed to standard institutional practice. Thus far, women's insights have frequently been ignored as leadership continues to be defined with an overwhelming preference for masculine values.

Helgesen begins with a comparison of traditional masculine leadership values and her research findings with female leaders. Mintzberg's (1968) research on the characteristics of leaders is used as the representative of male leadership styles. Mintzberg found that managers:

- Work at an unrelenting pace, with no breaks in activity during the day
- Have days characterized by interruption, discontinuity, and fragmentation
- Spare little time for activities not directly related to their job
- Exhibit preference for live action encounters
- Maintain a complex network of relationships with people outside of their organization
- Lack time for reflection because of immersion in the day-to-day needs of their organization
- Tend to identify themselves with their jobs
- Have difficulty sharing information

The bulk of Helgesen's book is an in-depth look at four female leaders and their leadership styles. These leaders are: Frances Hesselbein, former national executive director of the Girl Scouts and now executive director of the Peter Drucker Institute; Barbara Grogan, president of Western Industrial Contractors; Nancy Badore, president of Ford Motor Company's Executive Development Center; and Dorothy Brunson, president of minority-owned Brunson Communications. In chapters on each of these women, Helgesen details their leadership styles and highlights one particular strength or theme in their approach. She concludes that women:

- Work at a steady pace, but with small breaks scheduled throughout the day
- Do not view unscheduled tasks and encounters as interruptions
- Make time for activities not directly related to their work
- Prefer live action encounters, but schedule time to attend to mail
- See their own identities as complex and multifaceted
- Schedule time for sharing information

Helgesen concluded that both men and women maintain a complex network of relationships with people outside the organization. Also, she noted that women tend to focus on long-term visions, but that current male leaders are also more likely to do this.

In a chapter entitled "The Web of Inclusion," Helgesen draws from her own research and the work of Carol Gilligan (1982) to make the case that women tend to lead from the center of an organization. Males, by contrast, are more likely to form hierarchies and lead from the top. Helgesen likens leadership from the center to the formation of a **web of inclusion,** in that the goal is the formation of interrelated teams linked by the central leader. The primary strategy of the web is drawing people together; the primary strategy of the hierarchy is looking out for one's own interests. Leading from the center has the advantage of allowing the leader to solicit information directly, rather than sending information through a chain, which carries a greater likelihood of distortion. Not only does placement in the center allow the leader a wider range of input, it also provides a means for testing proposed solutions before a final decision is made. In contrast, Gilligan points out that the most desired space in a hierarchy (on top) is the least desirable space in the web, because one is then out of the information loop.

Helgesen also discusses the recent emphasis on vision in the management literature. Citing prominent scientist Evelyn Fox Keller (quoted in Belenky et al., 1989), she points out that while men may emphasize vision, many women connect more closely to the principles of voice. Visual metaphors presuppose detachment, which Keller links to a traditional "masculine" approach to science, but vocal metaphors suggest interconnectedness, a "feminine" approach to science advocated by Keller. Gilligan extends this analogy beyond science, writing that males tend to view truth as abstract and objective, while women tend to view truth as contextual. Belenky et al., in *Women's Way of Knowing*, discuss hearing and seeing in terms of communication. Seeing is a one-way process while hearing involves an interaction between sender and receiver.

The ultimate conclusion is that women have much to offer to organizations and that they have traditionally had a difficult time having their voices heard and respected. However, as Jean Baker Miller (1976) discusses in *Towards a New Psychology of Women*, in recent days the "female" values of community and inclusion, historically devalued by American organizations, are exerting broader appeal as organizations begin to recognize the limitations of rampant individualism and have begun to embrace cooperative approaches.

JOHN P. KOTTER, *A FORCE FOR CHANGE: HOW LEADERSHIP DIFFERS FROM MANAGEMENT*, 1990

As the title suggests, the primary theme of this book is that there are many distinctions between leadership behaviors and management behaviors. Kotter argues that a balance of leadership and management is necessary for an organization to run effectively, citing examples of incidences when an organization has much management and little leadership and vice versa and the disastrous consequences that may follow such an imbalance.

Kotter cites a number of core processes that come into play in modern management. These are: (1) planning and budgeting, (2) organizing and staffing, and (3) controlling and problem-solving. The ultimate goal of a manager is to produce a degree of predictability and order. The core processes of leadership, by contrast, are identified as: (1) establishing direction, (2) aligning people, and (3) motivating and inspiring. The primary goal of leadership is producing change.

Throughout the text, Kotter continues to contrast characteristics of managers and leaders. Leaders establish direction by creating a *vision* and a *strategy* for achieving the vision. This vision is specific enough to provide guidance, yet vague enough to encourage initiative and remain relevant across conditions. Managers do not develop a vision; they develop *plans*. These plans are designed to obtain predictable results on pertinent dimensions valued by important constituencies (i.e., customers).

Leaders and managers also differ in their methods for promoting their agenda. Managers *organize*. They create specific groups to enact specific plans in a predictable manner. Leaders engage in a process of *alignment*, communicating the vision and encouraging organization members to line up behind the vision and the strategies to facilitate change.

Finally, in terms of executing a course of action, managers engage in a process of *controlling* and *problem-solving*, while leaders *motivate* and *inspire*. Again, the primary goal of managers is to minimize deviations from the plan and to strive for predictable results, while leaders are primarily interested in overcoming obstacles to change.

In the end, managers keep a system stable and leaders keep an organization moving forward. Kotter notes that "little" acts of leadership that include practical responses to minor crises are underappreciated and are ultimately very important to the success of an organization. These little acts of leadership give employees energy and direction.

Kotter also touches on the issue of whether leaders are born or made. He points out that while it is generally accepted that one can be trained at a number of certified institutions to be a manager, there is still considerable controversy as to what characteristics comprise a leader and whether or not leadership can be taught. He identifies a number of core characteristics that appear common to all leaders: (1) high energy level, (2) high intellectual ability, (3) mental/emotional health, and (4) integrity.

Kotter also identifies a number of factors that may promote or inhibit the development of leadership skills over the course of one's career. Among the experiences that promote leadership are:

- Challenging assignments early in a career
- Visible leadership role models who are very good or very bad
- Assignments that broaden

Among the factors that may inhibit leadership skill development are:

- A long series of narrow and tactical jobs
- Vertical career movement
- Rapid promotions
- Measurements and rewards based on short-term results only

JAMES M. KOUZES AND BARRY Z. POSNER, *CREDIBILITY*, 1993

Modern American society has become increasingly cynical, according to Kouzes and Posner: Whereas corporate executives were once able to lead from the top and command large salaries with little dispute, today's world places a higher value on proving one's worth. Employees are tired of hearing lectures on the need for fiscal restraint while the CEO commands a seven-figure salary.

The authors state that in today's organizations leaders must be skilled in meeting the needs of their employees, as shown in a comparison of studies about modern leaders and leaders of ten years ago. Ten years ago, honesty and competence emerged as the most important characteristics of leaders. Today, honesty is still equally valued, but competence, although still valued highly, shows a reduction in importance. By contrast, supportiveness showed the most marked increase in reported value for leaders.

Honesty combined with competence and supportiveness make up the criteria for what the authors term **source credibility.** They postulate that in an era of cynicism, a leader's success is largely determined by that person's perceived credibility among followers.

How is credibility enhanced? One way is through how one expresses values. Leaders enhance their credibility through three primary mechanisms: clarity (are the values understood?), unity (do employees share in the values of the leader?), and intensity (is the leader committed to the values he/she espouses?). Leaders who master these skills tend to inspire and unite their employees behind a common goal and establish tremendous credibility within the organization.

Another way of looking at potential for credibility is to examine the personal characteristics of a leader. The authors believe that persons who display capacities in the following aspects are most successful in establishing credibility:

- Self-discovery
- Appreciating diversity
- Affirming shared values
- Developing and empowering others
- Serving a purpose
- Sustaining hope

The authors warn that any of these traits can be harmful to credibility if overused. That is, the credible leader is not one-dimensional. For example, it would be counterproductive to spend a lot of time developing and empowering employees if their efforts did not serve a particular purpose.

CHARLES C. MANZ AND HENRY P. SIMS, JR., *SUPERLEADERSHIP: LEADING OTHERS TO LEAD THEMSELVES*, 1989

Traditional thinking has placed leaders in the role of charismatic hero. Historical examples abound, from Napoleon Bonaparte to Winston Churchill to Golda Meir. According to Manz and Sims, however, the true measure of a leader is not simply the ability to lead others, but the ability to help others to lead themselves. They term leaders who have this ability **superleaders.**

Superleaders promote **self-leadership.** Self-leadership is defined by Manz and Sims as "the influence we exert upon ourselves to achieve the self-motivation and the self-direction we need to perform." Superleaders engage in a number of strategies to promote self-leadership. These strategies can be broken down into two classes. **Behavioral-focused strategies** aim to reinforce desired behaviors and discourage undesired behaviors. **Cognitive-focused strategies** are geared toward changing negative and/or counterproductive thought patterns.

Superleaders treat every member of the organization as a valuable resource and take the optimistic view that people, if properly motivated, will rise to the occasion. Superleaders thus take wise risks and give their employees room to make errors and then to learn from their mistakes. Manz and Sims list a number of methods useful in cultivating the resources of employees.

The first, and perhaps most important, method is to model self-leadership. If one desires employees with a positive outlook, one must also take on a positive outlook. It is the important task of the superleader to model constructive thought patterns and behaviors. One should attempt to avoid pessimistic expressions and to reward employees for thinking constructively.

The second step towards promoting self-leadership is to help subordinates to set reasonable and relevant goals, including those related to developing self-leadership skills.

The third step is providing encouragement and guidance directly or indirectly to subordinates. Ultimately, employees must adopt their own style, but encouragement is necessary for this ideal personal style to reach fruition.

The fourth step is reinforcing desired behaviors. When an employee engages in self-leadership, rewarding that behavior increases the likelihood of future self-leadership acts.

Finally, all of the above steps are part of the final step: developing a self-leadership culture. This involves creating a structure where self-leadership is encouraged, supported, and rewarded.

Superleadership is considered the cutting edge of leadership theory in terms of its emphasis on self-leadership and personal responsibility. Future trends may be unclear, but Manz and Sims's work provides a framework for a theory of leadership that transplants responsibility from a centralized leader to individual employees working directly on a problem.

BERT NANUS, *VISIONARY LEADERSHIP*, 1992

Geared toward organizational leaders, this book claims that although there are many texts that discuss methods of *implementing* vision, few address methods of *forming* a vision. Nanus begins his discussion by writing: "There is no more powerful engine driving an organization toward excellence and long-range success than an attractive, worthwhile, and achievable vision of the future, widely shared."

He defines a vision as a realistic, credible, attractive future for an organization and leadership as the ability to develop a vision, communicate it to others, and motivate others to commit resources and energy toward a shared goal. As with other texts examined, he distinguishes leaders from managers primarily by their end goal: managers are interested in preserving the status quo and leaders are interested in fostering change. Among the roles Nanus cites as critical for effective leadership are: (1) direction setter, (2) change agent, (3) spokesperson, and (4) coach.

Thus, leadership incorporates creating and communicating a vision. What are the steps in developing a vision? The first step involves taking stock of your organization via examining the basic nature of the organization, how the organization functions, and conducting what Nanus terms a *vision audit*, in which the leader researches whether the organization has a clearly stated vision, whether the organization is headed in the right direction, and whether the key people in the organization know and agree with that direction.

The second phase of developing a vision is drawing boundaries. One must have an understanding of the roles and values of the stakeholders and have an ability to target the vision in a manner consistent with organizational priorities.

The third phase involves positioning the organization in its future external environment. Ask yourself: What are the relevant future trends and what are the possible scenarios for your organization? What are all the potential scenarios that may play out and what is the probability of each of these scenarios? Which potential trends could have a great impact on your organization? All of these questions are important, as a vision must be flexible enough to anticipate and adapt to the future.

Finally, the last phase is choosing a vision. Nanus counsels that this step must not be rushed. Give yourself time to brainstorm and run differing scenarios through your mind. Make notes and discuss your ideas with trusted colleagues. Write down the vision in as clear a manner as possible and revise it if it cannot be written clearly.

In terms of implementing a vision, Nanus sees the role of the leader as being both the spokesperson and the personification of the vision, inspiring others to share in the vision. An essential ingredient for a shared vision is empowerment of employees. Nanus expresses the criteria for successful visionary leadership in a formula:

Vision + Communication = Shared Purpose

Shared Purpose + Empowered People + Appropriate Organizational Changes + Strategic Thinking = Successful Visionary Leadership

WILLIAM G. OUCHI, *THEORY Z: HOW AMERICAN BUSINESS CAN MEET THE JAPANESE CHALLENGE*, 1981

There has been considerable discussion throughout the last decade about the differences between Japanese and American management techniques. Although there can be no disputing the success of several Japanese companies and their subsequent influence on the way Americans view management, considerable debate exists whether Japanese management principles can be applied to American companies. In his text, Ouchi takes the position that American companies can draw on the success of their Japanese counterparts without necessarily duplicating their internal structures and organization. He terms his prototype for this hybrid approach as **Theory Z.**

The primary objective of a "Theory Z" organization is a commitment to people. The most important task of managers in this system is coordinating and organizing people. In terms of policy and structure, a Theory Z organization abides by the following principles: (1) a policy of long-term employment; (2) a great emphasis on training and career development across functional areas, with a deemphasis on early specialization; (3) a policy of slow evaluation and promotion, encouraging new employees to think long-term; and (4) a practice whereby decisions are still influenced by quantitative considerations, but not as prominently as many American businesses today.

Ouchi notes several successful American organizations that have adopted a Theory Z approach. By placing a higher value on people, organizations who adopt this approach can gain increased performance and loyalty from their employees.

PETER SENGE, *THE FIFTH DISCIPLINE: THE ART AND PRACTICE OF THE LEARNING ORGANIZATION*, 1990

To Senge, the primary determinant of an organization's potential for long-term success is its ability to learn faster than its competition. Organizations can only develop a capacity to learn if its members are capable of and committed to embracing a systems perspective, an ability to see and to value individual components of an organization as it relates to the organization as a whole. Too often, people get too caught up in viewing situations from a limited frame of reference. He highlights this tendency in an exercise titled "The Beer Game." In this exercise, he presents a scenario where the demand for a regional beer increases dramatically after it is mentioned in a popular rock video. Disaster ensues for retailers, the area wholesaler, and the brewery because a lack of communication causes a lack of supply in stores while the demand is high and then an oversupply after demand for the beer levels off. Senge relates this story from the individual perspective of each of the three players in this drama (retailer, wholesaler, and brewery) and then articulates how this problem could have been avoided had a broader systems approach been recognized and the three groups been working together.

Individual organizations also tend to foster overspecialization by breaking down the organization into numerous pieces that lack clear linkages. Senge likens this phenomenon to breaking a mirror into many pieces, putting the pieces back together and then attempting to produce a complete reflection.

Thus, systems thinking is viewed as the crucial "component technology" needed to build learning organizations as it links together the other four components (thus, the title, *The Fifth Discipline*). The first of the other components is personal mastery. Senge believes that individuals need to find positions within an organization that have personal meaning, deriving satisfaction from a process of continually clarifying and deepening personal vision, developing patience, and seeing reality clearly. Personal mastery thus forms the spiritual foundation of an organization.

Other components include the formation of appropriate mental models, which are the assumptions that guide our interpretations and behaviors. Building a shared vision is vital to learning in terms of its contribution to motivation. When a vision is shared, employees are driven to excel, not because they are told to excel, but because they *want* to excel. Finally, team learning is the final component. Senge notes that, although many organizations have recently begun to place increasing emphasis on groups, forming groups just because that is the trend is not a useful tactic: As the saying goes, "group IQ" is often lower than the IQ of the least intelligent member of the group. That is, formation of teams without an emphasis on learning may result in stifling of energy and resources in an attempt to be a "team player."

Remaining chapters address common practical issues faced by prototypical learning organizations. The chapters attempt to bridge Senge's theories into meaningful applications and are useful in further understanding both the importance of the ability to learn and how the five disciplines relate to the formation of a culture conducive to learning.

HENRY P. SIMS, JR. & PETER LORENZI, *THE NEW LEADERSHIP PARADIGM: SOCIAL LEARNING AND COGNITION IN ORGANIZATIONS*, 1992

Contrasted with many of the other books evaluated in this section, Sims and Lorenzi devote much of their text to a system rooted in psychology theory and recently adapted into management theory. In a book geared toward managers and/or leaders, they examine the roots of motivation theory and advocate including **social learning theory** in the thought processes of modern managers.

The central premise of social learning theory, they write, is that, "People think, learn, and perform in a social context. The relationship between managers and employees—leadership—is the focus of social learning and cognitions in organizations." Sims and Lorenzi define leadership as the portion of the job of a manager that involves motivating others, with the ultimate goal of improving efficiency while maintaining freedom and dignity.

The notion of motivational leadership has evolved considerably over the past fifty years. Reinforcement theory tells us that the most effective method of improving efficiency is simply to provide incentives for desirable behaviors and disincentives for undesirable behaviors. The first step in this process is pinpointing target behaviors. This involves: (1) observing the behavior, (2) counting or otherwise measuring the behavior, and (3) defining the situation where the behavior occurs. Once both the specific behavior in need of modification and the situation in which it occurs have been clarified, the crucial step is to link this behavior to a desired outcome. This can involve positive management, where one emphasizes rewards when an employee engages in a desirable behavior (such as exceeding a stated goal) or perhaps aversive management, where undesirable behavior is punished. In either case, when the behavior in question is clearly linked to a consequence, the leader has the ability to increase desired behavior and decrease undesirable behavior.

But must all motivation derive from external forces? A limitation of reinforcement theory is that it sees persons as passive recipients of feedback. A social cognitive model expands beyond learning obtained through direct experience and theorizes that motivation is also influenced by cognitive processes such as modeling, self-efficacy, and self-management. In modeling, persons, through observing the behaviors and consequences of that behavior in others, form expectations of the likely consequences for certain behaviors. Self-efficacy is defined by Sims and Lorenzi as a set of internal beliefs about one's ability to organize and execute courses of action. Self-management is a set of strategies a person uses to influence him/herself. All of these mechanisms involve internal attributions about potential contingencies and one's ability to be successful. The authors argue that one of the primary tasks of leadership is to facilitate positive internal attributions, particularly in the area of self-management. They view the highest level of leadership as superleadership, which they define as the process of leading others to lead themselves. They outline a number of steps toward becoming a superleader:

1. Become a self-leader
2. Model self-leadership
3. Encourage self-set goals
4. Create positive thought patterns
5. Develop self-leadership through rewards
6. Treat mistakes as learning opportunities
7. Promote self-managed teams
8. Facilitate a self-leadership culture

Thus, a superleader must have empowerment as his/her goal. Also, in order to achieve self-management, one must understand the impact of both direct and internal experiences of employees as they relate to motivation. The central premise of social cognitive theory is that the way employees think influences the way they behave and perform.

One criticism of utilizing these approaches in leadership is that there is the potential that leaders will utilize reinforcement and punishment principles simply to control their employees and force them to comply with the leader's agenda. The authors argue that this would not be in the spirit of superleadership, in which leaders inspire others to lead themselves. Ultimately, motivation principles must be utilized to reward effectiveness and promote personal freedom and dignity.

PETER B. VAILL, *MANAGING AS A PERFORMING ART*, 1989

Similar to DePree's work but unlike most of the other texts reviewed in this chapter, *Managing as a Performing Art* takes more of a narrative approach to leadership. Vaill decries the abundance of checklist and cookbook approaches in the management literature. Instead, he strives not to advocate for absolute solutions, but to stimulate discussion in areas warranting further reflection.

Vaill worries that in the rapidly changing world, the individual has no time for reflection: "To the extent that the imperatives of action are disconnected from the musings of thought, we are in considerable peril."

Two primary themes weave throughout the book. The first, the metaphor linking leadership to the performing arts, reflects the dynamism, fluidity, and significant complexity of organizational action. Vaill notes that managers often find themselves in the position of juggling many conflicting personal, organizational, social, and other values in making decisions, but *ultimately, they must act*. The second theme is that of chaotic change, a term he uses to describe a constantly unstable system. Although most managers are trained as if they will be paddling a canoe through a peaceful river, Vaill believes that the reality of organizations more closely resembles a state of permanent white water. His **systems perspective** says that systems constantly fluctuate, and calmness is rarely the context for making decisions.

Throughout the book, he challenges old assumptions on management. For example, he discusses the commonly held view that in times of crisis leaders must be "smarter" by asking what it means to be a "smart" leader in today's world. Previous notions equated "working smarter" with working harder, more intelligently, and more shrewdly. Today, "working smarter" might mean working more collectively, reflectively, and spiritually.

With each chapter, he challenges old assumptions and attempts to address problems in a manner that avoids the theoretical aloofness of other texts. Instead of asking, "How?" he asks "Why?" Focusing on the common dilemmas facing managers, he searches for solutions that address the complexity and inherent paradoxes involved in trying to produce control in a constantly changing system. He talks about the differences between knowing and doing and explains how concern over meeting performance goals may obscure human needs.

In his final chapters, he addresses the issue of managers' underlying assumptions via a fictitious "discussion" with people coming from an economic (Adam Smith), technological (Frederick Winslow Taylor), communal (Elton Mayo), sociopolitical (John L. Lewis), and transcendental (Ralph Waldo Emerson) frame of reference. Through this discussion and a following chapter on spirituality, Vaill argues that managers tend to underappreciate the effect of their personal frames of reference on decision-making. He equates **visionary leadership** with a spiritual process through which people seek ways to bring out the best in themselves and, consequently, the best in others. Furthermore, he says, this process is natural and ongoing, as shown in the apparent human need to find spiritual dimensions to events, other persons, and themselves.

In conclusion, we stress that these are but a few of the major works and theories on leadership. We challenge the reader to think about some of the views held by each author, noting consistencies with your own experiences and world view. Remember that while we have presented the views of some of the leading "experts," the leadership journey is different for each individual.

KEY TERMS

"command and control" paradigm
intellectual capitalism paradigm
one minute goals
one minute praising
one minute reprimands

stewardship model
structural frame
human resources frame
political frame
symbolic frame

charismatic leader
"web of inclusion"
credibility
superleaders
self-leadership
behavioral-focused strategies

cognitive-focused strategies
Theory Z
social learning theory
systems perspective
visionary leadership

FOR DISCUSSION AND REVIEW

1. Describe Belasco and Thayer's intellectual capitalism paradigm. What is the leader's role in this process?

2. What does Belasco identify as potential obstacles to change? How can these obstacles be overcome?

3. What do you see as some of the more favorable aspects of Blanchard and Johnson's "one-minute" approach? What are some potential drawbacks?

4. What are some potential advantages and disadvantages of Block's stewardship model? Are there certain types of organizations or cultures that it may be particularly suited for?

5. Which of Bolman and Deal's four frames do you fall into? Does this vary across situations? What are some situations in which your responses would fall into different frames?

6. What does Conger identify as the four stages in the development of a charismatic leader? Who are some of the charismatic leaders that you have interacted with? What made them so?

7. In *Leadership Is an Art* and *Leadership Jazz*, DePree advocates that leaders should take a personal interest in the lives of their employees. Do you agree with his view? Why or why not?

8. In what ways do organizations resemble permanent white water, as Vaill suggested?

9. What are some of the advantages of having a sense of community in the workplace? How often do you feel this is achieved? How about in society at large?

10. Do you agree with Helgesen's analysis on *Women's Ways of Leadership*? Why or why not? What do you predict the future will hold for female leaders?

11. What are some of the key differences between a "web" style of leadership and a hierarchical model?

12. What are some of the distinctions Kotter makes between leadership and management?

13. What are some of the mechanisms through which leaders can enhance credibility, according to Kouzes and Posner? Why is this important?

14. Who are some modern-day superleaders? Do you agree with Manz and Sims's assertion that the primary tasks of leaders should be to promote self-leadership? Why or why not?

15. To what extent do you feel that management techniques associated with Japan can and should be incorporated into American organizations?

16. How does embracing a systems perspective differ from other leadership approaches?

17. To what extent do you believe people learn from modeling, as opposed to direct experience?

18. What characteristics are shared by all the books reviewed in this chapter? What are some of the key differences?

CRITICAL INCIDENT

The president of the United States, sensing a vacuum of leadership among CEOs in major American organizations, has appointed you to be a special consultant. Your task is to meet with major executives across the country and advise them on ways to enhance their leadership skills. At your disposal as advisors are the authors of the books summarized in this chapter. Which authors would you consult with, and why? What would be your primary messages upon meeting with the CEOs?

Pre-Industrial Paradigms of Leadership

**The Leadership Journey:
A map of the terrain
Chapter 3**

Words/names to recognize
Greeks Aquinas
Plato   Machiavelli

Pre-industrial paradigms
of leadership

You are here

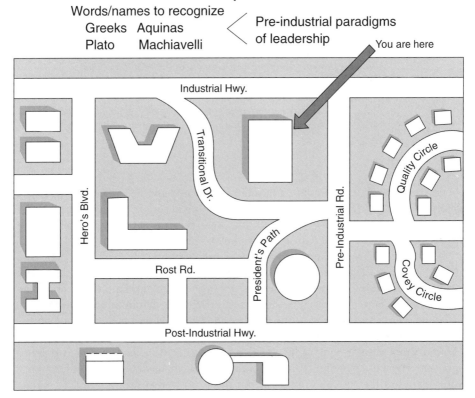

Juanita is talking to Ray, Mike, and Terri in Leadership 101: "I hate to say it, but my philosophy class is really interesting. Like, it's making me see all kinds of connections. Take Socrates, for example. He was really ahead of his time. Right before he killed himself, he . . ."

"Why'd he kill himself?" Mike asks.

"The government accused him of harming the youth. All he did was ask questions, but it started to get people really irritated, you know. They didn't have the answers, and it made them feel foolish, I guess."

"I like the other guy, Mack something," interjects Ray. "He basically said, it doesn't matter how you get there, as long as you do."

"Sounds like he'd say it didn't matter how we come up with this leadership paper, as long as we do," Terri says.

"Right. Why? Do you have some ideas?"

"Yeah, this kid I know took this class two years ago. Said he'd sell me his project stuff. His group did this really involved thing. They got a good grade."

"But is that right?" Juanita asks.

Terri and Ray look at Juanita. "Give me a break, I don't care about 'right'," says Ray. "Is it right for us to keep worrying about this dumb project and never getting anywhere with it?"

"So to stop worrying is what's really important?" Juanita says.

"Well, it'd be nice," Terri says. "I've got lots of other things to do."

"And using this other kid's project would help you do them?"

"What's with you, Juanita? Why are you acting like this? And will you please stop asking all these questions? What do you think?"

"I think it's more important to keep asking questions."

"Good," says Mike. "We can do our project like a big 'Jeopardy' game about leadership. Juanita will always remember to give her answer in the form of a question."

The conception of leadership, especially as defined by the current text, is intimately connected with the evolution of business organizations that do not originate far back in history. Chandler (1977), in fact, sees the rise of a professional class of business leaders as a nineteenth-century phenomenon.

The Greeks of the classical age had no shortage of great leaders, and they even made the matter of leadership an explicit issue for detailed inquiry, but they were specifically addressing military, moral, and political leadership. The profile of human excellence that emerges from these inquiries is useful for determining what the ideal leadership characteristics are in the abstract, however, whenever they occur on the battlefield, in daily life, or in the corporate board room.

Our proposal is to look at how leadership is treated in the moral and political sense, since that is a paradigm case of leadership that can be detected in philosophical works as old as the discipline itself. From these studies we will attempt to extract the abstract qualities that make a person an effective leader. Indeed, we shall title these sections to reflect the primary attributes that the thinker argued are central to effective leadership.

THE GREEKS: THE LEADER AS HARMONIZER AND TEACHER

Leadership became an issue in Greece first and foremost in the military sense with the *Iliad* of Homer. That document, set against the epic struggle of the Trojan War, provides many personifications of how leadership was understood in a society presided over by a warrior nobility. The warrior was different from the farmer because he served a different function. What is more, one can perform this function well or poorly. To perform one's function well, one must cultivate the appropriate *arete*; that is, the appropriate virtue or excellence that enables the possessor to perform well. Homer's multiple characters provide a dimension of the warrior's excellence. As Werner Jaeger (1965) writes, "the ideal of decisive action and physical prowess belongs to Ajax, cunning and warrior's guile to Odysseus, the unity of both of these qualities, as well as the possession of many other attributes belonging to the ideal warrior, are found in Achilles."

Yet, by the time of the Classical Age of Athens several centuries later, life had changed significantly from that of the Homeric heroes. No longer a warrior society, the Athens of Pericles was an accomplished economic power with a bustling seaborne foreign trade. What's more, aristocracy had given way to democracy, empowering many more people from many different social classes. To these people, the heroes of the *Iliad* led lives very unlike their own. Thus, this ideal of leadership needed to be supplemented.

This was the Athens of Socrates (470–399 B.C.). As a philosopher, Socrates' pupil Plato made the problems of morality and politics central. In his treatment of the ideal city, the subject of the **ideal leader** becomes a dominant issue.

Plato's *Republic:* Ideal Leader in the Ideal City

In the multilayered dialogue of the *Republic*, **Plato** engaged a wide range of issues central to the moral and political life of human beings. His treatment in the *Republic* of justice, politics, morality, and education, as well as the more speculative issues of the nature of knowledge and reality, provide an excellent summary statement of Plato's thought at that point in his life.

Before presenting the ideal city presided over by ideal rulers, Plato articulated a portrait of the political status quo. What emerges is a vision of a cynical society that has turned its back on traditional religious values and replaced them with a thorough-going relativism based on the primacy of power and self-interest.

The fundamental premise is that it is human nature to be self-interested. People are motivated by the desire to expand their power over other people and over desirable objects—wealth, influence, position, and so on. The population can be divided into those who are weak and those who are strong. The strong take their opportunities as they arise, while the weak are reluctant to do so. Laws are fabricated restraints placed upon human desire and are created in the attempt to introduce some degree of order into this chaotic situation. Since laws run contrary to human desire, in that laws serve as obstacles to human will, they are selectively obeyed: the strong will obey the law only when they must—when the fear of being caught and punished is real. When such threat is not present, the strong will break the law and thus satisfy their desires.

Assuming a self-interested human nature, coupled with the conviction that there are no absolute meanings to core value conceptions, the leader is that individual who is cunning enough to dupe others into entrusting him with power. As the shepherd, the leader appears to have the best interests—the comfort and security—of the flock at heart. In reality, and unbeknownst to the flock, the leader's real concerns are to advance his or her own interests at the people's expense.

Thus, the qualities of the ideal leader in this view are strength, cunning, and the ability to cultivate a believable facade. Such leaders manipulate the public for their own advantage. The public believes that their leaders love them and genuinely want their safety, security, and happiness. Yet, in the end this ruler desires nothing different than the shepherd, and the public is like so many unknowing sheep.

This is the position that **Socrates** must refute. In the course of his construction of the ideal city, we find that the exceptional few who will be its leaders are distinguished by certain talents that are then refined by a specially tailored education, with the result being a cultivation of wisdom.

It is clear that in Plato's opinion, not everybody is suited for this leadership role. Potential rulers are chosen from the population because they possess certain inborn traits and because of the lessons they have learned from experience. Consequently, Plato selected those who love unchanging truth, hate untruth, are moderate with money, are neither petty nor mean, do not fear death, and have a good memory. This is the philosophical nature that serves as the basis for the true leader's character. On their own, these characteristics do not guarantee a good leader; rather, they are the starting point for cultivating the quality of leadership.

The proper education can refine these qualities to the point where the excellence of wisdom emerges. Such truth is found only in the realm of abstract thought, which requires the development and exercise of the highest intellectual capacities found in the human mind. The educational curriculum relies on mathematics and philosophy, which orient the mind toward the abstract, the universal, the unchanging; in short, the Truth. These abstract ideas, called **Forms,** are the carriers of universal and immutable truth.

The ultimate Form for Plato, however, was the Form of the Good. Knowledge of the Good is the most abstract and difficult knowledge to master. It is so complex that in a dialogue, Socrates admitted to his friends that he himself was incapable of providing a ready definition of this Form.

Yet so much hangs in the balance. Without knowledge of the Good, the rest of our knowledge will come to little. Our deliberate actions will be foiled.

Thus, the ideal city constructed by Plato is an intellectual aristocracy, governed by the elite who, in contemplating the Good, have acquired the virtue of wisdom. Wisdom is viewed as the ability to make sound judgments, not about particular matters, but rather "about the city as a whole and the betterment of its relations with itself and other states." The men and women who possess this wisdom will translate their abstract knowledge of the Good into concrete practices: good laws, good public policy, a coherent and excellent program of education, all to the benefit of those who live in the city.

Socrates meant to illustrate that the truly wise ruler leads in order that those who are led can develop their potential as human beings and thereby prosper. In one metaphor, the ruler is compared to the physician, who alone among all people is permitted to administer harsh medicines to sick patients to effect a cure. The physician is permitted to do this because it is only the physician who possesses the special knowledge required to administer such drugs. The leader must likewise attend to the benefit of the led. This daunting task may require that the ruler does things that, like medicine, result in short-term pain. The ultimate goal, however, is the same as that of the physician: the well-being of those to whom the leader attends.

Plato depicted the leader as harmonizer of people, as the improver of those whom he or she leads, and as an individual of rare intellectual qualities.

THOMAS AQUINAS: THE LEADER AS PROVIDER OF RESOURCES AND GUIDE TO OTHERS

Conspicuous on the intellectual scene of the thirteenth century was **Thomas Aquinas** (1225–1274). Christianity had become the official religion of the late Roman Empire, and thus was also an intellectual focal point for the world that had succeeded the Roman era. Early Christian authors, such as St. Augustine (354–430), had developed philosophies incorporating Platonic ideas within the framework of the Christian religion. The result was a rich lineage of Christian Platonism that numbered among its company such figures as Augustine, Anselm, and Bonaventure. Theirs was a hierarchical universe with God standing at the summit. In many ways, the human world was a microcosmic version of the universe, and the traveler in that universe, the human soul, must by its own choices proceed to union with God.

Aquinas drew from this tradition, as well. However, unlike his predecessors, he had to reconcile the Christian and Platonic threads of his thought with the newly-recovered works of Aristotle, which had been lost to the Christian West since the emperor Justinian closed the Greek philosophical schools in the sixth century. During this period, the great Arab thinkers of the Middle Ages had studied the works of Aristotle closely. Much of Aristotle was not as compatible with Christian ideas as was Plato. Thomas Aquinas came of age in this period of cultural turmoil, and his great achievement was creating a new Christian philosophy that accommodated the obvious genius of Aristotle.

His writing on politics offers an insight into the qualities to be found in the ideal leader. His ideal monarch has the qualities derived from the divine model. A determinate feature of reality is that there is always a distinction between the part that rules and that which is ruled. Aquinas wrote that

> in all things that are ordained towards one end, one thing is found to rule the rest. So, too, in the individual man, the soul rules the body. Likewise among the members of a body, one, such as the heart or the head, is the principle and moves all the others. Therefore in every multitude there must be some governing power.

Thus, he wrote, "Let the king recognize that such is the office which he undertakes, namely, that he is to be in the kingdom what the soul is in the body, and what God is in the world." In discovering what God does in the universe, one discovers what "it is incumbent upon a king to do."

The king emerges as a teacher of virtue as well as the caretaker of human needs. The effective leader "should have as his principal concern the means by which the multitude subject to him may live well." Cultivation is crucial to living well, and the monarch must undertake this as a primary task. Beyond providing the goods needed for a comfortable life, the king must do what is necessary to cultivate virtue in his subjects. His efforts must lie in the direction of the continual improvement of his subjects. The ideal leader gives his subjects what they need to be as fully human as they can be. The result is the happiness of this world and the divine bliss of the next.

The ideal leader, given Thomas Aquinas's political ideas, assumes the role of teacher, improver, and moral paradigm for the people who are led. By embodying the highest standards of behavior in terms of goodness and nobility, leaders contribute to the improvement of those who look to them for leadership. The overall result is a community that approximates the ideal of a self-sufficient and thriving union of individuals, each of whom enjoys the resources needed to function in an optimally human manner.

MACHIAVELLI'S *PRINCE*: THE LEADER AS CONTROLLER OF FORTUNE

In sharp contrast to the God-centered, Christian world-view of Thomas Aquinas are the very worldly, realistic and unflinching views of **Niccolo Machiavelli** (1469–1527), a career diplomat immersed in the political intrigues of the Florence of his day. He wrote *The Prince* during his enforced leisure following the expulsion of the Medici as a summary of what he learned during his years of practical experience. Machiavelli addressed the work to Lorenzo de'Medici to exhort him to unify Italy.

With Machiavelli we pass into a world more familiar to the modern reader. Like ours, his society was commercial, with the primary form of wealth no longer land but money. The powerful were those who engaged in commerce in some manner as merchants, traders, or bankers. Indeed, what he says about the political life of the prince is readily applicable to the uncertain and risky world of commercial affairs.

Machiavelli's name has become synonymous with one who delights in manipulation, without scruples in doing what it takes to achieve an apparent good. Suggestive of calculation, manipulation, and the desire for power, *The Prince* does not disappoint upon a cursory first reading. He describes the prince, who would establish a new principality not by inheritance, but rather through force. The leadership qualities Machiavelli set down figure against this backdrop.

First of all, Machiavelli was loath to construct any ideal city or ruler who lived solely in the imagination. His gaze was directed purely and without apology at this world. He spoke not about human failings, nor did he lament that humans are not better than they are. Rather than creating utopia, Machiavelli sought to give the future ruler the best possible advice about dealing with friends, enemies, conflict, flatterers, and the ever-changing tides of fortune.

Human beings reveal themselves as less than the image of God. Governed by desire and greed, they take offense at minor injuries, break faith without regret, and switch loyalties with startling speed. The prince, he said, who would be successful in such a world must be a student of military affairs and must comb history for the appropriate role models to emulate:

> imitate the fox and the lion, for the lion cannot protect itself from traps, and the fox cannot defend himself from wolves. One must therefore be a fox to recognize traps, and a lion to frighten wolves. . . . Therefore, a prudent ruler ought not to keep faith when by so doing it would be against his interest, and when the reasons which made him bind himself no longer exist. If men were all good, this precept would not be a good one; but as they are bad and would not observe faith with you, so you are not bound to keep faith with them.

Gone is the inclination to view the successful leader as a microcosmic god, as Aquinas had, or as the optimally human philosopher-ruler, as Plato had. Machiavelli asserted that there are times when others must be pampered and times when they must be crushed, times when one must be kind and times when one must be cruel. The prince who learns this will be successful; the prince who insists upon being virtuous rather than merely appearing to be so will come to ruin.

In terms of the personal qualities of the prince, Machiavelli was no less cynical in his approach. While Plato spent much time defining the virtues necessary for the proper functioning of human beings and Aquinas stressed the cultivation of virtue among the vital projects the monarch must undertake to lead the people, Machiavelli offered a startling alternative view. In the turbulent world of political power and intrigue, the actual possession of virtues may be less advantageous than vice. Addressing the qualities of mercy, faithfulness, humanity, sincerity, and piety, Machiavelli wrote that it is not necessary for the prince to actually possess these qualities,

> but it is very necessary to seem to have them. I would even be bold to say that to possess them and always observe them is dangerous, but to appear to have them is useful. Thus it is well to seem merciful, faithful, humane, sincere, religious and to be so; but you must have the mind so disposed that when it is needful to be otherwise you may be able to change to the opposite qualities.

Neither Plato nor Aquinas could have put another end above the pursuit of the Good. In stating that the end justified the means, Machiavelli subordinated the Good to some other, more attractive end. This end includes power, order, and stability.

Fortune, what Machiavelli called "the ruler of half our actions," also assumes significance for the leader. He called fortune the chance element in events, and in colorful, sometimes notorious metaphors, likened it to a river raging out of control and a woman who can only be brought under control by the bold and impetuous young man who will conquer her by force. Above all else, he asserted, the effective prince must be able to foresee future contingencies so that he can bring them under control. The successful prince will be able to do this most of the time; nevertheless, even the most successful can't completely control fortune.

With Machiavelli, we experience the beginnings of the passage to modernity. Neither the transcendent values of the ancient world, the religious values of the medieval world, nor the artistic values of the Renaissance worlds are prized here. Leadership, instead, lives within a complicated matrix of greed, faithlessness, power, and chance. The task of the leader is to secure some degree of stability, order, and control in this swirling maelstrom of experience. Even the most effective leaders live precarious existences that are only as secure as their control over the ultimately unforeseeable.

HOBBES AND LOCKE: THE LEADER AS MEDIATOR OF INDIVIDUAL SELF-INTEREST

The seventeenth century was a period of turmoil in England. Along with the international conflicts with the Dutch, the domestic scene saw the scourge of civil war, the execution of the king, the turbulence of Cromwell, and ultimately, the victory of Parliament over the monarch in the Glorious Revolution of 1688–89. During this period of upheaval, England nurtured two of her greatest political theorists, **Thomas Hobbes** (1588–1679) and **John Locke** (1632–1704). The problem of legitimate and effective political leadership stood at the core of their respective philosophies.

Thomas Hobbes

Despite England's insularity, Thomas Hobbes followed the Continent's intellectual developments closely, especially regarding the new science being fashioned by Galileo and Descartes. Hobbes's insight was that human beings likewise emerge as material bodies in motion, with a native desire for power. Human life becomes, then, a ceaseless quest for power, and the pursuit of those things that accrue greater power. He concluded that such a nature will, in the absence of strong laws and governmental authority, convert social life into the war of each against all.

In his most celebrated chapter of *Leviathan*, Hobbes described the natural human condition as one of universal war, a world of perpetual violence and fear in which the life of human beings is "solitary, poore, nasty, brutish, and short." Just as the moving material bodies in nature, he saw human beings in motion in the political world, inevitably colliding over the pursuit of objects that promise to expand power. Without a powerful leader, political society, he said, cannot avoid the cataclysm of civil war.

However, Hobbes offered a solution: the **Laws of Nature,** which reason is able to discover, lay down the precepts that rescue humans from the civil war of their natural condition and pave the way to the peace of civil society. These laws instruct humans to seek peace, to fight with every advantage of war should peace not be possible, and to be content with that amount of liberty that one will allow all others to possess as well. His solution was to create sovereign power by a contractual agreement made by all those who live in society.

Yet, the peace that these laws establish is fragile. Human desire for power, and their willingness to dominate others in its pursuit, is simply too strong.

The primary attributes that the effective leader must possess, according to Hobbes, are strength and the ability to instill sufficient fear to keep the subjects obeying their agreements. Recall that human nature is self-interested, and that in the absence of a strong sovereign there is nothing but chaos.

John Locke

Locke proceeded from a statement of human nature in which humans are capable of reason yet also susceptible to passions. Reason, he said, indicates to all who consider it that all human beings have a right to life, liberty, health, and possessions.

The Law of Nature goes on to counsel respect for each other human being as a locus of reason and these rights. However, humans are not unfailingly rational. Passion encourages some to desire what others possess, and in the absence of organized society and political authority, humans will soon slide into a state of war. Passion will incline some to violate others' rights to life, liberty, and possessions. The legislative power is the primary function of governmental leadership, which he defined as the power "which has a right to direct how the force of the commonwealth shall be employed for preserving the community and the members of it." The executive power that carries out the laws must reside somewhere else and is "visibly subordinate and accountable" to the law-making function of government.

For Locke, fundamental decisions about policy should be made at a broadly based level with much participation. The executive leader acts on the decisions thus made and carries them out in the interest of the community. Failure to do this effectively results in the recall of the executive power.

Both Hobbes and Locke envisioned leadership in terms of keeping peace among the members of society, although the difficulty of doing this varies. Hobbes paints a more cynical picture in which the desire for power is so fundamental and overpowering that the leader must resort to fear as the primary mechanism for leadership. Locke, on the other hand, sees humans in more rational control of their lives, capable of rectifying the disruptions that are sparked by passion. The leader, according to Locke, guarantees that each respects the rights of others and refrains from their violation. Beyond that, leadership remains outside of people's lives, allowing them to pursue their own interests without undue interference.

VACLAV HAVEL: PLAYWRIGHT/PRESIDENT

Vaclav Havel was considered Czechoslovakia's foremost dissident and human rights champion during the twenty years his country was ruled by communism. His plays ridiculed communism and portrayed the inner crises of people struggling to deal with totalitarianism.

It is this moral authority that he brings to the presidency of the Czech Republic, following the events of the so-called velvet revolution of 1989.

Asked about his path from protest to politics, Havel disclaimed any plan, asserting that he "never consciously decided to become a dissident, much less a politician. We just happened to. We don't know how. And we started landing in jails—we also don't know how. We just did some things that seemed the decent things to do."

In his 1992 book, *Summer Meditations*, he said that he was simply "pulled forward by Being to become an instrument of the time."

He explained: "With no embarrassment, no stage fright, no hesitation, I did everything I had to do. I was capable of speaking extempore (I, who had never before spoken in public!) to several packed public squares a day, of negotiating confidently with the heads of great powers, of addressing foreign parliaments, and so on . . . not because historical opportunity suddenly uncovered in me some special aptitude for the office, but because . . . that special time caught me up in its wild vortex and—in the absence of leisure to reflect on the matter—compelled me to do what had to be done."

What had to be done was daunting: "To help this country move from totalitarianism to democracy, from satellitehood to independence, from a centrally directed economy to market economics."

Yet he saw the pivotal task as a moral one, calling communism "a monstrous, ramshackle, stinking machine" that left the country in a spoiled moral environment.

His televised address on New Year's Day, 1990, called the nation to a moral reawakening: "We have become morally ill because we are used to saying one thing and thinking another. We have learned not to believe in anything, not to care about each other. . . . Love, friendship, mercy, humility, or forgiveness have lost their depths and dimension. . . . They represent some sort of psychological curiosity, or they appear as long-lost wanderers from faraway times."

A recurrent theme in his writings and speeches is the importance of using language truthfully and the damage wreaked when official lies are promulgated, eventually putting an end to freedom.

U.S. writer Steven Schiff comments on Havel's forthrightness and generosity of spirit: "There's something exhilarating about the dogged way Havel sniffs and digs at his ideas until every bony chip has been unearthed. . . . That paradoxical combination of heartfelt humility and brick-wall moral conviction is as plain in his written voice as in the public man, and it's enormously appealing."

Havel sums up his philosophy with these words from *Summer Meditations:* "Some say I'm a naive dreamer trying to combine the incompatible: politics and morality. . . . My experience and observations confirm that politics as the practice of morality is possible [although] not always easy. . . . What I would like to accentuate . . . in my practice of politics is culture. . . . I am convinced that we will never build a democratic state based on law if we do not at the same time build a state that is . . . humane, moral, intellectual and spiritual, and cultural."

MARIAN WRIGHT EDELMAN: WORKING FOR A GOOD AND JUST SOCIETY

The daughter of a Baptist minister, Marian Wright Edelman grew up in racially segregated Bennettsville, South Carolina. Her parents were intensely involved in improving the conditions for the African Americans in the community, and those values became second nature to Marian.

"I was taught that the world had a lot of problems; that I could struggle and change them; that intellectual and material gifts brought the privilege and responsibility of sharing with others less fortunate; and that service is the rent each of us pays for living," she said.

Although she had a secure and happy family life, she witnessed the results of prejudice and discrimination time and time again, as when a childhood friend stepped on a nail and died after he couldn't get proper medical care because he was black and poor.

In 1954, her father suffered a heart attack, and among his final words to Marian in the ambulance were that she could do anything, be anything; that she must not let anything interfere with getting an education and being everything she could be.

As a senior at Spelman College in Atlanta, she took a stand in support of the black students picketing at the lunch counter in Greensboro, North Carolina. She was arrested for picketing the Atlanta City Hall cafeteria in a demonstration she had planned.

Her plans to go into foreign service (she had earlier traveled and studied in Europe and Russia) changed after volunteering at a local NAACP branch where she witnessed the numbers of poor and black people who could not get legal help for the discrimination they faced.

After receiving a fellowship to Yale Law School, she worked with groups such as the Student Non-Violent Coordinating Committee to promote voter registration in Mississippi. While there, she and a group of other activists seen as "outsiders" were attacked by the local police department's German shepherd police dogs. She became more resolved than ever to finish her studies and promote the civil rights of blacks.

After graduating, she became one of the first interns in the NAACP's Legal Defense and Education Fund in Jackson, Mississippi. There she faced threats of violence against herself and her clients. She passed the Mississippi bar, becoming the first black female to practice law in Mississippi.

She grew increasingly concerned about the effects of poverty, especially on young children. When Mississippi refused to accept federal funds for children as part of President Johnson's War Against Poverty, Marian helped form an organization that would seek federal funds for the children of Mississippi. She served as general counsel for the group, which provided educational programs for children throughout the state.

During Senate subcommittee hearings on hunger, she caught the attention of Senator Robert F. Kennedy, who joined her in an effort to do something about hunger. She met and eventually married Peter Edelman, a lawyer on Kennedy's staff. Their wedding marked the first interracial marriage in Virginia since the Supreme Court struck down state laws that made such marriages illegal.

After helping draft a major piece of legislation that offered health and education aid to preschool children, she was devastated by then-President Richard Nixon's veto. Marian had nevertheless found a direction for her energy: to look at children and their needs as a way to build a coalition for social change.

In 1973, she founded the Children's Defense Fund, an organization that identifies the problems facing children and then lobbies for legislation and programs to respond to the problems. In later years, the organization expanded its focus to include preventing teenage pregnancy, an increasing factor in the cycle of poverty, malnutrition, and neglect.

Although praised by many politicians (Senator Edward Kennedy called her the 101st senator of children's issues and noted that she uses the real power she has brilliantly), Marian claims that it all comes down to perseverance and commitment: "I'm a good pest is what I am," she says.

JOHN WOODEN: ON STAYING POWER*

John Wooden is the only man ever enshrined in the basketball Hall of Fame as both player and coach. He retired after forty years of coaching, leaving a record unparalleled in American sports.

During his twenty-seven years as a coach of UCLA, his teams never had a losing season. In his last twelve years there, they won ten national championships, seven of those in succession; they still hold the world's record for the longest winning streak in any major sport—eighty-eight games bridging four seasons.

Although retired now, he still conducts coaching clinics and basketball camps, and lectures widely.

"Like most coaches, my program revolved around fundamentals, conditioning and teaming, But I differed radically in several respects. I never worried about how our opponents would play us, and I never talked about winning.

Peaks Create Valleys

"I believe that for every artificial peak you create, you also create valleys. When you get too high for anything, emotion takes over and consistency of performance is lost and you will be unduly affected when adversity comes. I emphasized constant improvement and steady performance.

"I have often said, 'The mark of a true champion is to always perform near your own level of competency.' We were able to do that by never being satisfied with the past and always planning for what was to come. I believe that failure to prepare is preparing to fail. This constant focus on the future is one reason we continued staying near the top once we got there."

Develop Yourself, Don't Worry About Opponents

"I probably scouted opponents less than any coach in the country. Less than most high school coaches. I don't need to know that this forward likes to drive the outside. You're not supposed to give the outside to any forward whenever he tries it. Sound offensive and defensive principles apply to any style of play.

"Rather than having my teams prepare to play a certain team each week, I prepared to play anybody. I didn't want my players worrying about the other fellows. I wanted them executing the sound offensive and defensive principles we taught in practice.

There's No Pillow as Soft as a Clear Conscience

"To me, success isn't outscoring someone, it's the peace of mind that comes from self-satisfaction in knowing you did your best. That's something each individual must determine for himself. You can fool others, but you can't fool yourself.

"Many people are surprised to learn that in twenty-seven years at UCLA, I never once talked about winning. Instead I would tell my players before games, 'When it's over, I want your head up. And there's only one way your head can be up, that's for you to know, not me, that you gave the best effort of which you're capable. If you do that, then the score doesn't really matter, although I have a feeling that if you do that, the score will be to your liking.' I honestly, deeply believe that in not stressing winning as such, we won more than we would have if I'd stressed outscoring opponents."

Strength Through Adversity

"Why do so many people dread adversity, when it is only through adversity that we grow stronger? There's no great fun, satisfaction or joy derived from doing something that's easy. Failure is never fatal, but failure to change might be.

"Your strength as an individual depends on, and will be in direct proportion to, how you react to both praise and criticism. If you become too concerned about either, the effect on you is certain to be adverse."

The Main Ingredient of Stardom

"I have always taught players that the main ingredient of stardom is the rest of the team. It's amazing how much can be accomplished if no one cares who gets the credit. That's why I was as concerned with a player's character as I was with his ability.

"While it may be possible to reach the top of one's profession on sheer ability, it is impossible to stay there without hard work and character. One's character may be quite different from one's reputation.

"Your character is what you really are. Your reputation is only what others think you are. I made a determined effort to evaluate character. I looked for young men who would play the game hard, but clean, and who would always be trying to improve themselves to help the team. Then, if their ability warranted it, the championships would take care of themselves."

°From an advertisement by Panhandle Eastern Corporation, *Wall Street Journal,* 1986.

SUMMARY

In this chapter, we have traced the evolution of Western philosophical views of leadership, beginning with the Greeks. Plato's notions of leaders as harmonizers and teachers are discussed, followed by St. Thomas Aquinas's views that leaders must embody the highest standards of behavior. In marked contrast are Machiavelli's writings, steeped in the political intrigue of his day. The chapter ends with a discussion of the views of Hobbes, Locke and three contemporary leaders.

KEY TERMS

Plato

Socrates

Thomas Aquinas

Niccolo Machiavelli

Thomas Hobbes

John Locke

ideal leader

Forms

Laws of Nature

FOR DISCUSSION AND REVIEW

1. What are some of Plato's views on the nature of human beings and the characteristics of the ideal leader?
2. How did Socrates' conceptualization of a leader differ from that of Plato?
3. How did Thomas Aquinas's work contribute to our understanding of leadership? What characteristics did he equate with the ideal leader?
4. According to Machiavelli, why should leaders imitate foxes and lions?
5. What are the Laws of Nature, and how are they beneficial, according to Hobbes?
6. How do Hobbes and Locke differ in terms of their views on the amount of control people have over their lives?
7. How are the views of each of the individuals presented in this chapter reflective of the culture and historical time period in which they lived?

CRITICAL INCIDENT

Imagine that you are the campaign manager for a mayoral candidate. In order to win the election, it is imperative that your candidate gain the support of the prominent intellectuals in your community: Plato, Socrates, Thomas Aquinas, Niccolo Machiavelli, Thomas Hobbes, and John Locke. You have arranged individual thirty-minute meetings between your candidate and each of these philosophers. How would you prepare your candidate for each of these meetings? What leadership characteristics would be valued most by each intellectual?

EXERCISES FOR CHAPTER 3

Exercise 3.1   Summarizing Four Views of Leadership

GREEKS	HOBBES
1. Leaders were:	1. Leaders were:
2. Leaders were leaders because:	2. Leaders were leaders because:
3. Leadership qualities included:	3. Leadership qualities included:
4. A leader's primary task was to:	4. A leader's primary task was to:
AQUINAS	MACHIAVELLI
1. Leaders were:	1. Leaders were:
2. Leaders were leaders because:	2. Leaders were leaders because:
3. Leadership qualities included:	3. Leadership qualities included:
4. A leader's primary task was to:	4. A leader's primary task was to:

Directions: Using the options given in the following "Matching Choices," please choose the most appropriate way to complete each of the four categories above.

Exercise 3.1   Matching Choices

1. Leaders were:
    A. Princes who establish new principalities by force
    B. An elite intellectual aristocracy
    C. Warrior nobility
    D. Ideal monarchs

2. Leaders were leaders because:
    A. They derived their qualities from the divine model and functioned as a microcosmic god
    B. They had a different function and because they cultivated the appropriate arete
    C. They excelled at calculation, manipulation, and were driven by a desire for power
    D. They possessed certain inborn traits—through proper education these qualities were refined and excellence of wisdom emerged

3. Leadership qualities included:
    A. *Seeming* to be merciful, faithful, humane, sincere, religious, *but* with the ability to switch to opposite qualities if necessary
    B. A contemplative wisdom and love of truth, being moderate with money and being neither petty nor mean
    C. Decisive action, physical prowess, and cunning, with a warrior's guile
    D. Embodying the highest standards of behavior in terms of goodness and nobility

4. A leader's primary task was to:
    A. Demonstrate the virtue of wisdom, to make sound judgments—good laws, good public policy, and an excellent program of education
    B. Be a teacher of virtue as well as a provider of resources
    C. Protect society by their prowess as a warrior
    D. Subordinate the good to another, more attractive end (power, order, stability)

Exercise 3.1   Summarizing Four Views of Leadership

Answer Key:

GREEKS	PLATO	AQUINAS	MACHIAVELLI
1. C	B	D	A
2. B	D	A	C
3. C	B	D	A
4. C	A	B	D

The Disciplinary Roots of Leadership: Part I

**The Leadership Journey:
A map of the terrain
Chapter 4**

Words/names to recognize

Trait theories	Reinforcement
Maslow	Selective perception
McGregor	Listening
Equity theory	Semantics

Disciplinary Roots of Leadership: Part One

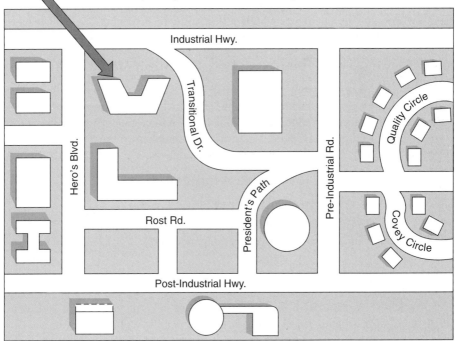

You are here

Industrial Hwy.

Transitional Dr.

Hero's Blvd.

President's Path

Pre-Industrial Rd.

Quality Circle

Covey Circle

Rost Rd.

Post-Industrial Hwy.

Juanita joins the other group members in the planning session at the Student Union. She opens her psychology text, which is filled with yellow slips marking certain passages. "Psychology is all about leadership. You know, who is task oriented, who is not, who is. . . ."

"Well, we could use a little orientation to this task," Terri says. "How are we going to get this done? I've got way too much other work to do!"

"It's not really that bad," Ray says, sounding a little unsure. "Is it? I mean, all we have to do is break it up so we all do a certain part. . . ."

"Yeah, but I don't even have time to do that. You guys will just have to do most of this without me." There's a silence. "I mean, I'll help as much as possible. But I can't make any promises."

"You're saying you're really busy, right?" Terri asks the other woman. "And you need, as Ray says, to break your section down so you can get going on it, and meet the deadline by next Tuesday. Right?" Terri looks challengingly at Juanita.

"Um, well," Juanita looks from Ray to Terri. "Well, yes. That's what I said. Let's all figure out our parts so we can get this done."

Ray has been watching the interaction carefully. "Great. So Juanita, you'll review the psychology section on leadership, and Terri—what part do you want?"

"You might as well give her the communication part. She's a master at getting people to say things they didn't really mean to say," says Juanita with a smile.

PSYCHOLOGY

Psychology is the study of human behavior. To practice leadership, it is critical to understand behavior—others' as well as our own. Mary and Dean Tjosvold go further: "Leaders are psychologists whether they want to be or not. . . . all leaders must work *with* and *through* other people to accomplish goals." (1995).

Trait Theories: Great Men (And They Did Mean *Men*) Are Born, Not Made

Sir Francis Galton asserted in 1869 that those qualities that make great leaders are inherited. Although later discredited by researchers, the notion still persists in some form. More fruitful for our purposes here, however, are discussions of the qualities ascribed to leaders. Typically, the characteristics of great leaders were thought to include:

- Intelligence, including judgment and verbal ability
- A record of achievement in school and athletics
- Emotional stability and maturity
- Strong achievement drive, persistence, dependability
- People skills and social flexibility
- Drive to find status and socioeconomic position

Others have broken down leader characteristics in terms of physical and mental attitudes, such as energy level, height, general cognitive ability, and, to a lesser extent, particular technical skills and knowledge about a group's task. Table 4–1 highlights the traits and skills most commonly associated with successful leaders.

TABLE 4–1   Traits and Skills Associated with
Successful Leaders

Traits	Skills
Adaptable to situations	Clever (intelligent)
Alert to social environment	Conceptually skilled
Ambitious and achievement-oriented	Creative
Assertive	Diplomatic and tactful
Cooperative	Fluent in speaking
Decisive	Knowledgeable about group task
Dependable	Organized (administrative ability)
Dominant (desire to influence others)	Persuasive
Energetic (high activity level)	Socially skilled
Persistent	
Self-confident	
Tolerant of stress	
Willing to assume responsibility	

Source: Leadership in Organizations, 3/E by Yukl, Gary. © 1994. Adapted by permission of Prentice-Hall, Inc., Upper Saddle River, N.J.

Personality Characteristics

Some evidence, though by no means conclusive, links leadership with several classes of personality characteristics: locus of control, self-efficacy, authoritarianism, dogmatism, self-motivating, self-esteem, and risk propensity. See Table 4–2 for a description of each of these attributes.

Nevertheless, it has been said that for every personality characteristic that does appear to be related to leadership potential, skill, or effectiveness, there are probably ten others for which no such evidence exists. So it was back to the drawing board for leadership researchers, who now looked to leader *behaviors* rather than universal personal characteristics.

Motivation

Hierarchy of Needs   You may have already learned about Maslow's **Hierarchy of Needs.** Psychologist Abraham Maslow claimed humans possessed certain levels of needs. The primary needs—for food, shelter, sex, and safety—have to be met before the higher order needs for esteem and self-actualization could be satisfied. The lower needs, he said, must be met before the higher needs would motivate someone's behavior. As Table 4-3 shows, **motivation** can be accomplished in a variety of ways.

For example, say you're in a volunteer group, attempting to coordinate efforts for a fund-raiser. The other members of the group have rushed to the meeting without any chance for dinner. Maslow's theory suggests you won't be able to motivate them by appealing to their self-concepts if their stomachs are growling.

TABLE 4–2   **Major Personality Attributes**

Personality Attribute	Description
Locus of control	The extent to which an individual believes that his or her behavior has a direct impact on the consequences of that behavior.
Self-efficacy	A person's belief about his or her capabilities to perform a task.
Authoritarianism	The extent to which an individual believes that power and status differences are appropriate within hierarchical social systems like organizations.
Dogmatism	Reflects the rigidity of a person's beliefs and his or her openness to other viewpoints.
Self-motivating	The extent to which a person pays close attention to and subsequently emulates the behavior of others.
Self-esteem	The extent to which a person believes that he or she is a worthwhile and deserving individual.
Risk propensity	The degree to which an individual is willing to take chances and make risky decisions.

ERG Theory   The **ERG theory** refined parts of the Maslow model. Alderfer postulated that *existence, relatedness,* and *growth* are humans' major needs, (see Figure 4–2), comparable to Maslow's five areas. Yet Alderfer suggested that we do things to satisfy more than one kind of need at a time, and not in the strictly hierarchical sense. For example, a person who has unmet relatedness needs (esteem needs in Maslow's model) may still look toward growth experiences (Maslow's self-actualization). In addition, the ERG theory notes that when an individual is frustrated in achieving a higher level need, he or she may look to satisfying a lower level one. This is termed a **frustration regression hypothesis.**

Although both Maslow's and Alderfer's theories are applicable to organizational

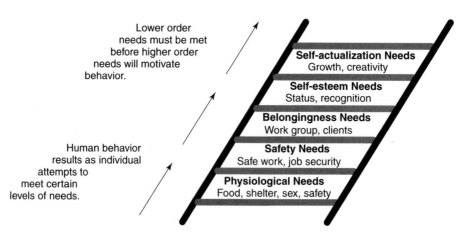

Figure 4–1   Maslow's Hierarchy of Needs

TABLE 4–3 Forms of Gratification for the Six Needs

Need for Achievement

Doing better than competitors

Attaining or surpassing a difficult goal

Solving a complex problem

Carrying out a challenging assignment successfully

Developing a better way to do something

Need for Power

Influencing people to change their attitudes or behavior

Controlling people and activities

Being in a position of authority over others

Gaining control over information and resources

Defeating an opponent or enemy

Need for Affiliation

Being liked by many people

Being accepted as part of a group or team

Working with people who are friendly and cooperative

Maintaining harmonious relationships and avoiding conflicts

Participating in pleasant social activities

Need for Independence

Assuming responsibility for your own life and how you live it

Being free from control by authority figures

Reducing dependence on others for resources and support

Working without close supervision or elaborate restrictions

Being your own boss

Need for Esteem

Being respected by people whose opinion you value

Receiving praise and recognition from coworkers and superiors

Having high status and visibility in an organization or community

Being treated like a celebrity or VIP

Collecting appropriate status symbols

Need for Security

Having a secure job

Being protected against loss of income or economic disaster

Having protection against illness and disability

Being protected against physical harm or hazardous conditions

Avoiding tasks or decisions with a risk of failure and blame

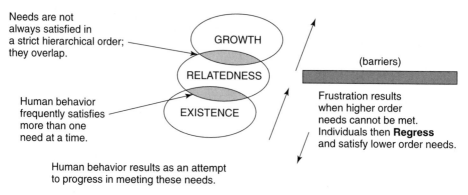

Needs are not always satisfied in a strict hierarchical order; they overlap.

Human behavior frequently satisfies more than one need at a time.

Human behavior results as an attempt to progress in meeting these needs.

GROWTH

RELATEDNESS

EXISTENCE

(barriers)

Frustration results when higher order needs cannot be met. Individuals then **Regress** and satisfy lower order needs.

Figure 4–2   ERG Theory

settings, their work was primarily fueled by the desire to understand human needs across all settings. On the other hand, however, there are a number of theories that have placed primary emphasis on examining work-related needs. The most notable are the works of Frederick Herzberg and Douglas McGregor.

Herzberg's Dual Factor Theory   Herzberg began his research by asking a simple question: What do people want from their jobs? After surveying accountants and engineers, he concluded that certain factors tended to be associated with job dissatisfaction while a separate set of factors was linked with job satisfaction. He called this the **Dual Factor theory.** See Figure 4–3.

Herzberg termed the factors whose absence can lead to dissatisfaction **hygiene**

Satisfaction		No satisfaction
	Motivation factors • Achievement • Recognition • The work itself • Responsibility • Advancement and growth	
Dissatisfaction		No dissatisfaction
	Motivation factors • Supervisors • Working conditions • Interpersonal relations • Pay and security • Company policies and administration	

Figure 4–3   The Two-factor Theory of Motivation

factors. They included job security, quality of supervision, interpersonal relationships, working conditions, and adequacy of pay and fringe benefits. If these factors are present in an organization, employees are not necessarily satisfied; however, Herzberg contended that their absence would be associated with high levels of dissatisfaction reported by many employees.

Those factors that portend satisfaction he called **motivational factors.** Among them were opportunity for achievement and advancement, responsibility, job challenge, and recognition. Although these factors in and of themselves do not predict job satisfaction, Herzberg noted that highly satisfied employees tended to report the presence of these factors in their organizations.

Despite some disagreement about the accuracy of Herzberg's theory, it is nevertheless among the most widely read and cited theories, and as such, is highly relevant to our discussion. Leaders need to examine an organization in terms of these factors so they can better understand the motivational forces that underlie people's satisfaction or dissatisfaction.

McClelland's Trichotomy of Needs

Drive for Power.   According to McClelland, individuals differ in their needs to control events and influence people. Those with high power motives, he suggests, are characterized by three traits:

- Vigorous action and determination to use their power
- Thoughtfulness (some would call it scheming) about how to influence others' thinking and behavior; and
- Concern about their standing with others (McClelland, 1982).

As we will see in the discussion about power (chapter 6) , both those who are leading and those who are following exert power at different times. Some theorists draw a further distinction between different types of power drive—personalized, in which people want power for their own reasons, and socialized, in which people look to use the power for the good of others.

IMPLICATIONS FOR PRACTICING LEADERSHIP

As you engage in both leader and follower behavior, it's instructive to understand why you are making the effort to influence others. Those with personalized power drives are less likely to act to be effective leaders, less emotionally mature, and more apt to try to manipulate others for their own goals. Those with socialized power drives, on the other hand, tend to be more open to questioning and advice and less defensive. They also tend to see the bigger picture rather than the short-term snapshot.

Drive and Achievement Motivation   Again, both followers and leaders can exhibit drive, or a strong "pull" toward getting things done. Some people demonstrate a high achievement motivation; that is, they love to be challenged and enjoy accomplishment for its own sake. People with strong achievement motivation have been described as consistently taking responsibility for success or failure, competitive, looking for feedback on their performance, taking moderate risks, and planning and setting goals for themselves.

By contrast, people—again, both leaders and followers—with weak achievement orientations are less motivated by solving problems, not as satisfied by accomplishing the assigned tasks, and looking for easier tasks.

Need for Affiliation   The third drive or need is for belonging, love, and connection with others. People with high affiliation needs work well with others and may be motivated by the interaction. Although people exhibit all three needs to varying degrees, according to McClelland, only one usually motivates the individual at any one time.

McGregor's Theory X and Theory Y   Assumptions about what motivates collaborators can significantly affect the decisions that leaders make. Influenced by Maslow's work, Douglas McGregor proposed a continuum of beliefs held by managers about the motives of employees. At one end of the continuum, which he named **Theory X,** is the belief that people are motivated primarily by basic needs. Theory X leaders and managers hold the following assumptions:

People inherently dislike work, and whenever possible will try to avoid it.

Since people dislike work, they must be coerced, controlled, or threatened with punishment to achieve goals.

People will avoid responsibilities and seek formal direction whenever possible.

Most people place security above all other factors associated with work and will display little ambition.

A **Theory Y** leader, on the other hand, thinks that people are motivated by higher-order needs. Theory Y leaders base their behaviors on the following four assumptions:

People can view work as an activity as natural as rest or play.

People will exercise self-direction and self-control if they are committed to the objectives of the task.

The average person can learn to accept and even seek responsibility.

The ability to make innovative decisions is widely dispersed throughout the general population and is not necessarily the sole province of those in management positions.

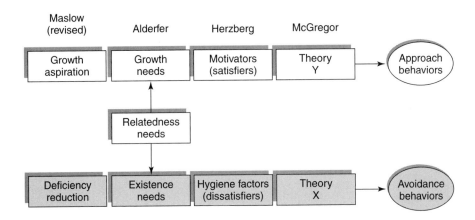

Figure 4–4 Parallels Among Popular Theories of Motivation

Leaders should constantly evaluate their assumptions about others' motivation. Although no individual is likely to be a "true X" or a "true Y," the assumptions one makes can significantly affect the ability to practice leadership and inspire others.

For an interesting comparison of the major motivational theories we have discussed thus far, consult Figure 4–4.

Equity Theory   In this approach, people are thought to be influenced by their perceptions of the fairness of rewards for certain performances. Based on social comparison theory, the **equity theory** suggests that people evaluate their own performance and their attitudes by comparing them to others. Developed by J. Stacy Adams at the University of North Carolina, the equity theory of motivation posits that people consider two primary factors in evaluating equity:

- The ratio of their outcomes to their inputs
- The ratio of another's outcomes to inputs

Notice that these judgments are based on perceptions rather than objective data. A problem arises when a leader puts into place policies that are intended to be equal and fair, but that employees may see as preferential for some. This theory challenges leaders to consider the policies from the standpoint of the workers, both individually and collectively, in terms of fairness. Leaders will ask themselves whether some sectors are rewarded more than others, and in which situations resentments are likely to occur.

Equity theory further proposes that people will seek to equalize the ratios of outcomes (such as pay, recognition, job status) to inputs (such as effort, age, gender, experience, and level of productivity). Thus, if people feel they have been working

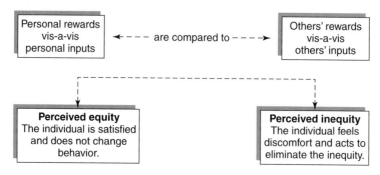

Figure 4–5   Equity Theory

very hard without receiving enough recognition for their efforts, at some point they will likely begin to produce less, moving the outcome/input ratio closer to 1. Conversely, when people feel they are being rewarded too much (a rare occurrence!), they will start to work harder so they can offset the inequity. Figure 4–5 outlines the basic tenets of this theory.

Expectancy Theory   Psychologist Victor Vroom first proposed the expectancy theory of motivation in 1964. Leaders benefit by having an accurate sense of the expectations employees bring to specific situations, for they can use the information to help motivate performance.

As depicted in Figure 4–6, Vroom claimed that three principal components influence motivation:

1. Expectancy—an individual's perception of the likelihood that effort will improve performance

2. Instrumentality—an individual's perception of the likelihood that specific outcomes will be linked to their performance

3. Valence—an individual's perception of the worth of certain outcomes

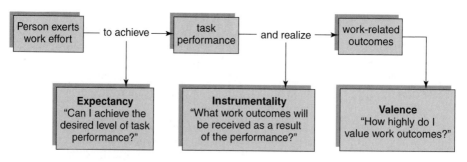

Figure 4–6   Expectancy Theory

IMPLICATIONS FOR PRACTICING LEADERSHIP

Leaders can influence each component. For example, leaders can help collaborators improve their skills and abilities, thereby influencing expectancies. Leaders can affect instrumentalities by offering support and advice. Finally, leaders can influence valences, or perceptions, by listening to others and helping them achieve the specified outcomes.

Reinforcement Theory   Based on the notion that behavior results from consequences, **reinforcement theory** looks at the role of positive and negative reinforcers, not at people's needs or reasons for choices. Classical conditioning was highlighted by Pavlov around the turn of the century through experiments in which he trained dogs to salivate when a bell was rung, thus associating two normally unrelated stimuli. (See Figure 4–7.)

B. F. Skinner and others claimed that this type of conditioning could not explain more complex learning. Skinner asserted that rewards are the major determinant of behavior; that is, behavior that is reinforced will tend to recur. Seen in this light, motivation can be thought of as finding the appropriate reward for the behavior that's desired. Obviously, this conditioning can go both ways. For instance, teachers have long known that praise or good grades—or, in some cases, more concrete rewards such as stickers or candy or opportunities to engage in favorite activities—can shape a student's behavior.

However, canny students have learned that looking incredibly interested, asking questions, and general "brown-nosing" can help shape instructors' attitudes, and per-

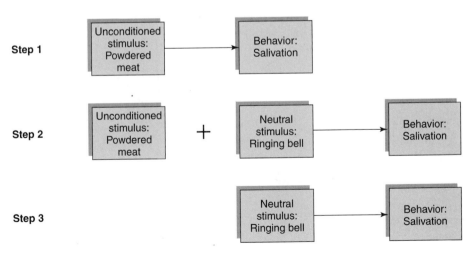

Figure 4–7   Pavlov's Conditioning Experiments

haps even their grading. The same operant conditioning dynamic exists between followers and leaders.

Modern behavioral learning theory has expanded on the classical and operant models to produce **social learning theory.** According to proponents, including Albert Bandura, learning is more active and the learner has more control than classical or operant conditioning would suggest. A person's cognitive processes affect his or her responses to the environment. In social learning theory, reinforcements or incentives are also seen to affect behavior. Most complex learning takes place via observing others and then imitating them.

To influence the desired behavior, leaders can apply this principle: Behavior that results in a pleasant outcome will likely be repeated, while that which results in an unpleasant outcome will not likely be repeated. Manipulating the consequences to control behavior, sometimes called behavior modification, has its critics, who cite the dangers of control and manipulation and denigrate the reliance on such external rewards as money and prizes.

An Integrating Model of Reinforcement: The Porter–Lawler Model Psychologists Lyman Porter and Edward Lawler developed a model (see Figure 4–8) that combines elements of the hierarchy of needs, expectancy theory, and reinforcement theory to account for the relationship between process and content. The model links performance, satisfaction, and rewards, while also stressing the importance of fitting people to the tasks that best suit their traits, skills, and abilities.

The Effects of Human Differences on Motivation As if understanding the aforementioned intricacies of motivation weren't difficult enough, the range of human dif-

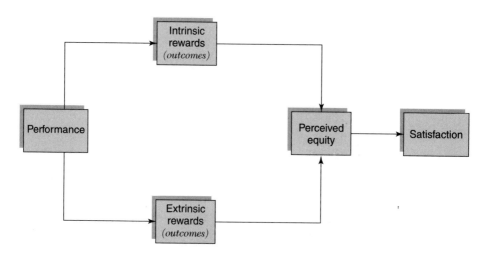

Figure 4–8 The Porter-Lawler Extension of Expectancy Theory
Source: Edward E. Lawler, III, and Lyman W. Porter, "The Effect of Performance on Job Satisfaction," *Industrial Relations,* October 1967, p. 23. Used with permission of Blackwell Publishers.

ferences adds significantly to the mix. With our increasingly diverse population—including differences in race, gender, religion, physical ability, country of origin, age, personality style, and sexual orientation—the overwhelming interplay of factors becomes obvious. Not that we can understand and predict all of the effects of these differences on motivation, but we can at least recognize their presence and seek advice about the implications.

Cultural preferences, for example, can turn what is intended as friendly eye contact into what is perceived as rude and offensive behavior. A reward that is clearly motivating for a young adult may be meaningless or denigrating to an older person. And expecting the same degree of effort from a person who may be weak from religious fasting but who prefers not to mention it is doomed to failure.

IMPLICATIONS OF UNDERSTANDING MOTIVATION FOR PRACTICING LEADERSHIP

Grasping some of the factors involved in motivation—and their interaction—is essential for leaders. For instance, leaders may examine the situation in which they and others perform, noting whether and how they can affect the consequences of certain efforts, as well as how, in general, they can help others achieve desired outcomes. Consider the depiction in Figure 4–9 of the factors involved in bringing out an individual's best performance.

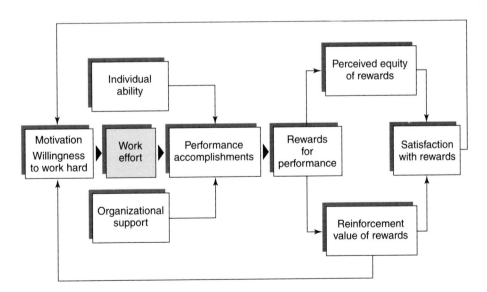

Figure 4–9   Factors Involved in Promoting Optimum Performance
Source: John R. Schermerborn Jr. *Management for Productivity.* 1981. Reprinted by permission of John Wiley & Sons, Inc.

The Leader's Role in Motivation

In *Tough-Minded Leadership,* management consultant Joe D. Batten says, "We must get rid of the old idea that a leader can *give* motivation. All motivation is self-motivation. We simply cannot and should not want to install motivation externally. The excellent leader goes all out to provide the climate, the stimuli, and the example, but all real motivation is self-generated. Only growing, actualized individuals can reach out beyond themselves in ways essential to true synergistic teams. . . . *We can know and lead others only when we are progressively learning how to know and lead ourselves.*"

The Dale Carnegie folks know all about this kind of motivation. In their book, *The Leader in You,* Stuart R. Levine and Michael A. Crom discuss an employee going the "extra mile" in satisfying a customer:

> And people will only want to perform like that if they feel like an important part of the organization. That's why employees need to be respected and included in a corporate vision they can embrace. That's why people need a stake in their work lives. That's why their successes need to be rewarded, praised, and celebrated. That's why their failures need to be handled gingerly. Do these things. Then stand back and watch the results roll in. (pp. 51–52)

They go on to list three underlying principles that must be addressed for motivation to be effective:

1. Employees must be included in all parts of the process, every step of the way. Teamwork is the key here, not hierarchy.

2. People must be treated as individuals. Always acknowledge their importance and show them respect. They're people first, employees second.

3. Superior work must be encouraged, recognized, and rewarded. Everyone responds to expectations. If you treat people as if they are capable and smart—and get out of the way—that's exactly how they'll perform. (p. 52)

Attitudes

Successful leadership demands an understanding of attitudes and their manifestations in an organization. For our purposes, we'll define **attitude** as a series of beliefs and feelings held by people about specific situations, ideas, or other people. As shown in Table 4–4, three main aspects of attitudes include *affect,* the emotional content of a situation; *behavior,* specific actions taken in response to or in anticipation of a situation; and *cognitions,* an individual's thoughts or perceptions of a situation.

In general, it is believed that people try to maintain a balance between these three components as they form attitudes. In some situations, the three components come into conflict, and a skilled leader will consider feelings as well as behaviors in the attempt to promote positive attitudes.

TABLE 4–4   The Components of Attitudes

Components	Definition	Example
Affective	Favorable or unfavorable feelings	The workers' feelings about the new regulations
Behavioral	Human actions	The workers' performance
Cognitive	Beliefs, knowledge, understanding	The workers' beliefs about performance standards and supervision

Cognitive Factors and Personality

"Leaders," say Dean and Mary Tjosvold (1995), well-known authorities on leadership and team building, "help people care." If followers are not motivated to accomplish a task, they suggest that leaders should be "psychologically savvy": They must have the kinds of interpersonal skills that let them get others involved and working together in what they call the "cooperative bottom line."

Effectively pulling in others to participate in a shared effort addresses the individuals' needs to work towards self-actualization. But the Tjosvolds point out that it also is a good business strategy. "Life is aspiration. Learning, striving people are happy people and good workers. They have initiative and imagination, and the companies they work for are rarely caught napping" (1995).

Personality Differences

As if leadership itself did not present enough difficulties in definition, we now look at *personality*, a term that has engendered as much, if not more, disagreement. We'll define personality as how people affect others and understand themselves. Personality traits are important aspects to consider in terms of leaders and followers. Five traits have been recognized as major affectors of task performance:

1. Extroversion—Sociable, talkative, and assertive

2. Agreeableness—Good-natured, cooperative, and trusting

3. Conscientiousness—Responsible, dependable, persistent, and achievement–oriented

4. Emotional stability—Viewed from a negative standpoint: tense, insecure, and nervous

5. Openness to experience—Imaginative, artistically sensitive, and intellectual

(Luthans, p. 114)

In the same way, leaders and followers are certainly affected by their own and their colleagues' self-concepts, or their attempts to understand themselves. Despite much of the hype surrounding self-esteem, research on its value has been ambiguous and contradictory, according to Luthans, (p.115). What is clear, however, is that people with high self-esteem feel empowered, competent, and connected to their colleagues. People practicing leadership should be sensitive to, and strive to increase followers' sense of themselves.

Perception and Attribution

We pay attention to people and objects in such a way that gives them meaning to us. That idiosyncratic aspect of perception can mean that two people can form two different impressions of the same evidence, as the classic illusion in Figure 4–10 shows.

Figure 4–11 shows how our perceptions of people—our **social perceptions**— are affected by a number of elements, including the characteristics of the person we perceive, such as physical appearance, clothing, and verbal and nonverbal communication, as well as the ascribed attributes, including status, occupation, and personal characteristics.

Social perceptions have much to do with our impressions of people who are different from ourselves. Upon meeting a disabled person, for instance, we may react by speaking too loudly, asking questions of others instead of speaking directly to the disabled person, or not knowing what to say for fear of saying the wrong thing. Similarly, our first impressions of people whose accent is different from our own—or whose height, or clothing, or even vehicle is not like ours—may be erroneous. (Would you expect a nun to drive a pickup?)

Our perceptions can be inaccurate for three main reasons: **stereotyping, selective perception,** and **perceptual defense.** In the preceding examples, we might stereotype the person with an Italian accent by inferring connections to organized

Figure 4–10   The Old Woman/Young Woman Illusion

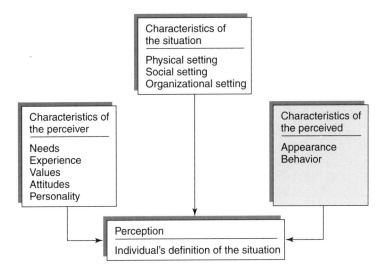

Figure 4–11   Factors Affecting Perception

crime; the disabled person by assuming she is unable to respond to conversation. A stereotype can also be positive, as hearing a Scandinavian's accent and assuming the person must be a good skiier. Frequent workplace stereotyping occurs with differences in age and gender.

Selective perception occurs when we hear or see only what we want to. Teenagers have marvelous powers of selective perception when they screen out parental requests. We select on the basis of our own experiences, needs, and orientations.

The third way to block perceptions is through perceptual defense. Typically, defense takes place when we distort or deny something that is too difficult to acknowledge.

Yet it is not only how we perceive people and events that affects our response to them; **attribution,** or the reasons we ascribe for our behavior, plays an important role. We interpret an event and then try to uncover its cause. Much depends on our view of ourselves and the world—seeing ourselves on a continuum as having a great deal of control over events or as being powerless.

Leader as Learner

If we accept the Tjosvolds' assertions, leaders are not those people who are always certain of themselves and their direction for the organization. Rather, leaders are people who are open-minded learners. What's more, they're not afraid to let others see them in this light. In fact, creating an environment in which learning—and its natural by-product, mistakes—are OK can be a potent tool to unite a group and inspire creativity, risk-taking, and effort.

Today those who practice leadership must be open to learning about their colleagues and followers. That includes their differences in personality and work styles, their lifestyle as it affects the effort, and the interplay of such factors as age, race, religion, and gender. No one can be expected to grasp all the implications of such a wide range of differences, so leaders especially must show they are willing and able to learn. But interpersonal skills in understanding the group members don't stop with the leader. The leader must promote such understanding among group members themselves, so they can empower each other, and call forth and recognize each other's contributions.

We'll let the Tjosvolds have the last word here:

> Leadership is a "we" thing that requires both leader and employee. So too does using psychology. You will be more efficient if you involve your employees, colleagues and friends in helping you develop your psychology skills and strengthen your leadership competence. Learning unites leaders and followers in a common journey of self discovery and team development. . . . Leadership today is too complex and challenging to be left to one person; it's only successful when done together.

GENE CHELBERG: DISABLED AND PROUD

Gene Chelberg never started out to be a leader in the disability community. The 28-year-old remembers, in fact, that his whole purpose in going to college at the 40,000-student Twin Cities campus of the University of Minnesota was to get lost in the crowd.

"I was trying to figure out who I was, from the inside out. My entire life before that had been telling me who I was from the outside in—Gene, the blind kid."

Now the project director of Disabled Student Services at the University of Minnesota, Chelberg says that he probably wouldn't have been so conscious of the need to find his identity had he not been born with blindness. The value of disability—in Gene's case, its fueling of the search for personal identity—is becoming central to current thought in disability issues.

"To a large extent, we are taught that disability is inherently negative," Chelberg says. "Now we're trying to look at our disability in a new light—as something that has added to our lives. It's not all of who we are, but it's a central piece of it."

Chelberg's life modeled the leadership steps he now teaches to disabled college students through Project LEEDS, Leadership Education to Empower Disabled Students. First, reflection: "We need to take time to think of where we've been and where we're going," he says.

Chelberg maintains that reflection must take place individually as well as within a group, that no one can exercise leadership without first having some sense of his or her identity. And for disabled people, he stresses, that means coming to an understanding—and an appreciation—of the disability that sets them apart. It reverses the traditional medical/rehabilitation model of disability by proclaiming that the individual, not the doctor or rehab specialist, is the "agent of remedy."

Yet once the individual reflection has begun, community becomes vital. "Disabled people have fought for the past twenty years or so to secure their rights, and we must continue to make sure they're available. But now we also have to think of our responsibilities, not only to the disabled community but to the nondisabled as well," he says.

His affiliation with the Disabled Student Cultural Center at the University of Minnesota helped him and other disabled students understand the power of creating alliances, as well as the importance of recognizing the dynamics behind sharing the power. These are among the issues he will address in a new project designed to acquaint students and Student Affairs personnel with ways to hold accessible events and to welcome disability.

"Leadership has sort of happened within the disabled community," he says, citing the case of a man who wanted to go to college when few disabled people had enrolled. This man's actions started the Independent Living movement at Berkeley. "Rather than being thrust into the middle of things all the time," Chelberg says, "we need to take our time, step back, and chart our course." He thinks reflection is a central piece of teaching leadership.

Chelberg helped arrange a ground-breaking event for disabled students: "Disabled and Proud: The 1993 national gathering of college student leaders with disabilities." Attended by people from across the country, the event, he says, "was unbelievable. I still hear people refer to it and say that it changed their lives."

DAVID KORESH: CHARISMATIC CULT LEADER

The leader of the religious sect known as the Branch Davidians, Koresh was originally named Vernon Wayne Howell. He chose the new name to reflect King David. *Koresh* is the Hebrew name of a Persian leader. After a schism in the sect, Koresh moved his followers to a primitive camp in east Texas, where he gathered his "family" every day for lessons and sermons.

Koresh's rule was absolute: He not only owned everything in the camp but he also had the right to have numerous wives and mistresses. An articulate speaker with a reportedly phenomenal knowledge of the Bible, Koresh traveled across the country recruiting followers to join the "family" in Texas.

He preached that Armageddon was imminent, and he and his followers dug tunnels, built watchtowers, and heavily armed the camp. They began referring to the camp as "Ranch Apocalypse."

Alcohol, Tobacco, and Firearms agents eventually found out that the camp contained more than 8,000 pounds of ammunition that included M16 rifles and grenade launchers.

After a 51-day standoff between the ATF forces and the Branch Davidians, the federal agents tried to smoke Koresh's group out with tear gas. Although the events are disputed, the FBI maintains that Koresh ordered his followers to ignite the lamp fuel. Whatever the cause, a horrible fire swept through the compound killing 78 people, among whom were 17 children. Many were the children of Koresh.

COMMUNICATION

Just as psychologists think leadership—indeed, almost every aspect of life—can be understood through psychology, communication theorists believe that their field yields a comprehensive way to consider leadership. The interpersonal skills we touched upon in the psychology section are central to communication skills, as are two additional significant aspects of practicing leadership: oral presentation and written communication.

Basic Communication Theory

In the past, we saw communication first as a *linear* process in which a message went from sender to receiver. As people began to see that the interaction between sender and receiver affected the message, an *interactional* model was proposed. The most contemporary view, however, is that communication is a *transactional* process. Figure 4–12 outlines the core elements of this process. This view builds on the interactional model, but also includes the nonverbal aspects as well as the entire range of factors in the relationship between sender and receiver.

When a **communication** is made, it passes through several points between the sender and receiver (see Figure 4–13). When information is communicated, the first step toward interpreting that information is called *encoding*.

The encoding process translates the communication into a set of meaningful symbols (language) that express the communicator's purpose. The resulting message is then transmitted through an available **channel**. Among the many channels of communication within organizations are face-to-face communications, memos, computer messages, and nonverbal cues, such as facial expressions.

When a communication is received by another, that person then decodes the message. Decoding is a process of interpretation performed by the receiver of the message. Based on that interpretation, the receiver may structure a response, which then goes through the same process of encoding, transmitting, and decoding.

We communicate to bring about six outcomes: understanding, pleasure, attitude, influence, improved relations, and action. But, as we all know, the original intent can be affected by a variety of factors, such as filters and sets.

Filters are the physical and psychological factors that affect the message. Perceptual filters refer to the biological aspects of our senses that limit how we hear and process the message.

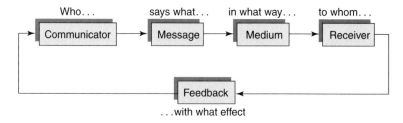

Figure 4–12   The Communication Process

Source: J. Ivancevich, and M. Matterson, *Organizational Behavior and Management.* 1996, Richard D. Irwin Inc. p. 489. Reprinted with permission.

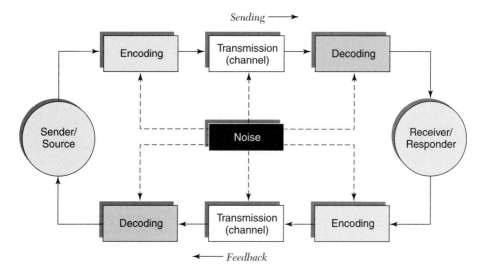

Figure 4–13   A Model of the Interpersonal Communication Process
Source: P. L. Hunsaker and C. W. Cook, *Managing Organizational Behavior,* Reading, Mass.: Addison-Wesley, 1986, p. 197. Copyright 1986 by Phillip L. Hunsaker. Reprinted by authors' permission.

Sets describe a predisposition to respond in a certain way. Cultural sets, for example, may interfere with a message. For instance, people from the Middle East stand much closer to each other (6 to 12 inches) than people from the United States (18 to 36 inches). The distance cultural set had major implications during a series of negotiations about the Middle East. One Egyptian diplomat complained to the press that an American diplomat must not have been truly concerned about the negotiations. He explained that when the American talked to him, he stood far away, a clear sign to the Egyptian that he was withdrawing. The American, of course, was surprised by this accusation, asserting, rather, that he stood where he was comfortable.

What we communicate—the *communicative stimuli*—can be grouped into several types of stimuli:

intentional verbal stimuli—our conscious attempts to communicate through words

unintentional verbal stimuli—things we say without meaning to

nonverbal stimuli—all the nonspeech factors that influence communication, including tone of voice, gestures, eye contact, and posture

intentional nonverbal stimuli—the nonverbal stimuli we want to transmit

unintentional nonverbal stimuli—the nonverbal stimuli we are unaware of or unable to control, which nevertheless influence our communication

At this point, then, we know why we are communicating (outcome), and what verbal and nonverbal messages we may be sending. The channels we use include the telephone, the computer (e-mail), and, in face-to-face communication, our senses, especially hearing, sight, and touch. The more channels we use, the greater the chance for interference. For instance, speaking on the phone deprives us of seeing the other's facial cues. Communicating via e-mail involves its own set of established protocols, but alleviates tone of voice as well as facial cues and gestures.

Culture affects our choice of channels: With messages of emotional content, some cultures ascribe more import to tone of voice than to facial expression. Others, such as some African cultures, may place a higher value on touching while conveying a message.

A story about a Turkish friend illustrates the disastrous effects possible when cultural differences interfere with communication. Gungor was an extremely outgoing, friendly person I had met in the Peace Corps. He came to visit in New York City, and was particularly excited about seeing the United Nations. I showed him how to use the bus and told him I'd see him that evening.

When I returned to my apartment that evening, my usually high-spirited pal was in the dumps. He told me how he had been so bitterly disappointed. It was then that I realized I should have given him some pointers.

First, I should have told him not to sit next to someone else on the bus if other seats were empty. Nor to look at anyone else in the eyes, much less try to engage them in conversation. He thought that people disliked him, while they were actually protecting their space and their sense of safety—two elements vital to anyone who has ever ridden public transportation in New York City.

Individual preferences, of course, exist as well. Some people, for example, are self-confessed "phone-a-phobics" who dislike telephone conversations and thus may give abrupt responses that can be interpreted as unfriendly.

Interference, or **noise,** refers to anything that distorts the message or distracts the receiver from accurately hearing the message. Beyond the usual kinds of noise we experience, such as loud music or the sound of jackhammers on the street, interference can include nonsound factors such as the room's stuffiness or lack of light, or other people's distracting behavior or strange dress.

All of these factors—the input, the types of filters and sets, communication channels, and interference—are different for communicator number two, the receiver, because of individual and perhaps cultural and other factors. Only recently have we begun to focus on the critical importance of listening in effective communication. We all know that listening and hearing are quite different: hearing involves physiologically receiving the sound waves and neurologically processing the stimuli. Listening, on the other hand, involves *understanding*—assigning meaning to what we hear—and *remembering* (short-term or long-term).

Also affecting communication are the variables of *time* as it affects the intensity of the relationship and the communication style.

Formal and Informal Communication

We can distinguish between types of communication in a number of ways. One common method is to compare formal versus informal information channels. A formal information channel is built within the framework of an organization and follows a stated procedure. For example, posting memos in many organizations is a formalized procedure. Such formal communications take place in many ways. In the work-place, for example, **upward communication** consists of feedback given by employees to others higher in the corporate chain of command. Further, the feedback can be given via direct communication, surveys, memos, e-mail, and so on. Managers who place rigid guidelines on upward communication and discourage feedback from lower-level employees hinder their ability to share in common goals and thus inhibit their own leadership effectiveness.

Downward communication is feedback given by managers to their subordinates. Examples include performance evaluations, memos, policy statements, and so on. This information must be presented clearly and its relevance to the audience highlighted so that they don't ignore it. Again, managers and leaders who do not share the goals of their employees/collaborators hinder their leadership ability, as well as their effectiveness in communicating.

Lateral communication is organized communication with peers. When done effectively, it serves to heighten the efficiency, clarity, and quality of information and further strengthen existing communication networks.

Figure 4–14 displays some of the core objectives for using upward, downward, and lateral communication.

Informal communication channels are not formally sanctioned or created by the organization. Rather, they emerge within its everyday life. Similarly, informal groups in the workplace may emerge both across and within levels and departments and serve the interests of the members.

Among the more common manifestations of informal communication is the **grapevine.** Rumors and beliefs—sometimes given more credence than those passed down by higher management—are passed along the grapevine. This channel serves the social needs of group members but may be disliked by those managers or leaders whose communications are inadequate. These leaders may see the grapevine as

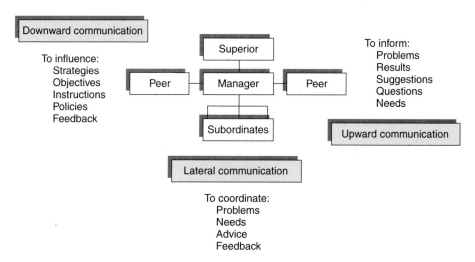

Figure 4–14   Directions of Communication and Their Objectives

TABLE 4–5   Observations about the Grapevine

1. The grapevine is a significant part of an organizational communication system with regard to (a) quantity of information communicated and (b) quality of information, such as its importance and its effects on people and performance.

2. The quality of management decisions depends on quality of information inputs that management has, and one useful input is information from the grapevine.

3. Successful communication with employees depends on (a) understanding their problems, (b) understanding their attitudes, and (c) determining gaps in employee information (the grapevine is a valuable source of these kinds of inputs).

4. The quality of management decisions is significantly affected by management's success in listening to and interpreting the grapevine.

5. The quality of management communication programs is significantly affected by management's capacity to understand and to relate to the grapevine.

6. The grapevine cannot be suppressed or directly controlled, although it may be influenced by the way management relates to it.

7. The grapevine has both negative and positive influences in an organization.

8. The grapevine can provide useful inputs even when information it carries is known to be incorrect.

9. In normal organizational situations, excluding situations such as strikes and disasters, the grapevine on the average carries more correct information than inaccurate information.

10. The grapevine carries an incomplete story.

11. Compared with most formal communications, the grapevine tends to speed faster through an organization, so it can affect people very quickly.

12. Grapevine communications are *caused.*

13. Men and women are approximately equally active on the grapevine.

14. Nonverbal communication is significant in interpreting verbal grapevine communication.

15. Informal leaders often serve as message centers for receiving, interpreting, and distributing grapevine information to others.

16. Typical grapevine activity usually is not a sign of organizational sickness or health; that is, grapevine activity is a normal response to group work.

Source: From P. V. Lewis, *Organizational Communication: The Essence of Effective Management,* 3rd ed. (New York: Wiley, 1987), pp. 47–48. Reprinted by permission of the publisher.

creating much noise and distorting their messages. Table 4–5 describes some primary characteristics of the grapevine.

Social gatherings are another informal channel for meeting social needs and reducing communication barriers within the organization through a lighter atmosphere.

Effective Communication for Practicing Leadership

On the day of the 1995 "Million Man March" in Washington, DC., President Clinton urged Americans to take the time to talk—and listen—to people of different races. Corporate executives are admonished to do as much listening as talking. Parents snap up books by the hundreds with such titles as *How to Talk So Your Kids Will Listen and Listen So Your Kids Will Talk.* Women tell men they "just don't get it." The Japanese language has seven words that describe levels of listening. Try to think of any synonyms in English!

Once we look at all the factors involved in communicating just one message to one receiver, the complexity of speaking and understanding appears overwhelming. Looking at the business application of communication, the Tjosvolds describe these traps for leaders and employees: leader arrogance by dominating meetings, interrupting, being unwilling to see others' perspectives; and employee avoidance of controversial topics for fear the boss will blame them and lack of appreciation for the burdens and stresses facing the leader.

IMPLICATIONS FOR PRACTICING LEADERSHIP

Here's a great chance to lead by example. Leaders can take classes or get training to improve their communication skills—and let the others know they're trying to improve. Showing concern for others and listening helps others hear what you're trying to say.

Levine and Crom (1993) assert that listening is the "single most important of all the communication skills. More important than stirring oratory. More important than a powerful voice. More important than the ability to speak multiple languages. More important even than a flair for the written word." (p. 985)

But **active listening** is far from easy. It takes not only sustained concentration on what the other person is saying, but also attention to nonverbal cues such as gestures or other body language. Nonverbal cues convey the message that you are listening and concentrating on what the other person is saying. Active listening can produce huge benefits. People everywhere love to be listened to, to find a receptive audience for their thoughts and concerns. Active listening does much to nourish a relationship and convey the sense that you respect that person. Table 4–6 provides key guidelines for active and effective listening.

Dean Rusk, former secretary of state under President Lyndon Johnson, understood the power of listening. His experiences in negotiating with political leaders across the globe convinced him that listening is "convincing people with your ears."

Within any organization, a number of factors can cause noise and thus contribute to the breakdown of communication. We will highlight several key factors among the wide variety cited by writers and theorists (as identified by Donnelly, Gibson & Ivanecevich in *Fundamentals of Management*):

- Differing frames of reference
- Selective perception
- Semantic problems
- Filtering

TABLE 4–6   Guidelines for Effective Listening

1. Stop talking. It is impossible to listen and talk at the same time.
2. Listen for main ideas.
3. Be sensitive to emotional deaf spots that make your mind wander.
4. Fight off distractions.
5. Take notes.
6. Be patient. Let others tell their stories first.
7. Empathize with other people's points of view.
8. Withhold judgment.
9. React to the message, not the person.
10. Appreciate the emotion behind the speaker's words.
11. Use feedback to check your understanding.
12. Relax and put the sender at ease.
13. Be attentive.
14. Create a positive listening environment.
15. Ask questions.

Source: Phillip L. Hunsaker and Anthony J. Alessandra. *The Art of Managing People.* New York: Simon and Schuster, 1986. Copyright 1986 by Phillip L. Hunsaker and Anthony J. Alessandra. Reprinted by authors' permission.

- Constraints on time
- Communication overload

Differing frames of reference refers to the fact that senders and receivers bring to any communication diverse experiences and expectations, offering the potential for message distortion. What the sender intended to convey may not be interpreted in the desired manner because the receiver is approaching the message from a different perspective.

Selective perception occurs when the receiver attends to a certain portion of a message and ignores the rest. People particularly attend to statements that reconfirm their beliefs and often ignore or distort disconfirming statements.

Poor listening skills may derive from a host of sources and can lead to a great deal of frustration on the part of the sender, who does not feel heard or validated. When people make value judgments, they are selectively attending only to those portions of communication that are important to them. If people have poor source credibility, their message may be distorted or ignored by the receiver because the receiver does not find the senders to be a reliable source of information. Do we always believe what the boss tells us?

Sometimes poor communications can be attributed to semantic problems, a particularly salient problem when the sender and receiver hail from different cultures. Words with double meanings or culturally specific meanings run the risk of being misinterpreted by the receiver. Along the same lines, words can take on special meaning within a group and then be misunderstood by those outside the group because the sender has not clearly communicated its special meaning.

The process of filtering involves manipulating information with the goal of structuring it to be more pleasing to the receiver. Filtering can occur for a number of reasons, the most common being to cover up for a mistake or to try to impress another.

Time pressures can also contribute to distortion, because important words or steps in the communication may be omitted to obtain a desired outcome more quickly.

Finally, communication overload occurs when a person simply has too much information to decode in a reasonable time frame. The recent explosion of the electronic media often results in arriving at one's office to find dozens of messages waiting on the computer! A deluge of information limits our ability to absorb and respond effectively.

Expressing Feelings and Solving Conflicts

People express their feelings in a variety of nonverbal ways: by laughing, yawning, complaining, gritting their teeth. A goal of effective communication is to set a climate in which it is permissible, even expected, for people to express their feelings directly and openly. When people stop suppressing their feelings, others can understand more of what is going on and speculation shrinks. To do this, we must feel safe. We must trust that others will value what we say and try to understand our feelings and reactions from our perspective.

IMPLICATIONS FOR PRACTICING LEADERSHIP

Learning to use "I" statements is important for all group members. Doing so enables the individual to pinpoint personal feelings and avoids blaming others. Practice using I statements and letting others know you appreciate their I statements.

Nonverbal Communication

It is said that a message is conveyed more by nonverbal means than by actual words. When someone smiles all the while saying he is angry, it's common to discount the anger. Yet nonverbal cues can also be ambiguous and open to disparate interpretations. A smiling angry person, for instance, could be squinting, trying to soften the anger by smiling, or expressing contempt. Cultural and gender differences come into play regarding nonverbal cues.

Learning to Express Anger

Few of us, however, are really comfortable expressing strong emotions, especially anger. Women may have a particularly difficult time doing so, because they may have been taught that it is not ladylike to get mad, or that women should never be angry with men, or they may be afraid they will cry from their anger.

Helpful hints:

- Ventilate. Release your strong feelings of anger in other ways when direct expression may not be wise or useful.
- Check interpretations.
- Challenge unrealistic assumptions.

Improving Communications

Just as there are a number of potential impediments to communication, so too are there a number of ways to improve communication. The first step is to create a **supportive communicative climate.** According to Gibb (1965), this involves:

1. Using descriptive, as opposed to evaluative, speech
2. Taking a collaborative approach to problem-solving
3. Communicating with spontaneity, rather than from hidden strategies or agenda
4. Demonstrating empathy—beyond hearing what someone says, but attempting to view the situation from the other's frame of reference
5. Promoting equality across and within levels of an organization
6. Trying to hear all sides of a debate rather than simply sticking to one's own agenda

Another important aid to communication beyond effective listening (discussed earlier in this section) is using **feedback** to increase understanding. Organizations with a highly hierarchical structure or limited opportunities for interaction across levels frequently have communication problems because no feedback is given. People in these cases are falsely assuming that their messages are being heard in the manner intended, when it is likely that just the opposite may be occurring. In other cases, people may not feel free to offer accurate information, so they filter their message to obtain a more positive response.

Leaders must understand the importance of both giving and receiving feedback. Table 4–7 offers guidelines on giving and receiving feedback. Leaders need to model giving effective feedback—that is, feedback that will help others to increase their performance. See Table 4–8 for a comparison of effective and ineffective feedback.

RACHEL CARSON: WRITER, SCIENTIST, CRUSADER

When Rachel Carson journeyed to a summer job at Woods Hole Oceanographic Institute in Cape Cod, it was the first time she had even seen the ocean. The sea had captivated her interest for years, however, even as a young girl on a farm north of

TABLE 4–7   Guides for Giving and Receiving Feedback

Criteria for Giving Feedback

1. Make sure your comments are intended to help the recipient.

2. Speak directly and with feeling, based on trust.

3. Describe what the person is doing and the effect the person is having.

4. Don't be threatening or judgmental.

5. Be specific, not general (use clear and recent examples).

6. Give feedback when the recipient is in a condition of readiness to accept it.

7. Check to ensure the validity of your statements.

8. Include only things the receiver can do something about.

9. Don't overwhelm; make sure your comments aren't more than the person can handle.

Criteria for Receiving Feedback

1. Don't be defensive.

2. Seek specific examples.

3. Be sure you understand (summarize).

4. Share your feelings about the comments.

5. Ask for definitions.

6. Check out underlying assumptions.

7. Be sensitive to sender's nonverbal messages.

8. Ask questions to clarify.

Source: Phillip L. Hunsaker and Anthony J. Alessandra. *The Art of Managing People.* New York: Simon and Schuster, 1986: pp. 202–213. Copyright 1986 by Phillip L. Hunsaker and Anthony J. Alessandra. Reprinted by authors' permission.

TABLE 4–8   Characteristics of Effective and Ineffective Feedback

Effective Feedback is...	Ineffective Feedback is...
• Meant to help	• Meant to disparage
• Clear, specific	• Vague, ambiguous
• Immediate (if possible)	• Slow in coming, not tied to event
• Sensible and appropriate	• Inaccurate, inappropriate

Pittsburgh. She had studied diligently enough to win a scholarship in marine zoology at Johns Hopkins University in Baltimore. She earned her M.S. in 1932.

She was warned repeatedly to pursue some other field: women did not become scientists in the first half of the twentieth century. And if they insisted on getting their degrees, there would be no jobs for them. Nevertheless, Carson persisted, fueled in part by her overwhelming passion for the natural world and by her mother's support. She later recounted how much it meant to her when FDR appointed the first woman in the history of the United States to a cabinet position. (Frances Perkins became FDR's secretary of labor.) To top it off, Eleanor Roosevelt was becoming a national figure.

She found a job that combined her loves of language and science through writing scripts for the weekly radio show "Romance Under the Waters." The sea became her touchstone as she began to explain in graceful, nontechnical terms much of what scientists knew about the ocean and its life.

Carson went on to write several books about the natural world, including *The Sea Around Us, Under the Sea Wind,* and *The Edge of the Sea.* In between caring for her mother and raising children of relatives who had died, she wrote a moving book, *A Sense of Wonder,* to help young people appreciate the natural world.

A much-awarded and highly praised writer, she retired to her cottage off the coast of Maine. She could easily have lived a contented life producing more of the same type of writings. However, she took a gamble and began to research not the beauties of nature, but the spoilers of nature. Her landmark 1962 book, *Silent Spring,* charged that rampant use of pesticides was devastating the environment, killing birds and other animals and potentially affecting humans as well. Further, she charged that government scientists had known of the damage from the chemicals but had been prevented from speaking out.

Ironically, shortly before the book was published, she was diagnosed with breast cancer. At the time scientists were just beginning to uncover links between environmental influences and diseases such as cancer.

It's hard to appreciate the commotion the publication of *Silent Spring* unleashed. Many scientific associations, including the American Medical Association, attacked the book, and much of the media went after Carson personally. *Time* magazine called the book "an emotional and inaccurate outburst." The chemical industry spent large sums of money ridiculing her arguments in print. Some suggested she was a communist.

Upset at the unfairness of these attacks, the normally shy woman agreed to a nationally televised interview with Eric Sevareid on CBS April 3, 1963. Her soft-spoken, articulate remarks convinced millions of viewers and swung public opinion to her side. Legislation passed the next year that tightened requirements for chemical companies.

More significantly, however, Rachel Carson had helped people understand the ramifications of tampering with the environment. As her comments on television showed, she was able to convey the bigger picture:

> We still talk in terms of conquest. We still haven't become mature enough to think of ourselves as only a tiny part of a vast and incredible universe. Man's attitude toward na-

ture is today critically important simply because we have now acquired a fateful power to alter and destroy nature. But man is a part of nature, and his war against nature is inevitably a war against himself.

She won many honors and awards for her efforts. Upon receiving the Audubon Medal (the first woman to be so honored), she asserted that "Conservation is a cause that has no end. There is no point at which we will say 'our work is finished.'"

Ms. Carson succumbed to cancer just over one year after her remarkable television appearance. She had become well-known and greatly admired for her courage and dedication. She acknowledged her real reward, however, in this passage written shortly before her death: "It is good to know that I shall live on even in the minds of many who do not know me and largely through association with things that are beautiful and lovely."

MICHAEL DORRIS: NATIVE AMERICAN WRITER AND ACTIVIST

Michael Dorris has drawn from his life as a Native American, a professor of anthropology and Native American studies at Dartmouth, and father to produce a distinctive array of fiction and nonfiction. He and his wife, the noted author Louise Erdrich, have collaborated on several novels that illuminate the Native American experience.

Perhaps Dorris's major contribution—the arena in which he has practiced a great deal of leadership—is in acquainting the world with the dangers of Fetal Alcohol Syndrome. FAS is the set of physical, psychological, and emotional problems resulting from even light or moderate drinking during pregnancy. FAS, as he showed in *The Broken Cord,* has had a particularly devastating effect on many Native American children and their families.

The mix of scientific research on the syndrome and personal experience about his own family's struggles with FAS—his oldest child, Adam, was finally diagnosed with the condition after Dorris persisted in investigating the bewildering array of behavior and physiological problems—made the book a bestseller and influenced public attitudes about the problem. He has spoken across the country on the topic and consulted on a prize-winning television adaptation of the work.

The upshot of his leadership on the issue was the 1990 federal law requiring that all bottles of wine or liquor sold in the United States carry this warning: "According to the surgeon general, women should not drink alcoholic beverages during pregnancy because of the risk of birth defects."

Using part of the advance money for *The Crown of Columbus*, Dorris and Erdrich established a fund for FAS research.

In another, lesser known writing project, Dorris brought attention to the personal consequences of hunger. After a trip to Zimbabwe in 1992 as a board member of the Save the Children Foundation, he published a moving booklet titled *Rooms in the House of Stone*.

BARBARA JORDAN: HER WORDS WORE BOOTS*

My first thought upon hearing of Barbara Jordan's death was, "She was too young."

She was only 59 when she died. Yet she long ago became one of our society's elders, a wise woman for our national village, a deeply rooted moral touchstone for an increasingly rootless nation.

She had always been wise beyond her years. She was only 29 when she became the first black woman elected to the Texas Senate, elevating the collective IQ of that chamber by several hundred points simply by showing up.

She was only 37 when, on the House Judiciary Committee, her eloquence lifted the squalid mess of Watergate out of the shadows of petty partisan politics and into the sunlight cast by our Constitution. As the measured tones of this stolid young black woman pealed across this nation, the oh-so-powerful white men of Watergate began to shrink into a foul-mouthed smallness totally unworthy of the offices they held. As she said then, Barbara Jordan was not willing to be an idle spectator of our nation's government. She knew to her bones that she was the government, she and the rest of us—We the People. She was that truly rare thing: a thinking patriot.

Why did she touch us so? I think it was because she always connected her prose to this passion, and thereby exalted both. Her words always wore boots, treading powerfully into our hearts and minds.

Blacks and women especially were enlarged and empowered by her words and example, but her wisdom and humor transcended race and gender. No one ever mistook Barbara Jordan for some mere token. She was wholly and completely herself. Moreover, she did not suffer fools gladly. I often saw her silence buffoons with a look—a skill that came in handy in the Texas Senate.

When her illness struck her in the late '70s, we were bereft, mourning what might have been—perhaps even the first female and first African-American president.

But to mourn then was to underestimate Barbara Jordan. She had just come home, she hadn't given up. As she assumed the mantle of elder stateswoman and scholar, her influence continued to be felt in Texas and in Washington. Powerful men and women flew into Austin to sit at her feet, and she gave them all the same thing: unsparing honesty.

Her vast intellect was matched by her courage and integrity and, often, tempered by her wit. Even as her illness attacked her body, that magnificent voice went on. When he was about four years old, my nephew Nicholas heard her on the radio and asked me, "Is that God?'"

I replied, "No, but it should be."

I think the idea of God as a black woman would have tickled Barbara Jordan. Now I find myself imagining all the great conversations going on up there on heaven's front porch—Barbara and God, voices rolling like thunder, laughter sparkling like rain.

We're gonna miss her for a long, long time.

°Written by Katie Sherrod, 1996.

SUMMARY

This is the first of three chapters that trace the contributions to leadership theory of various disciplines. We focus on psychology and communication in chapter 4. Because psychological approaches to motivation are critical to the study of leadership, the chapter introduces a variety of motivational models, including Maslow's Hierarchy of Needs, the ERG theory, equity theory, and expectancy theory. Also addressed are attitudes, personality differences, perception, and attribution. The importance of seeing the leader as a learner is stressed.

The section on communication begins with a review of basic communication theory. Implications of effective communication for practicing leadership are discussed in terms of listening, expressing feelings, and solving conflicts.

KEY TERMS

PSYCHOLOGY SECTION

motivation	Theory X and Theory Y	social perceptions
Hierarchy of Needs	Trichotomy of Needs	stereotyping
ERG theory	equity theory	selective perception
frustration regression hypothesis	classical conditioning	perceptual defense
Dual Factor theory	operant conditioning	attribution
hygiene factors	social learning theory	
motivational factors	attitude	

COMMUNICATION SECTION

transactional communication	downward communication
channels	grapevine
filters	active listening
interference	supportive communicative climate
noise	feedback
upward communication	lateral communication

FOR DISCUSSION AND REVIEW

1. What are some of the traditional assumptions about the characteristics of great leaders? Have these assumptions been borne out over time? What assumptions do you make when you hear the term *leader*?

2. What does Alderfer consider to be the primary human needs?

3. What are some of the distinctions between Theory X and Theory Y leaders? Do you know anyone who meets the criteria for either of these styles?

4. What is the primary difference between personalized and socialized power drives?

5. Compare and contrast Bandura's social learning theory with Skinner's operant conditioning and Pavlov's classical conditioning.

6. What do you consider to be the leader's role in motivation?

7. What five personality traits are recognized as major effectors of task performance? For each of these traits, give an example of a leader you know who exemplifies that characteristic.

8. What are some of the elements that influence our perceptions of people? What are some common misperceptions made about people in the workplace? How about in society at large?

9. What is interference? Give some examples of potential sources of interference.

10. What cultural differences in communication styles have you observed?

11. What steps might an organization take to enhance upward communication? Downward communication? Lateral communication?

12. What are some methods of creating a supportive communicative climate?

CRITICAL INCIDENTS

You have recently been promoted to the position of plant manager at Leupen's Textiles, Inc. While you are excited about this promotion, you are somewhat wary of the task before you, as morale is reportedly very low at your new plant. Production has dropped off over the past several months, necessitating fairly significant layoffs. There have also been many reports of heated arguments between plant employees. Your directive from upper management is to boost morale and productivity. What questions might you ask employees at this plant upon arrival, and what types of interventions might prove useful in boosting employee motivation?

You are a mid-level manager at Peter's Pencils, Inc. You have just received an e-mail message from your boss. She is very upset because she has just received the results of an employee satisfaction questionnaire and the employees have reported a high level of dissatisfaction with communication. She is particularly irritated because she has scheduled several open forums over the past few months for employees to air their complaints and no one has attended. Given a chance to complain in written form, however, the employees' complaints are overwhelming. She has charged you with getting to the bottom of this situation and devising a system where communication is enhanced. What principles might you follow in developing an enhanced degree of communication in your department?

EXERCISES FOR CHAPTER 4

Exercise 4.1   Evaluating Reinforcement Theories

Directions: Please evaluate the following theories in terms of their usefulness to you as an aspiring leader. Rate each theory on a scale of 1 (low) to 10 (high) by writing the appropriate number next to each of the questions shown below:

QUESTIONS	CLASSICAL AND OPERANT CONDITIONING 12345678910	SOCIAL LEARNING THEORY 12345678910	PORTER–LAWLER MODEL 12345678910
1. Easy to understand.			
2. Easy to think of real-life applications.			
3. Generally helpful in understanding how to motivate people.			
4. Information that I might actually use in attempting to influence.			
5. I have experienced others' attempts to influence my own behavior in this way.			
6. These attempts by others were successful in influencing your behavior.			
7. Attempts to deal with the demographic differences among people (gender, ethnicity, age, etc.)			
8. Attempts to deal with the individual differences among people (traits, skills, abilities, etc.)			
9. Generally useful as a model to influence behavior in the twenty-first century.			

The Disciplinary Roots of Leadership: Part II

**The Leadership Journey:
A map of the terrain
Chapter 5**

Words/names to recognize

Scientific mgt.	Deming	Yukl	
Mgt. science	Ishikawa	Empowerment	Disciplinary Roots
Systems approach	Juran	Ethics	of Leadership
Contingency theory	French/Raven		You are here

Industrial Hwy.

Transitional Dr.

Hero's Blvd.

President's Path

Pre-Industrial Rd.

Quality Circle

Covey Circle

Rost Rd.

Post-Industrial Hwy.

MANAGEMENT

Peter Drucker (1974) wrote:

> The emergence of management in this century may have been a pivotal event in history. It signaled a major transformation of society into a pluralistic society of institutions, of which managements are the effective organs. Management, after more than a century of development as a practice and as a discipline, burst into public consciousness in the management boom that began after World War II and lasted through the 1960s. (p. 2)
>
> [Every developed society,] has become a society of institutions. . . . Every major task, whether economic performance or health care, education or the protection of the environment, the pursuit of new knowledge or defense is today being entrusted to big organizations designed for perpetuity and managed by their own management. On the performance of those institutions, the performance of modern society—if not the survival of each individual—increasingly depends.

Although the effects of management were first felt more than two hundred years ago during the Industrial Revolution as factories developed, it is only in this century that we have begun to systematically study its impact. **Management** has been defined as the coordination of human, material, technological and financial resources needed for the organization to reach its goals (Hess and Siciliano, 1996, p. 7). Or, to return to Drucker (1954, p. 17), management is "a multipurpose organ that manages a business *and* manages managers *and* manages workers and work." Figure 5–1 illustrates the way in which the classical approach to management has served as a foundation for the development of leadership.

With such far-reaching definitions, just what is it that managers do? It is commonly agreed that five functions make up a manager's job: planning, controlling, organizing, staffing, and leading. For examples of what each of these functions entails, see Figure 5–2. The addition of continuous improvement as a sixth function of management is a relatively new phenomenon.

Although these charts seem fairly straightforward, defining management becomes much more difficult because none of the functions is really discrete; they are all interconnected. Further, not every manager is involved in each of the functions. One way to distinguish between management functions is to designate different levels of managers. Top-level managers, for instance—the chief executive officers, presidents, and senior vice presidents—spend most of their time in the two functions of planning and organizing. They are overseeing the "big picture."

First-line, or front-line, managers, on the other hand, are typically involved in the "nitty gritty" of daily operations. These are the foremen, crew chiefs, and supervisors. Thus, first-line managers tend to spend much of their time in leading and controlling.

Leadership versus Management

Perusing Figure 5–2 prompts a very basic question for this text—indeed, for any participant of a class in leadership. Is leadership merely a subset of management? Just as we see with other disciplines—psychology, communications, political science, and

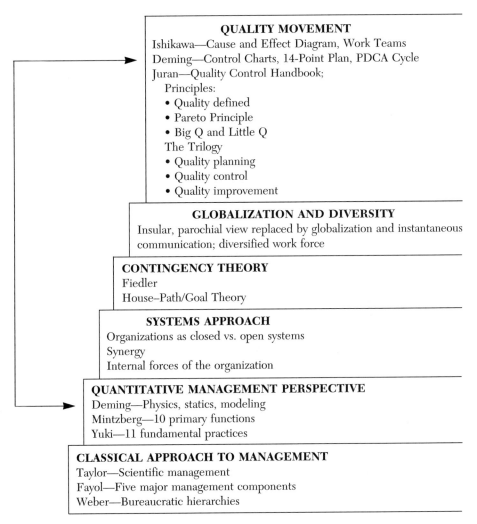

Figure 5–1   Evolution of Leadership from Management

military science—some management proponents might argue that, yes, leadership is one facet of management. The military, for example, asserts that leadership is a totally definable skill, a science that can be learned. Their training manuals outline the behaviors that typify leadership, so that to lead one must simply acquire those skills and behaviors.

We disagree. Along with other leadership theorists, we maintain that leadership is a piece of the pie, a part of management, but that there is a good bit of leadership that cannot be considered a subset of management. Leadership and management share some characteristics, but each is also separate and distinct. For a useful depiction of the distinctions between leadership and management, see Tables 5–1 and 5–2.

Figure 5–2 Traditional Functions of Management (including Leadership)

These tables do not define leadership and management, as neither is synonymous with nor a subject of the other. They describe leadership as both a process and a property (Jago, 1992). The process of practicing leadership is integral to this text, because it envisions leadership as a noncoercive influence that shapes an organization's culture and people and motivates participants toward a common goal. The property is the characteristic attributed to the people who are perceived as leaders (Yukl, 1995).

A person, then, may be skilled as a leader or manager or both—or neither. The skilled leader definitely needs to understand the principles of management. Which brings us to the question: What is doing management all about?

Mintzberg (1979) lists the ten primary roles of a manager (Table 5–3).

In the same way, Yukl (1990) includes eleven fundamental management practices in his model (see Table 5–4).

The Evolution of Leadership from Scientific Management

Most management historians see leadership theory evolving from classical management work in the 1890s as defining scientific management. Leadership theory developed in part from the classical approaches to management, specifically the work of Taylor, Fayol, and Weber.

In the 1890s, **Frederick Taylor,** the father of scientific management, felt that workers performed below their true abilities and that what they needed was proper direction and support. He drew on his engineering background to find the most efficient way to perform specific tasks. Applying his scientific management principles to the task of loading slab steel onto railroad cars, he meticulously analyzed each component of the job, then trained a hand-picked man to follow his directions precisely for each part of the task. Further, Taylor agreed to pay this man on a per-piece

TABLE 5–1   Distinctions Between Management and Leadership

Activity	Management	Leadership
Creating an agenda	**Planning and budgeting.** Establishing detailed steps and timetables for achieving needed results: allocating the resources necessary to make those needed results happen.	**Establishing direction.** Developing a vision of the future, often the distant future, and strategies for producing the changes needed to achieve that vision.
Developing a human network for achieving the agenda	**Organizing and staffing.** Establishing some structure for accomplishing plan requirements, staffing that structure with individuals, delegating responsibility and authority for carrying out the plan, providing policies and procedures to help guide people, and creating methods or systems to monitor implementation.	**Aligning people.** Communicating the direction by words and deeds to all those whose cooperation may be needed to influence the creation of teams and coalitions that understand the vision and strategies and accept their validity.
Executing plans	**Controlling and problem solving.** Monitoring results vs. plan in some detail, identifying deviations, and then planning and organizing to solve these problems.	**Motivating and inspiring.** Energizing people to overcome major political, bureaucratic, and resource barriers to change by satisfying very basic, but often unfulfilled, human needs.
Outcomes	Produce a degree of predictability and order and has the potential to consistently produce key results expected by various stakeholders (e.g., for customers, always being on time for stockholders, being on budget).	Produces change, often to a dramatic degree and has the potential to produce extremely useful change (e.g., new products that customers want, new approaches to labor relations that help make a firm more competitive).

Source: Reprinted with permission. by The Free Press, a Division of Simon & Schuster Inc. from *A Force for Change: How Leadership Differs from Management* by John P. Kotter. Copyright © 1996 by John P. Kotter, Inc.

basis, a significant departure from standard practices at the time and one he predicted would encourage greater productivity. As a final step, Taylor arranged for the worker to focus only on the specific task of loading the steel, and Taylor, as the manager, oversaw related aspects, such as when and how the railroad car would be moved. The productivity gains were remarkable: productivity for this worker increased nearly fourfold. Taylor's experiment won over many who had been skeptical about such scientific approaches to work.

Specifically, Taylor called for:

1. A "science" for every job, including standardized work flow and work conditions

2. Carefully selected workers with the right ability to do each job

3. Careful training with proper incentives

4. Clear planning by managers

TABLE 5–2   **Distinctions Between Managers and Leaders**

Personality Dimension	Manager	Leader
Attitudes toward goals	Has an impersonal, passive, functional attitude; believes goals arise out of necessity and reality	Has a personal and active attitude; believes goals arise from desire and imagination
Conceptions of work	Views work as an enabling process that combines people, ideas, and things; seeks moderate risk through coordination and balance	Looks for fresh approaches to old problems; seeks high-risk positions, especially with high payoffs
Relationships with others	Avoids solitary work activity, preferring to work with others; avoids close, intense relationships; avoids conflict	Is comfortable in solitary work activity; encourages close, intense working relationships; is not conflict averse
Sense of self	Is once born; makes a straight-forward life adjustment; accepts life as it is	Is twice born; engages in a struggle for a sense of order in life; questions life

In 1916, **Henri Fayol** helped to further delineate the principles of management by setting forth the five major management elements: planning, organizing, commanding, coordinating, and controlling. In the 1920s, sociologist **Max Weber** brought to the study of management the concept of bureaucracy, including a clear division of labor, a hierarchy of authority, formal rules and procedures, impersonality, and merit-based evaluations. Weber's notions of bureaucracy had none of the negative connotations of today.

After World War I, when there was a tremendous increase in the demand for consumer goods, the **Hawthorne effect** was conceptualized. Simply put, as Ellen Mayo (1953) explained, if management increased its attention to workers, productivity also increased. From these findings the human relations movement evolved (discussed in chapter 4), drawing on Maslow's hierarchy of human needs and McGregor's Theory X and Theory Y. Leadership theory continued to develop from these early works.

Beginning in the 1940s, the **quantitative management** perspectives (management science) emerged. This approach centers on applying mathematical models and processes to decision-making situations. **Operations management** focuses directly on applying management science to organizations. All leaders depend on information and management science as the basis for much of the information used by decision makers. One of the century's leading theorists on management, W. Edwards Deming, began his career as a physics instructor and then moved on to statistics. From this base, he molded the highly influential principles of quality. (Deming and the quality movement are discussed later in this chapter.)

Management information science, commonly referred to within organizations as

TABLE 5–3   Mintzberg's Roles

Role	Description
Figurehead	The manager, acting as a symbol or representative of the organization, performs diverse ceremonial duties. By attending Chamber of Commerce meetings, heading the local United Way drive, or representing the president of the firm at an awards banquet, a manager performs the figurehead role.
Leader	The manager, interacting with subordinates, motivates and develops them. The supervisor who conducts quarterly performance interviews or selects training opportunities for his or her subordinates performs the role of leader. This role emphasizes the socioemotional and people-oriented side of leadership and deemphasizes task activities, which are more often incorporated into the decisional roles.
Liaison	The manager establishes a network of contacts to gather information for the organization. Belonging to professional associations or meeting over lunch with peers in other organizations helps the manager perform the liaison role.
Monitor	The manager gathers information from the environment inside and outside the organization. He or she may attend meetings with subordinates, scan company publications, or participate in company-wide committees as a way of performing this role.
Disseminator	The manager transmits both factual and value information to subordinates. Managers may conduct staff meetings, send memorandums to their staff, or meet informally with them on a one-to-one basis to discuss current and future projects.
Spokesperson	The manager gives information to people outside the organization about its performance and policies. He or she oversees preparation of the annual report, prepares advertising copy, or speaks at community and professional meetings.
Entrepreneur	The manager designs and initiates change in the organization. The supervisor who redesigns the jobs of subordinates, introduces flexible working hours, or brings new technology to the job performs this role.
Disturbance handler	The manager deals with problems that arise when organizational operations break down. A person who finds a new supplier on short notice for an out-of-stock part, who replaces unexpectedly absent employees, or who deals with machine breakdowns performs this role.
Resource allocator	The manager controls the allocation of people, money, materials, and time by scheduling his or her own time, programming subordinates' work effort, and authorizing all significant decisions. Preparation of the budget is a major aspect of this role.
Negotiator	The manager participates in negotiation activities. A manager who hires a new employee may negotiate work assignments or compensation with that person.

Source: These roles are drawn from H. Mintzberg, *The Nature of Managerial Work* (Englewood Cliffs, N.J.: Prentice-Hall, 1979).

TABLE 5–4 Definitions of the Eleven Managerial Practices

INFORMING: disseminating relevant information about decisions, plans, and activities to people who need it to do their work, answering requests for technical information, and telling people about the organizational unit to promote its reputation.

CONSULTING AND DELEGATING: checking with people before making changes that affect them, encouraging suggestions for improvement, inviting participation in decision making, incorporating the ideas and suggestions of others in decisions, and allowing others to have substantial responsibility and discretion in carrying out work activities and making decisions.

PLANNING AND ORGANIZING: determining long-term objectives and strategies for adapting to environmental change, determining how to use personnel and allocate resources to accomplish objectives, determining how to improve the efficiency of operations, and determining how to achieve coordination with other parts of the organization.

PROBLEM SOLVING AND CRISIS MANAGEMENT: identifying work-related problems, analyzing problems in a timely but systematic manner to identify causes and find solutions, and acting decisively to implement solutions and resolve important problems or crises.

CLARIFYING ROLES AND OBJECTIVES: assigning tasks, providing direction in how to do the work, and communicating a clear understanding of job responsibilities, task objectives, deadlines, and performance expectations.

MONITORING OPERATIONS AND ENVIRONMENT: gathering information about work activities, checking on the progress and quality of the work, evaluating the performance of individuals and the organizational unit, and scanning the environment to detect threats and opportunities.

MOTIVATING: using influence techniques that appeal to emotion, values, or logic to generate enthusiasm for the work, commitment to task objectives, and compliance with requests for cooperation, assistance, support, or resources; also, setting an example of proper behavior.

RECOGNIZING AND REWARDING: providing praise, recognition, and rewards for effective performance, significant achievements, and special contributions.

SUPPORTING AND MENTORING: acting friendly and considerate, being patient and helpful, showing sympathy and support, and doing things to facilitate someone's skill development and career advancement.

MANAGING CONFLICT AND TEAM BUILDING: encouraging and facilitating the constructive resolution of conflict, and encouraging cooperation, teamwork, and identification with the organizational unit.

NETWORKING: socializing informally, developing contacts with people who are a source of information and support, and maintaining contacts through periodic interaction, including visits, telephone calls, correspondence, and attendance at meetings and social events.

MIS, is a fairly recent subset of the management science perspective. In MIS, problems are examined and solved via quantifiable analysis.

Since the 1960s, we have seen other developments in management that have directly affected leadership. For instance, leadership scholars have examined management skills at different levels with an understanding of the impact of technical, conceptual, interpersonal, and diagnostic skills on top managers, middle managers, and

	Management skills—different skills are needed at different levels			
	Conceptual	Technical	Diagnostic	Interpersonal
Top management	XXXXXXXXX	XXX	XXXXXXXXX	XXX
Middle management	XXXXXX	XXXXXX	XXXXXX	XXXXXX
Front-line management	XXX	XXXXXXXXX	XXX	XXXXXXXXX

Figure 5–3   Management Skills—Different Skills are Needed at Different Levels

first-line managers, as shown in Figure 5–3. The discussion has yielded useful information for both leaders and managers.

Similarly, the debate over whether management (and leadership) is a science or an art has also influenced the dialogue. Those who argue that leadership is a science believe that the issue can be approached in a logical, rational, objective manner. They stress the use of management science and "hard" data. Others, however, who feel that intuition, experience, and instinct are crucial, rely heavily on interpersonal and conceptual skills.

Contemporary Management Issues

Among the more contemporary management issues, the *systems approach* to organizations has had significant effects on leadership theory. This approach depicts a system as a set of interrelated parts that work together as a whole to achieve goals. In this view, organizations were originally considered **closed systems;** that is, they were not affected by outside events or situations. In reality, all organizations are **open systems.** They must deal with the environment to survive.

Clearly, then, individuals can't lead unless they have a thorough understanding of the organization as an open system, along with an appreciation of the make-up of the external and internal forces impinging on it. From the systems theorists came the word *synergy,* which describes the product of separate parts working together, making something more than merely the total of the separate parts by themselves.

The systems approach also suggests that managers consider the organization's internal forces, such as the subgroups and the effects of these subgroups on the entire organization. (For example, see chapter 4 for a discussion of the grapevine.)

Although classical management theory states that there is only one best way to resolve an issue, today there is widespread agreement with the **contingency theory,** which suggests that appropriate behavior in a given situation depends on a wide variety of variables and that each situation is different. What might work in one company with one set of issues, employees, and customers might not work in a different company with different issues, employees, and customers. See Figure 5–4.

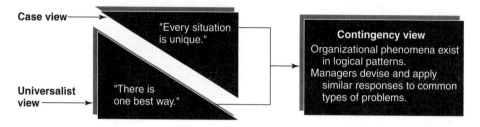

Figure 5–4   The Contingency View of Management

Source: Figures from *Management,* Third Edition, by Richard L. Draft; Copyright© 1994 by the Dryden Press. Reprinted with permission.

Although it is impossible to address the impact of globalization on management and leadership theory in a few short paragraphs, it's indisputable that the impact of markets across the world on U.S. business has meant a significant change in perspectives. Organizations are being affected by the increasingly broad sweep of day-to-day life. How can it not be a sea change when we can access electronically the latest figures on the Hong Kong stock market and in the next minute communicate via the Internet with a consultant in Eastern Europe? Never again can business ignore global implications for their organizations, as the U.S. auto makers learned to their peril in the 1980s.

Management has formed a key basis for leadership theory. Both classical and contemporary issues have provided vital data and insights for leaders and followers.

LEADERSHIP

BY JOHN E. PEPPER

Leadership is an intriguing subject for me, and I'm happy to offer my observations about its development. First, a definition. Leadership to me is the particular process of guiding, directing, and motivating an organization to outstanding achievement in the organization's fundamental purposes.

Leading, then, involves articulating the appropriate vision, helping to develop what I call "stretching" objectives, making the right strategic choices to achieve the objectives; and implementing effective deployment plans to ensure that the resources and other necessary means are available to reach those objectives.

Leaders must also set the standards that guide the growth of the organization's culture and its results. Further, leaders must communicate with people so as to inspire them to exceed their previous achievements.

Clearly, the kind of leadership I'm describing pertains to all manner of activities, including a football team, an industry, a city, a nation, a household.

In my experience, I've found that certain qualities characterize the most effective leaders. I've identified three major benchmarks.

A Compelling Vision

Every effective leader I've known has possessed a personally felt vision and goals. Deep commitments that they are not only willing, but anxious to share with others.

There's almost a spiritual dimension to the conviction these leaders have about the purpose of the organization for which they are responsible. Think about the great football coaches—Lou Holtz, George Allen. They both had unwavering commitments to their teams' excellence.

Simply put, if you don't believe in something passionately, you cannot be an effective leader. Yet it goes well beyond the passionate belief, to a concern for achieving the organization's basic purpose—its highest values—at the highest possible level. And then constantly improving that performance.

At P&G, this means serving the consumer, winning in the market place, and achieving both financial and share leadership. It also means building a place of employment that attracts the best people around and helps them fulfill their ambitions. This aspect of leadership focuses on one's belief in innovation, growth, continuing improvement, and contribution to the company.

The most effective leaders at P&G, then, are those who believe deeply in the aforementioned values and who continually define what they mean, as well as how best to achieve them. Of course, these central values are shared by others at the company.

The question becomes, how does one develop this compelling vision? Let me address that on a personal level. I've worked at defining my personal goals as well as those of my department/subsidiary, and as the years have gone by, the company.

I have found a personal mission and priority statement very helpful in defining my goals long before they became so trendy. More than twenty-five years ago, I started what has become a personal tradition. I write down on a piece of paper what I want to do and what I want to contribute; where I need to improve; and what lessons I've learned. For these twenty-five years I've pulled out that piece of paper every six months or so.

It's been more than just a reminder to me. It has helped me build a deeper commitment to certain purposes and values and priorities, including superior products for the consumer, innovation, taking the offensive, and respect for the individual.

Personal commitment to a mission is vital, and it simply can't be manufactured. No matter what area you pursue, the capacity to be completely dedicated to a career or mission or strategy or tactic is all-important to its success. For the capacity to be totally dedicated is the foundation of a compelling vision, one that can be shared by others.

The kind of true leadership that involves taking risks and putting oneself forward as an example requires that the individual have deep convictions about a set of principles or a project that needs to be done.

The Ability to Inspire

Once the vision is in place, a leader must then have the capacity to inspire others in its pursuit—not blindly or unquestioningly, but with enough fervor to achieve the goals.

In my experiences, I've found leaders with different characteristics that persuade others to pursue the vision. Part of this infectious nature of leadership is due to the importance of the mission itself. Yet part also comes from a burning desire within the most effective leaders for action—to win—to contribute—to serve.

This brings us to the question of appetite. The appetite for pushing oneself to be the best we can be and to help others be the best they can be. This drive springs from different sources within us, and from a mixture of sources. Many people's drive is sparked by a deep commitment to serving others.

All of us, I believe, are pushed by the drive to win, to be our best selves. To keep improving.

For me, the three greatest drivers in my work and life have been to serve, to be the best I can be, and to win.

Winning is something we all understand. In our highly competitive business, people won't succeed if they aren't winning against the competition. Competition provides a great benchmark, and, frankly, it spurs the adrenaline. Winning is fun.

Service is another great motivator—service to consumers, shareholders, our communities, and employees. Better service than before, better service than our competitors, better service in the absolute. That points to the quality of our products, and in having major preferences in consumer acceptance versus competition. It comes down to the value of our products.

Going into a country in Eastern Europe where we've never sold before, providing products of a quality consumers have never seen before—that's service. That's rewarding.

And it's service to employees, employees who stake their lives with the company, to offer them the training and the environment where they can grow to their fullest. In Eastern Europe, China, and Russia, young men and women can contribute in ways they've never before imagined.

It's service, too, to the communities where we work. We're involved in education and in other fields where the leadership of P&G can help. In addition, we serve the environment directly through our products and our processes.

That drive to be all you can be keeps you learning and growing. Each of the strongest leaders I've known would describe these drivers—the ones that enable them to inspire others in their vision—somewhat differently. Yet in all cases the drives are honestly felt and experienced. And ones we must nourish.

Initiative, Focus on Results, Courage, and Tenacity

The most effective leaders I've known take the initiative to make the biggest personal difference, the most significant personal contribution they can. Whatever action they're focused on, they're fully engaged in trying to make things better than they are at present. Real leaders don't wait for permission. And their willingness to jump into the situation makes work fun for them, and for those around them. Their initiative also produces results that are recognized and rewarded.

These men and women have a laser-like focus on results. Their inner drive propels them to make things happen and get things done, producing a better tomorrow than today. They display an enormous amount of energy and capacity.

True leaders have the kind of personal courage that fuels their pursuit of their convictions, even when this means persisting against significant opposition. They're unafraid to say and do what may be unpopular. To do what they're convinced is right. These leaders are transparent.

They are forceful advocates for what they believe in, even—indeed, especially—when that goes against the grain.

Most of the biggest decisions I've been involved in have been controversial. The decisions have come about because someone had the courage to persist with a point of view.

Many of P&G's largest brands today were subjects of controversy when they began. Take Bounce Dryer-Added Fabric Softener. There were many who wondered whether putting a sheet in a dryer would appeal to consumers. In fact, the patent was turned down by other companies and almost by P&G until someone with a strong conviction that this could be made into a high-performing, high-value product persuaded the company to proceed. And now Bounce is one of our most successful brands, highly accepted by consumers and providing excellent returns to Procter & Gamble.

In the same way, these leaders have the courage to take command, to be decisive, to ask for action. After they've reviewed all the options and the discussions and debates have run their course, these leaders reach the point where they must step out and exercise their own responsibility.

One example we encountered in the 1980s was the need to bring a regional focus to our operations in Europe. Through much of our history, we had operated almost as separate fiefdoms—each country on its own. That was fine in some respects, but it became clear that it was necessary to focus our research and development efforts against a narrower group of projects if we were to achieve true performance and value breakthroughs for the consumer. We also had to rationalize our production sourcing in Europe so that we could achieve greater reliability and lower costs for consumers. That required a major change in mindset in the way we operated. It was very controversial. Ultimately, as the head of European operations, I needed to make the decision that this was the right way to go in the future.

In order to carry out this responsibility for decision making, it is essential to deal with problems head-on and not avoid them. Overcome difficult obstacles rather than put them off. With that conviction, I've always aimed to tackle the toughest problems first.

Persistence

Finally, my great leaders don't give up. They push on and on. It reminds me of my favorite story about Winston Churchill. After he retired from public office, he was asked to address the students and faculty at his grammar school. As you can imagine, the headmaster was very excited and told the students to prepare to hear one of the greatest talks they'd ever hear in their lifetimes.

The day arrived and Winston Churchill walked out on the stage with a small piece of paper, on which was written a few notes. He peered down at the audience, over his glasses, and said:

"Never, never, never, never give up."

And with that, he turned around and went back to his seat. Initially, the audience was surprised and let down. They'd expected so much more. But in time, they came to view it as the most important talk they could have heard. It summarized a lifetime of experience in just six words.

I've never forgotten this. I never will.

SAM WALTON: THE WORLD'S BIGGEST SMALL-TOWN MERCHANT

A quintessential American business leader, Sam Walton demonstrated his fascination with retail sales early in life. In a *Time* magazine article (June 15, 1992), Walton recalled an early experience working at JC Penney when John Cash Penney visited the store: "I still remember him showing me how to tie and package merchandise, how to wrap it with very little twine and very little paper but still make it look nice."

The drive to do things inexpensively, yet with an eye to its customer appeal, framed Walton's career. The hallmark of Wal-Mart—their locations in small towns throughout America—was, he explained, more of an outcome of his wife's aversion to big cities.

Yet Walton was clever enough to understand the wisdom of maintaining that small-town base; indeed, the small-town flavor continues throughout the organization, including in the famous cheers and hog calls that Walton himself would lead on his visits to stores.

In typically straightforward fashion, Walton summarized "our key strategy, which was simply to put good-sized discount stores into little one-horse towns, which everybody else was ignoring."

His success is legendary, and he attributed a major part of it to the role of the employees, whom he called associates. He believed "there is absolutely no limit to what plain old working people can accomplish if they're given the opportunity and the encouragement and the incentive to do their best."

"Wal-Mart is a spectacular example of what happens when almost 400,000 people come together with a feeling of partnership. The decision to give the associates more equitable treatment in the company, through our profit-sharing and other incentive plans, was without a doubt the single smartest move we ever made at Wal-Mart. We're always encouraging them to push their good ideas up through the system."

He stressed the importance of remembering the company's roots in small-town America. "The bigger Wal-Mart gets," he wrote, "the more essential it is that we think like small town merchants. Because that's exactly how we have become a huge corporation—by not acting like one."

THE QUALITY MOVEMENT

In recent years several proponents of a more comprehensive approach to ensuring quality in products and services have emerged. The teachings of these quality gurus often contrast starkly with the prevailing beliefs of managers. In the 1950s, as Japanese business tried to rebuild after World War II, these quality teachers were well received, but they were shunned in the United States until the 1980s, when Japanese companies exerted tremendous pressure on American business. Apparently, necessity is also the mother of radically new approaches to leadership, as industrial leaders in both countries only adopted the new approaches when they were desperate.

Who were these quality proponents, and what was so different and challenging about their approach? Numerous quality leaders offer overlapping and sometimes contradicting ideas about leading organizations for quality results. We will focus on three of the early leaders whose path-breaking efforts form much of the currently accepted body of knowledge called **Total Quality Management** (TQM): Kaoru Ishikawa, W. Edwards Deming, and Joseph Juran.

Kaoru Ishikawa

The son of Ichiro Ishikawa, one of the most prominent engineers in Japan in the early part of the twentieth century, Kaoru Ishikawa, born in 1915, served first as an engineer and factory manager and then had a long, distinguished career as engineering professor at Tokyo University. Given his engineering background, Ishikawa's technical developments are easy to understand and accept. More amazing, however, are his innovative leadership practices. The real power of Ishikawa's ideas is that they combined technical and leadership practices into a unified system, which he called *company-wide quality control.*

Ishikawa's technical contributions centered on process improvement, based on the understanding that all work is accomplished by processes. That is, suppliers furnish inputs, certain steps and decisions add value to the product, and output is furnished to someone who needs it, called a customer. Often this "customer" is the next person in the company assembly line. In a manufacturing setting, process improvement proved to be fairly easy to understand, but for many years it did not translate well to service settings. Once one understands that all work is accomplished via processes, one then realizes that improving processes is the only way to improve quality and competitiveness. A basic way to improve processes is to recognize that all processes exhibit variation. If we can understand this variation and start to eliminate the unwanted portions of it, we can improve our processes.

Early on, Ishikawa advocated using analytical methods to understand variation and identified many tools for so doing, including some so complicated that only specialists such as engineers and statisticians should use them. However, one set, the *seven simple tools for quality,* was straightforward and simple, suitable for training everyone in a company. This was a radical departure from the standard approach that left analysis to specialists. It meant that hands-on workers, supervisors, even top management had to learn and use basic statistical tools.

Ishikawa convinced large numbers of leaders to start using these tools by relating them to the seven weapons of the Samurai. When a Samurai went to battle, he had seven weapons. Ishikawa said the Japanese products were the laughingstock of the world because of their poor quality; the seven simple tools for quality were the weapons with which Japanese industry was going to do battle. He stated that with effective use of these tools, 95 percent of all quality problems could be identified and eliminated. Although these tools were not the only way the Japanese improved quality, they certainly won many battles in the war against poor quality.

Most of the tools for quality had been developed by other engineers or statisticians. Ishikawa, however, devised the **cause and effect diagram** (also known as the Ishikawa diagram or the fishbone diagram, named for its shape). This tool, originally developed in 1943, allowed workers to identify and group large numbers of possible causes of problems. Other tools had allowed workers to identify many possible instances of variation, but did not help them understand the reason for the variation. The cause and effect diagram continually asks why some event may be occurring, creating for the first time a structured way to deal with the many possible causes of a problem without being overwhelmed. Ishikawa understood that workers were trying to use the other simple quality tools, but were frustrated by their inability to organize the multitude of possible causes they identified. The cause and effect diagram requires creativity and joint effort. Ishikawa said workers need to be able to work together sometimes.

This led to Ishikawa's second major contribution, that of *teamwork*. Originally, he had groups of volunteers meet on their own time to study the use of quality tools and then select problems to solve. In 1962, these teams were named **quality control circles.** Ishikawa stated that one of the main advantages of these teams was that now nonspecialists can contribute to improvement of their organizations. He edited the journal *Quality Control for the Foreman* so that people active in quality control circles could learn from each other. The success of these circles led to their widespread imitation all over the world by the late 1970s.

Actually, quality circles were initially far less successful in most other countries, requiring the help of other quality pioneers to apply these principles in different cultures.

W. Edwards Deming

The best-known quality pioneer worldwide was Dr. W. Edwards Deming of the United States. Deming (1900–1993) was raised on a homestead in Wyoming with a strong ethic not to waste anything. He was quite a scholar, studying engineering and math before completing a Ph.D. in physics. During summers between school sessions, the young Deming worked in sweatshop-style factories, where he developed a deep sympathy for the working person.

Deming met Walter Shewart, creator of quality control charts that separated variability caused by natural forces in a system from special occurrences outside the norm that require further investigation. With the War Department during World War II, Deming continued to refine these control charts. Thanks partly to Deming's influence, American defense contractors produced large quantities of high-quality arms and munitions in the war effort. After the war, however, American industry turned its back on Deming's quality leadership principles, instead producing large quantities of dubious quality goods, since anything they produced would sell to Americans with a pent-up consumer demand. Deming was extremely discouraged.

Meanwhile, across the Pacific, Japan was having a terrible time trying to rebuild. Many Japanese industries in 1946 were producing only 10 to 15 percent of their 1941 output, and the country's leaders were desperate. Among the most influential of the experts they consulted was Dr. Deming, who gave a series of lectures on statistical quality control to top executives in positions to lead the efforts within their companies. This early acceptance by leaders proved a key factor in Japanese companies obtaining impressive results from the modern approach to quality decades before American companies.

Although Deming started by teaching statistical quality control, he gradually developed a system of fourteen points. Fittingly, he tinkered with the wording and explanation of some of these points up to his death at age 93. Deming believed that while minor improvements might be possible by choosing to perform some of the points, skipping any of them would greatly diminish the total success. The fourteen points form a manifesto of what is wrong with traditional Western-style management (Deming would not call traditional practices *leadership;* he would call them *management*). Because many leaders initially found Deming's points counter to their normal way of thinking, they rejected them. Others willingly accepted some points, but disagreed with others. The fourteen points are shown here in Deming's own words, although many other writers have adapted them. Numerous books, articles, study groups, and seminars have been devoted to understanding Deming's ideas. For a man who had minor influence in his own country until age 80, Deming will long have a profound influence on the United States and the world.

Deming's Fourteen Points°

1. Create constancy of purpose toward improvement of product and service, with the aim to become competitive and stay in business, and to provide jobs.

2. Adopt the new philosophy. We are in a new economic age. Western management must awaken to the challenge, must learn their responsibilities, and take on leadership for change.

3. Cease dependence on inspection to achieve quality. Eliminate the need for inspection on a mass basis by building quality into the product in the first place.

4. End the practice of awarding business on the basis of the price tag. Instead, minimize total cost. Move toward a single supplier for any one item, on a long-term basis of trust.

5. Improve constantly and forever the system of production and service, to improve quality and productivity, and thus constantly decrease cost.

6. Institute training on the job.

7. Institute leadership. The aim of supervision should be to help people and ma-

°W. Edwards Deming, *Out of the Crisis* (Cambridge, Mass.: MIT Center for Advanced Engineering Study, 1986), pp. 23–24.

chines and gadgets to do a better job. Supervision of management is in need of overhaul, as well as supervision of production workers.

8. Drive out fear so that everyone may work effectively for the company.

9. Break down barriers between departments. People in research, design, sales, and production must work as a team, to foresee problems of production and in use that may be encountered with the product or service.

10. Eliminate slogans, exhortations, and targets for the work force asking for zero defects and new levels of productivity. Such exhortations only create adversarial relationships, as the bulk of the causes of low quality and productivity belong to the system and thus lie beyond the power of the work force.

11. Eliminate work standards (quotas) on the factory floor. Substitute leadership. Eliminate management by objective. Eliminate management by numbers, numerical goals. Substitute leadership.

12. Remove barriers that rob the hourly worker of his right to pride of workmanship. The responsibility of supervisors must be changed from sheer numbers to quality. Remove barriers that rob people in management and engineering of their right to pride of workmanship. This means *inter alia*, abolishment of the annual or merit rating and of management by objective.

13. Institute a vigorous program of education and improvement.

14. Put everybody in the company to work to accomplish the transformation. The transformation is everybody's job.

Joseph Juran

Dr. Joseph Juran was born in Rumania, came to the United States as a boy just before World War I, and spent his youth performing odd jobs to earn money for his family. Trained as an engineer, he worked for Western Electric Company in a variety of engineering and quality-related assignments. Juran and Deming were influenced by some of the same people and ideas early in their careers. Juran received a law degree working at night, then worked for the U.S. government during World War II and taught engineering for several years. In 1951, Juran published his acclaimed *Quality Control Handbook,* which many people still consider to be the quality "bible." On numerous occasions Juran traveled to Japan, where he taught middle and upper managers the importance of direct managerial involvement in improving quality. Management, he told them, was as important to quality as the statistical approaches they had already started to use. In fact, the combination of statistical and management approaches has proven exceedingly effective in Japan and elsewhere.

In contrast to Deming's demands for an overthrow of Western-style management systems, Juran focused on improving current management systems, thereby showing concern for practical quality improvement issues.

Of Juran's many contributions to quality, the most important can be summarized in several of his principles and in his trilogy. These include broad definitions of quality systems and quality itself, the Pareto principle, and organizational demands of quality.

Juran coined the terms **Big Q** and **Little Q** to demonstrate an important point regarding quality systems. Little Q, an emphasis on quality outputs, is necessary but far from sufficient, he said. Companies should exhibit Big Q, in which everything done in the company is done with an eye toward quality. He extended the scope to all products and services, including those for internal company use as well as all support and business processes.

Proposing a broad definition of quality, he claimed that four components are required: quality of design, conformance, availability, and field service. This means a company must work with potential customers in advance to ensure an appropriate design through the entire manufacture, sale, and use of the product or service. This life-cycle type concept sharply contrasted with the prevalent conception of a provider limited to meeting the current specification.

Having observed that the majority of quality problems in any system resulted from a few causes, Juran named this phenomenon after Vilfredo Pareto, an Italian economist who noted a similar phenomenon: that most wealth resided in a few hands. Juran's *Pareto principle* and the *Pareto chart* are significant because they help people concentrate on those quality issues that cause the most problems.

Juran made several organizational recommendations regarding quality, including a quality council of high-level managers to coordinating a top-down approach to obtain needed resources and commitment. Juran believed in devising and following annual goals and strategies for quality improvement as in finances.

One of his most acclaimed contributions is his **quality trilogy.** All organizations, he said, must perform three universal processes well: quality planning, control, and improvement.

Quality planning encompasses identifying customers and their needs, translating those needs into product design specifications, developing and optimizing a process to manufacture that product, and transferring responsibility for production to operations.

Quality control is intended to reduce variability and waste in operations by determining what to control, establishing standards, measuring actual performance, comparing that to the standard, and acting on the difference. Properly carried out, quality control will identify and eliminate special causes of variation. As Deming, Juran stated that most quality problems are *common causes*. To reduce common causes one must first eliminate most of the *special causes,* so quality control is necessary, but far from sufficient. What is also needed is a structured approach to reducing **common cause variation;** hence, Juran developed quality improvement.

Juran's quality improvement model, sometimes referred to as a breakthrough sequence, consists of the following tasks:

1. Convince important decision makers that the improvement is needed.

2. Set logical improvement goals based on a reasonable plan.

3. Organize a project team to reach the goals with specific guidance on what to do.

4. Provide the team adequate training.

5. Identify the causes of the problem.

6. Develop a set of possible approaches to solve the problem, select one approach, and implement it on a small scale.

7. Evaluate the results.

8. Improve the approach, if needed, and implement it.

9. Overcome the resistance that some people are bound to have concerning the new methods.

10. Standardize the approach to maintain the improvement through training, control charts, and so on.

Juran has proven to be very accurate in predicting the direction of quality. As far back as the middle 1960s, he warned the Western world that Japan would overtake them in quality and productivity because of their quality improvement efforts. Now Juran calls the twentieth century the Century of Productivity. As we approach the end of this century there is greater worldwide supply than demand of most products and services. The result, he says, will be that customers can increasingly demand excellent quality, and companies that do not produce it will go out of business. Juran believes this trend will be so strong that he has already named the twenty-first century the Century of Quality!

Now that we have scratched the surface of the ideas of three leading quality experts, what lessons for leaders can we draw from them? We envision the lessons grouped under the four headings of paradigms, commitment, using facts, and teamwork.

Paradigms

1. ***Quality must be a systematic approach.***
    Minor improvements may result from using some of the quality concepts and tools, but major improvement requires that they be used as an integrated whole. The Malcolm Baldrige National Quality Award in the United States has become the most common framework for describing the various parts of Total Quality Management. The Baldrige framework states that leadership is what fuels a quality effort. Without active, direct leadership, improvement will not happen (see Figure 5–5).

2. ***Customers are the reason we do everything we do.***
    Every time we answer the phone, fill out a piece of paper, cut metal, or answer a question it is because someone needs the output of that action. That someone is a customer, either external or internal to our organization. We need to identify that customer and his or her needs and treat satisfying those needs as our reason for existing.

3. ***Leaders must understand long-term thinking.***
    Because our goal must be the long-term viability of our organization, we must frequently make decisions that help in the long run, but may cost us money or inconvenience now.

4. ***Quality improvement requires a series of different thinking patterns.***
    Instead of always thinking in linear logic, we must frequently think first in a divergent manner such as brainstorming possibilities, then in a convergent manner such as prioritizing or selecting. See Figure 5–6.

Leadership

(Drives long-term improvement of organization as a system)

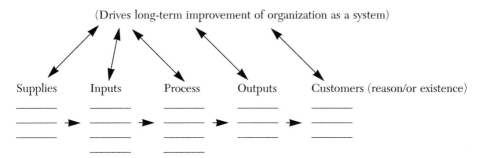

| Supplies | Inputs | Process | Outputs | Customers (reason/or existence) |

Figure 5–5   Paradigms 1–3

Each of these paradigms requires different thought patterns than many people are accustomed to, yet all are needed. In the same way, reading the works of quality experts reveals both commonalities and contradictions. In this book, we are stressing the similarities; however, leaders of an organization trying to implement quality must determine how to best reconcile different approaches for their company. In this regard, the quality demands placed on leaders are similar to the many leadership theories that leaders must sort through for commonality and applicability in their organization.

Commitment   TQM demands total commitment from everyone in the organization. Figure 5–7 shows that while top managers must lead the quality effort, they must also secure the active support of leaders at all levels of the organization to ensure success. To obtain this support, organization leaders must prove to be trustworthy and competent so as to inspire confidence, articulate the advantages of the quality approach, provide resources, remove barriers, and coach others. The leader must listen to and establish a cooperative win–win atmosphere with employees, customers, and suppliers. Understanding the needs and capabilities of each of these groups, leaders must learn to use influence rather than power to accomplish goals.

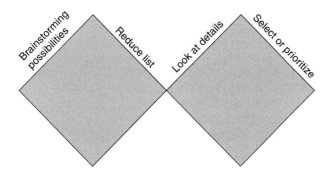

Figure 5–6   Expanding and Contracting Thought Patterns for Improvement

Commitment to Lead Quality Efforts

Tasks of Top Leaders

Top Management: Must be trustworthy and competent.

Tasks of All Leaders

Leaders at All Levels: Must actively support quality efforts by:
Articulating advantages
Providing resources
Removing barriers
Coaching
Establishing win-win atmosphere
Understanding
Influencing (not directing)

Figure 5–7   Tasks of Top Leaders

Describing the advantages and demands of quality from the perspectives of these groups makes it more understandable and acceptable.

Using Facts   The third major set of demands that quality places on leaders is to use facts to understand variation and to improve systems. Everyone in the organization must be trained how to use data gathering and analysis tools, and must then be encouraged to use them to improve the system rather than to reward and punish individuals. It must be understood that when something out of the ordinary occurs—**special cause variation**—workers need to be able to identify and correct it. The other type of variation, common cause, is inherent in the system, and management is responsible for reducing it. Everyone must be able to tell the difference between common and special cause variation. Finally, one major goal of quality is to improve our processes. To improve a process, first we must understand it. Next, we must eliminate special cause variation through quality control. Finally, we must use a structured quality improvement process to prevent mistakes in the first place rather than trying to find them via inspection. All of these steps place training needs on our entire organization, including leaders.

Teamwork   The final set of demands placed on leaders by quality is the requirement for using teams in our organization, as depicted in Figure 5–8. A leader must set up a steering team to coordinate all of the quality efforts in the organization. To make effective use of a team we must first "charter" the team by having leadership and the team members come to a common understanding of the goals, boundaries, methods, and so on under which the team will operate. Teamwork requires a set of roles to be played both outside the team by a "champion," as well as within the team by leader, facilitator, and others.

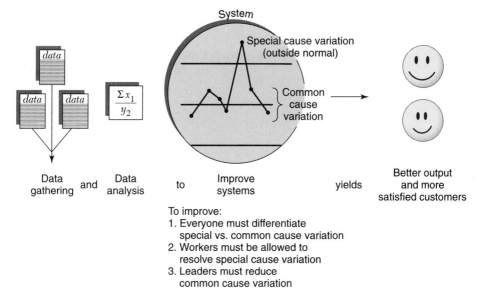

Figure 5–8   Using Facts

Teams develop in a predictable progression that leaders must understand and plan for. Leaders generally need to develop more influencing skills for dealing with teams rather than just directing them. For example, teams often make decisions using consensus for which all team members must truly agree. Teams also need to be empowered to make some decisions that previously may have been made at levels higher in the organization. If leaders suggest teams will get to make decisions, but then do not actually let them because the decision does not conform to what the leader wants, all efforts are likely to backfire. Finally, measuring team process and results and establishing appropriate reward and recognition systems place demands on leaders (see Figure 5–9).

This might seem like an unreasonable set of demands to place upon leaders; however, the alternative is to ignore quality at the peril of losing your career and/or your company. The good news is that leaders who fulfill these demands will have very full and rewarding careers.

ROBERTO CLEMENTE: QUALITY CHAMPION, HUMANITARIAN

This Hall of Fame baseball player started his baseball career in the major leagues unappreciated and misunderstood, largely because of his cultural and language differences. When sportswriters mocked his English, he retorted by telling them to come to Puerto Rico and see how good their Spanish was.

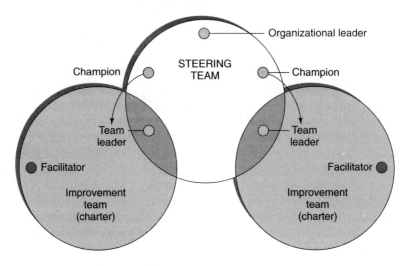

Figure 5–9   Teamwork Demands
Steering team "charters" improvement team by discussing and reaching shared understanding on goals, boundaries, methods, etc. To reach this common understanding, leaders must
influence (not direct). Teams must reach consensus, and teams will feel empowered to proceed to the full extent of their charters. The steering team guides, measures, and rewards
the improvement teams.

Baseball wasn't used to someone who was so sure of his ability—they saw him
as cocky—or so forthright and honest. When he didn't feel good, he said so: a bad
back nearly forced him to quit several times. Sportswriters and managers called him
a hypochondriac, claiming that he would talk about his aches and pains in the dugout
but then go on to play superbly. They didn't understand that his back did hurt, but
he couldn't give any less than 100 percent on the field. Long-time Pittsburgh manager Danny Murtaugh acknowledged that Clemente "was such a truthful man, it
backfired on him sometimes. If you asked him if his shoulder hurt, he'd say, 'Yes, it
does.' Then he'd go out and throw a guy out at the plate. That's how he got the
hypochondriac label."

And, in 1954, baseball was still very much afraid of race. True, Jackie Robinson
had broken the color barrier, but many players and managers were hostile to nonwhite
players. Even the Dodgers, who had the most black players on the roster, had an un-
spoken agreement never to have a majority of black players on the field at one time.

In Pittsburgh, the fans loved watching Clemente's dazzling plays, but for most
of his career he was called "Bobby," a name he never liked for himself, insisting that
Roberto was his real name.

After he won the MVP award in 1966, Clemente took up the cause of the Latin
players in the major leagues, asserting that he was happy to be an example for Latin
kids to follow.

Yet still his actions could be misunderstood. When he broke Pie Traynor's team
record for Runs Batted In in 1973, he refused to acknowledge the fans' standing ova-

tion. Only later did he explain, "The man whose record I broke was a great ballplayer, a great fellow. And he just died here a few months ago. That's why I didn't tip my cap."

His teammates looked to him for inspiration. Teammate Willy Stargell wrote about the 1971 World Series, in which Clemente racked up a staggering .414 batting average: "Each one of us wanted to be like Roberto. He taught us to take pride in ourselves, our team, and our profession."

Clemente's off-season actions were marked by service to others. When an earthquake devastated Nicaragua in 1971, he personally supervised gathering supplies in Puerto Rico and then insisted on accompanying the shipment so that the people, not the ruling dictator, obtained the help. The plane went down, and Roberto's body was never found.

At his death, contributions poured in to his dream—Ciudad Deportiva, Sports City, a sports facility where Puerto Rican children and young adults could learn the value of teamwork and sacrificing for the common good.

DEAN SMITH: TEACHER OF TEAMWORK

Since becoming head basketball coach at the University of North Carolina, Chapel Hill, in 1961, Dean Smith has fashioned one of the leading college athletics programs in the country. Not only are the Tarheels the most successful college basketball team of all time, but the program has also avoided scandal and managed to have an excellent record for graduating its basketball players.

Smith's teams are known for their cunning defenses, their discipline, and above all, their unselfishness. Coach Smith stresses teamwork as the highest priority. No matter how talented the players are individually—and he has coached Michael Jordan, James Worthy, and dozens of others who have gone on to successful NBA careers—Smith wants no part of a "star" system at UNC. Instead, he places a higher value on assists than points. As a result, few of his players have averaged 20 points per game, and that's more than OK with him.

He reportedly has never promised playing time, even to stellar prospects. When the newcomers arrive on campus, he assigns them an underling role to upperclassmen. For instance, they may be asked carry the film projector and chase loose balls in practice.

In addition to the stress on unselfish play and teamwork, Smith has instituted many other innovations, including huddling at the free throw line before foul shots and allowing tired players to take themselves out of the game.

Despite an incredible overall win–loss record (851–247) and coaching the 1976 U.S. Olympic team to a gold medal performance, Smith for years was dogged by the media for never winning an NCAA title, even though his teams made repeated trips to the Final Four and the championship game.

When asked about it, he said "If we win, I won't be a better coach."

When the 1981–82 team finally won the coveted NCAA title with a last second win over Georgetown, Smith's players were happy to have won for him. Guard Jimmy Black, who had endured his mother's death and his own near-fatal car accident, said, "In my times of tragedy, he [Smith] has always been there to lean on. This is our way of repaying him for being a shoulder."

Frequently deflecting praise to his players, Smith that night asserted that his protégé, Georgetown's John Thompson, had outcoached him. "And I don't think I'm a better coach now because we've won a national. . . . If we lost, I'd have another shot; I'd feel for those kids who wouldn't have another chance. Just because they won, I won't like them any more than last year's team," he said.

Despite the effect on future seasons, Smith has repeatedly counseled those juniors projected to be among the top five picks in the NBA to enter the draft. This has meant losing the services of such notables as Jordan, James Worthy, and many others, most of whom have returned to earn their degrees.

Long after they've left the team, the players frequently return to visit Smith and keep in close contact with him and with each other. Michael Jordan, for instance, gave Smith his 1991 NBA championship ring. They report that more than simply being a coach, he has been a friend and a teacher, concerned with their lives beyond basketball.

A shoe contract he recently signed with Nike was far different from the contracts many coaches sign: it covered the entire athletic department of the university, providing shoes and apparel for twenty-four university teams, funded the basketball team's international exhibition tour, and paid the university as well. Rather than pocketing the money himself, as most coaches do, Smith donated the entire signing bonus ($500,000) to charity. He also earmarked $45,000 of his annual $300,000 endorsement salary from Nike to a fund that helps former players finish their degrees and divides the rest among his assistants and office staff.

WILLIAM EDWARDS DEMING

The man who changed Japanese business—and as a result, American business—began his academic career in physics and mathematics. His groundbreaking research on sampling led him to consider the impact of quality control, first in manufacturing and then in other, non-manufacturing fields.

One of his most successful quality control projects was the US Census Bureau. As head mathematician and advisor in sampling, he led the Bureau into a new era of reliable and cost-effective data production.

As a consultant to the War Department after World War II, Deming made many visits in the 1940s. His stress on quality control was taken to heart by business and industry in Japan to such an extent that he was asked to award the Deming Prize, beginning in 1950. He continued to present the award up until his death.

All the while Deming was leading a quality revolution in Japan, he was virtually unknown in the US outside of a small circle. That changed in 1980 after a television news show entitled, "If Japan Can, Why Can't We?" featured him, bringing attention to his accomplishments and heightening his recognition as a management specialist.

Deming biographer Jose Aguayo summarizes the man's contributions:

> If we were to sum up the management lessons of Dr. Deming, what would they be? Let me first mention some things that they would not be. The lessons of Deming are definitely not that we have to set high standards and then stick to them. . . . The lessons are definitely not that gadgets and machinery are the way to improve our quality and productivity. Sometimes they help, but they are not enough. The lessons are definitely not that we have to get tough with our people and demand the impossible. The lessons are definitely not that we have to reward excellence and punish mediocrity.
>
> The main aim of the Deming philosophy is empowerment of the individual. The lesson is that we have to empower all our people with dignity, knowledge, and skills so that they may contribute. They have to be made secure so that they can contribute, trained so that they can do the work properly, and encouraged to grow so that the firm can develop and grow. The purpose of all management, the purpose of cooperation, is to bring out the best in each of us and allow each of us to contribute fully.

Aguayo adds a personal note about the man:

> I've known too many professors who seem to have trouble getting their heads through the door on their way to a class—professors who grace us with their presence and bring a fixed body of material to teach the students. God help the student who disagrees or even questions the sanctity of the professor's word. After all, students are only students.
>
> But from the very first class Deming was different. Here is a man of international prominence, who in fact has changed the world, but who believes every student has something to offer, something to teach. Deming goes to a class or seminar prepared to learn as well as to teach. Learning with him has been one of the great pleasures of my life.

Aguayo describes an example of Deming's philosophy in action—coaching Little League soccer:

> Several years after I began studying with Deming, I had the privilege of coaching a Little League soccer team comprised of my son and twelve other six-year-olds.
>
> As I was coaching, I realized that none of the coaches I had played for really understood teamwork. I had played three sports in high school, so I had had ample exposure to coaching styles.
>
> My own coaching methods began to differ radically from those of any coach I knew personally. I was applying Deming's teachings. My job as coach was not to criticize or distinguish between above-average players and below-average players. My job was to teach the skills, the game, and physical discipline; to make sure that every player had a really good time at each practice and at each game; to encourage continual improvement (which of course meant risk taking and occasional failure); and to encourage teamwork.
>
> I did everything I could to make practices fun and to turn the athletes on to soccer in particular and sports in general. Each practice ended with a scrimmage. I would pick

two captains, who would then choose sides. Each captain would then assign positions to each player on his scrimmage squad, and we would play for the balance of the practice.

Each athlete received a turn at being captain. No one had a second turn until everyone had been captain at least once. Many players looked forward to the practices as much as or more than the games. My thinking was that if they loved playing and practicing, they would do it often, and improve.

Before the games I would emphasize that I didn't care about scoring goals or winning, I just wanted them to have fun, to improve, and to play like a team, not a mob of unrelated individuals. For someone like myself, brought up under a system that constantly emphasized winning, this was not an easy thing to do.

After the games I would ask a question like "Who scored that first goal?" Initially one boy would raise his hand and I would respond, "No! We all scored that goal. Every person on a team is responsible for scoring a goal. The individual who touches it last is the one who may get the statistic, but scoring a goal starts with the goalie passing to a defender, who passes to a midfielder, who passes to a forward. If the forward scores, it is because of everyone else on the team, not just him.

"Now, who scored that goal?" All the athletes would raise their hands. All of them received credit for each goal scored. Unbeknownst to them, they had received their first lecture on common causes.

. . . It should be mentioned that in the four years I coached, my teams had the best record in the league each of the four years. In fact, in four years we lost all of one game. But more important, from my point of view, is that I turned on a lot of good athletes to team sports, soccer in particular. They were motivated by intrinsic motivation, the love of the game, the desire to play well, not higher pay or bigger trophies. My athletes improved considerably each year, to the point that each was a desirable player from any coach's point of view.

Source: Aguayo, Rafael. *Dr. Deming: The American Who Taught the Japanese about Quality,* New York: Simon and Schuster, 1990.

SUMMARY

This chapter has touched on two additional areas of study that have shaped the growing field of leadership. Management, like leadership, can be characterized by a variety of definitions. The ambiguity, in fact, has spawned some controversy over whether leadership is a subset of management or vice versa. The authors review this issue and assert that, although the two fields share many features, each has its own separate elements. The beginnings of scientific management are traced, and contemporary systems approaches are described.

Following John Pepper's remarks about leadership, the chapter continues with a discussion of the quality movement and three of its early quality leaders, Kaoru Ishikawa, Joseph Juran, and W. Edwards Deming. A final section on the implications of the quality movement for leadership addresses the topics of paradigms, commitment, using facts, and teamwork.

KEY TERMS

management	Total Quality Management
Frederick Taylor	cause and effect diagram
Henri Fayol	quality control circle
Max Weber	quality trilogy
Hawthorne effect	Big Q
quantitative management	Little Q
operations management	common cause variation
contingency theory	special cause variation
open systems	Pareto Principle
closed systems	

FOR DISCUSSION AND REVIEW

1. What does Fayol identify as the five key functions of management?

2. What are some key roles of managers as identified by Mintzberg? In which situations might each role be most effective?

3. What is the primary distinction between early management theories (i.e., Taylor, Fayol, Weber) and contemporary theories?

4. Do you see management as being more an art or a science? Why?

5. Describe Ishikawa's views on processes and process improvement.

6. What was the impact of Ishikawa's cause and effect diagram?

7. According to Deming, what were the key historical factors behind Japan's embracing of modern quality principles before U.S. managers did?

8. What are some common themes linking Deming's fourteen points? Which points seem particularly important to you, and why?

9. What are some differences between the approaches of Juran and Deming?

10. Describe Juran's quality trilogy. What are its primary components, and what are some of the assumptions underlying this model?

11. What are some of the paradigms that Total Quality Management demands of leaders?

12. To what extent do you feel that TQM principles will be a factor in leadership development and practices in the twenty-first century?

EXERCISES FOR CHAPTER 5

Exercise 5.1   Leading vs. Managing

You are the Regional Director of the American Heart Association. As such you are responsible for the 18 local offices in your territory. Listed below are a number of typical activities. Please identify them as management or leadership by placing a check mark in the appropriate columns. Some activities could fall in either category. In that case, identify which it *should be* based on the way you would actually perform the activity.

ACTIVITY/FUNCTION	MANAGEMENT	LEADERSHIP
1. Supervising the development of the budget at each of the local offices.		
2. Hiring, firing, and evaluating the 18 local directors.		
3. Conducting an annual retreat with the local directors to set specific objectives for the coming year.		
4. Preparing and submitting quarterly reports to the national executive director about the work of each chapter.		
5. Mediating conflicts at the local level and between the 18 directors.		
6. Visiting each chapter monthly in order to motivate and inspire each staff.		
7. Speaking at endless Rotary, Kiwanis, Lions' Clubs and other civic groups in the region in order to articulate the mission and need for the American Heart Assoc.		
8. Solving problems that local directors are unable to.		
9. Monitoring the budgets of the local chapters closely since there are few contingency dollars if budgets aren't met.		
10. Spending quality time on substantive, long-range plans for the association.		
11. Attempting to influence policy at the national level because of the changes observed locally.		
12. Forming ad hoc teams from various local offices to deal with unexpected/unusual or regional issues and opportunities.		
13. Reviewing and adjusting the fund raising time-line for each office.		
14. Participating in the selection of key leaders in each local fund campaign.		
15. Keeping local directors and staff members energized and excited as the long months of fund raising continue.		
16. Keeping the local directors and staff focused on final details after the fund campaign ends.		
17. Continually searching for new and innovative ideas about solving the age-old problems in not-for-profit organizations.		

ACTIVITY/FUNCTION	MANAGEMENT	LEADERSHIP
18. Developing and implementing the high-risk strategies if they have the potential for big pay-offs.		
19. Scheduling personal "thinking time" each week to try and remain focused on the big picture and removed from the flood of daily minutia.		
20. Reading and promptly responding to the numerous reports, correspondence and requisite forms from local offices, national headquarters, and constituent groups in your five-state region.		

KEY

1. M	6. L	11. L	16. M
2. M	7. L	12. L	17. L
3. M	8. M	13. M	18. L
4. M	9. M	14. M	19. L
5. M	10. L	15. L	20. M

Exercise 5.2   Leading vs. Management: Follow-up

1. Which activities/functions in the previous exercise could be classified as either management or leadership, in your opinion?

2. In two or three sentences, explain why each of those activities/functions could be an example of both management and/or leadership.

3. Briefly explain *why* you classified those particular activities/functions the way that you did.

4. Were there any activities/functions that you disagreed with the answer key's classification?

5. If so, why?

CHAPTER 6

The Disciplinary Roots of Leadership: Part III

The Leadership Journey:
A map of the terrain

Words/names to recognize

| The Disciplinary Roots of Leadership Part III | Power Influence Influence tactics Politics | Gender perspective Position power Empowering | Gandhi Military leadership Ethics |

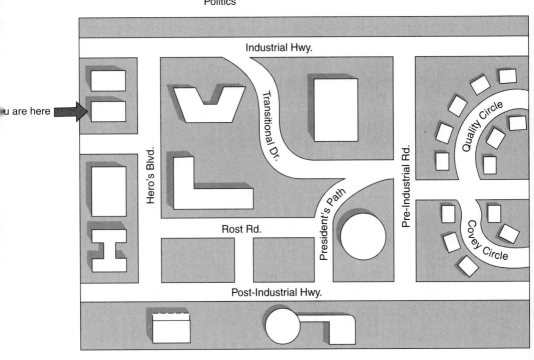

Ray has been researching the contributions of political science to leadership. He calls Terri to talk about the project.

"The funny thing is, I have a hard time seeing how poly sci relates to leadership at all. I mean, it's been five or six lectures already and each time at the end, the professor ends up with lots of circles and squares drawn on the board. And he keeps posing the same question: who shall rule? It's making me crazy."

"I know what you mean," Terri says. "Although my political science class is really great. We've been reading biographies of people like Benjamin Franklin, Golda Meir, and Colin Powell."

"That's a pretty amazing combination of people," Ray says. "How do they relate to the subject? I guess they all were pretty powerful people, in different ways."

"Yeah, and they each had a separate take on power—you know, what it means to develop it, how you can nurture it. As the prof says, 'etcetera, etcetera, so forth and so on.' I think it's neat to consider the different ways people think about power— like differences that some people say exist between men and women in using power."

"Oh no, here we go," mutters Ray. "Not this female superiority stuff again, please."

"Not what I meant at all," Terri says, miffed. "But now that you mention it, well, you've got something there." She slams down the phone.

As Ray hangs up, he wonders how this all came about. "All I really wanted to ask her," he says, half aloud, "Was 'Who shall rule?' "

POLITICAL SCIENCE

Political science's primary contribution to leadership is an explanation of the approaches to power. We'll consider where power comes from, how to use (and not use) it, how to share it, and how to increase it.

Power is central to leadership. As the ability or the potential ability to influence others or the ability to affect attitudes, power has been analyzed and discussed for centuries. (For instance, see Chapter 3, page 44 on Machiavelli.) For our purposes, we will discuss its sources, its uses, and its relationship to ethics.

The issue is not whether or not we have power—we all have some or can cultivate it. The issue, rather, is how—or even if—we choose to exercise it. (See the Ten Beliefs that Keep Us Powerless, Table 6–1.) John Gardner tells us that we need not exercise the power; it's enough to know we have it—"as any holdup man will tell you."

But first a message from our wordsmiths. Let's straighten out the definitions of power, influence, and influence tactics. Too often they're used interchangeably.

Power = potential influence over the attitudes and behavior of one or more other target people.

Influence = the degree of actual change in the target person's attitudes or behaviors.

Influence tactics = behaviors used by one person to affect another's attitudes or behaviors.

TABLE 6-1   Ten Beliefs that Keep Us Powerless

1. What I experience is not as important as what others experience.
2. To say what I want is selfish.
3. Power is wrong, so to want to be powerful is wrong.
4. If I try to be powerful, I will fail.
5. I don't need to be powerful; all I need to do is love.
6. Power should not be talked about directly, especially in intimate relationships.
7. People are born powerful; I can't help it if I wasn't.
8. It doesn't matter what I do, I can't affect those with power.
9. My failures in relationships have nothing to do with power.
10. Power corrupts anyone who has it.

Source: Wood, John Thomas, *The Little Blue Book on Power.* Winslow, Wash.: Zen'n'lnk Publishers, no date.

Examples of influence tactics include emotional appeals, rational appeals, inspirational appeals, consulting with the other person, ingratiating ("softening" the other person before making a request), exchanging favors, forming a coalition with others to influence a target, pressure tactics (threats and hard sells), and legitimizing tactics (requests based on one's position or authority).

Figure 6-1 portrays another way to view the distinctions between power and influence.

People choose a particular influence tactic based, in part, on their power. More powerful people have a greater range of tactics from which to choose. Within any organization people seek to influence the others around them. A workplace survey of 165 managers cited by Robbins (1993) notes that seven strategies were found to be the most common forms of obtaining influence:

- Reason (the most popular strategy)
- Friendliness
- Sanctions
- Bargaining
- Higher authority
- Assertiveness
- Coalition building

The survey also revealed that the influence tactic selected depended on four factors: the manager's relative power, the manager's objectives for desiring to influence, the manager's expectation that the other person would comply, and the culture of the organization.

Understanding that power tactics are present in any organization, leaders must be aware of their use and be able to analyze their intended use—either to simply

Basis of manipulation

		Power	Influence
	Positive	Inducement	Persuasion
Type of manipulation			
	Negative	Coercion	Obligation

Figure 6–1   Different Forms of Political Manipulation

Source: Reprinted from *Business Horizons,* March–April 1987. Copyright 1987 by the foundation for the School of Business at Indiana University. Used with permission.

further individuals' own ideas and status or to create a shared vision. Similarly, followers need to be aware of the influence tactics used so they have a clear understanding of how the leader is approaching the situation.

IMPLICATIONS OF INFLUENCE TACTICS FOR PRACTICING LEADERSHIP

We need to be aware of which tactic(s) we use and their effects. Relying on pressure tactics, for example, can affect the way we view others: we convince ourselves, in effect, that the others are less skilled and motivated, so we must use these tactics. By contrast, those influence tactics intended to increase others' morale and self-esteem usually are more effective in affecting behavior and attitudes.

Politics

And last, but certainly not least among our terms, is *politics*, the art of the possible. We'll use DuBrin's (1995) definition of organizational politics:

politics = the informal approaches to gaining power through means other than luck or merit.

Bellman (1992) has these pointers for the ethical understanding and use of politics:

1. **Know what your principles are.**
   Revisit them daily. Live by them. Make sure they are your own, what you really believe and are willing to defend.
2. **Acknowledge the reality of politics.**
   Do not waste all your time cursing the political realities. Instead, accept that they are a real, legitimate organizational force and seek to understand them. Test

your understanding on other people to see if they view the political world as you do.

3. **Know that you are a part of the political process.**
   You cannot declare yourself a nonmember. You may not be playing in the traditional sense, but you are a player.

4. **When you want to get something important done, know that it will be considered politically as well as objectively.**
   This is the reality of all important organizational actions. As you try to accomplish your goal, deal with the political support you need in order to succeed.

5. **Be clear about what you will and will not do in the politics of your organization.**
   Based on your observations of your company's politics, the help of successful players, and your own good judgment, decide how you will participate. . . . Be able to articulate what you see as more and less appropriate actions for you to participate.

The Nature of Power—a Gender Perspective

Traditional views equate power with strength and force, authority over others, getting others to do what you want. These "tough" characterizations of power reflect traditional masculine traits. How does this affect how women learn about and use power?

> Not only doesn't society attribute power to women, but women themselves have not been comfortable using power as long as it is defined in the classic terms. They don't think of themselves as powerful. And when women try to put on the mantle of male-style power—force and strength, devoid of the *feminine* [italics ours] caring aspect—they frequently feel extremely uncomfortable. They sense that power is 'not me.' . . . Society is finally beginning to appreciate the fact that women complement rather than compete with the strength of male managers. (Cantor and Bernay, 1992)

Psychologists Cantor and Bernay cite the definitions of power they obtained from interviews of twenty-five women holding various political offices in the United States:

> "Power in itself means nothing . . . . I think power is the opportunity to really have an impact on your community."

> "My goal is to be a powerful advocate on the part of my constituents."

> "Power is basically that sense of strength and understanding about how to pull together resources to get your agendas done."

> "To me power means being able to do something for others. I use the power of my office to help other people."

> From Senator Barbara Boxer, (D., Calif.): "More and more people look to me for ideas. I guess the ability to change people's lives and to have other people look to you for advice and assistance and leadership—I guess that's power."

Typically, say the authors, a woman who communicates directly and straight-forwardly risks being labeled "tough," bitchy" or "overbearing." Congresswoman Jo-lene Unsoeld of Washington said this is because "the public does not know what the 'proper' image of a woman with power is. Somebody in Washington who wrote an article a couple of years ago on people in power inevitably described the women as 'bitchy,' having tantrums and losing control. The men were described as 'tough,' not tolerating dissent, and this kind of thing. So the activities being described were iden-tical, but the perceptions were so different." Unsoeld further claimed that while many men and women assume men are effective because they are men, women are auto-matically assumed—by both men and many women—to be not powerful. "And they have to prove it."

A mother is a truly powerful figure in her children's lives, Cantor and Bernay note. "Society tolerates mothers' power, and women feel comfortable with it. But neither society nor mothers define what they have as *truly* powerful because its sphere of influence seems so small. As Jean Baker Miller has pointed out, the real world doesn't define power as enhancing other people's power, and that's what mothers' power is all about." (Miller, 1992.)

The Sources of Power

In seeking to determine the sources of power used by managers, French and Raven (1975) proposed that power arises from five sources. Traditionally, the French–Raven model of five sources of power has been well accepted. Because leaders are not the only parties to use power, we have also discussed how these sources relate to the power of followers. It's not an all-or-nothing proposition: Effective leaders and fol-lowers use power from several different sources simultaneously.

- **Expert**—based on knowledge or competence. The expertise could range from understanding how to make a strong presentation or how to get an invoice processed in an organization to demonstrating how to harness nuclear energy. Clearly, followers can also be experts, as in the professor whose class is rescued when a mechanically adept student fixes the video recorder.

- **Referent**—based on relationship and personal "drawing power." Leaders who attract others by their style or charisma are demonstrating referent power. A stu-dent dressed in a novel or unusual way may inspire others to dress similarly.

- **Legitimate**—bestowed by the formal organization. Also known as **position** power, this type comes with the sign on the door and the title on the letterhead. However, the real power may lie elsewhere in the organization. Sometimes the most powerful person in an organization is the administrative assistant who con-trols the schedule and access to the titular head.

- **Reward**—the ability to offer and withhold types of incentives such as status, promotions, salary increases, or interesting assignments. Followers can reward leaders' behavior through their praise, enthusiasm, or obvious support.

- **Coercive**—the ability to force someone to comply through threat of physical, psychological, or emotional consequences. Parents generally possess this power;

children do, too, which is why they often get favorable results from throwing a tantrum in a crowded store.

You might be saying to yourself, "Fine—there are five sources of power. So what? What is the most effective source?" As Nelson and Quick (1996) point out, the answers are somewhat surprising. Reward and coercive power are similarly effective, in that both produce the desired results, as long as the leader/manager is present. This requirement could make the leader something of a "Big Brother" watching over employees'/followers' shoulders. Another counterproductive effect of coercion and reward is the growing dependence they foster. Rather than showing initiative in related tasks or bringing a new insight to the task performance, those who are to be rewarded or coerced take their cues from the leader.

Legitimate power—the kind that arises from position and mutual agreement—is embodied in the T-shirt that proclaims: "Because I'm the mommy, that's why!" Legitimate power is not particularly effective in terms of organizations reaching their goals and employees reporting satisfaction. On the other hand, the remaining two sources of power have been associated with greater levels of effectiveness. Referent power is effective, with this caveat: Beware the charismatic leader who loses sight of common goals. Finally, expert power is the source most vigorously associated with task performance and employee satisfaction.

Position or Personal Power

Yukl (1994) views power through a different set of lenses. He describes two types of power—position and personal power.

Position power is derived from one's place in the organization. People with position power can have various kinds of power, including

- Authority (the right to influence other people in specific ways)
- Control over information
- Control over who does the work, and where
- Control over rewards and punishments

Position power is diagrammed in Figure 6–2.

Yukl points out that people can vary greatly in the amount of position power they have, depending on factors such as organizational policies and union contracts.

Personal power (Figure 6–3), on the other hand, arises from characteristics of the individual. Leaders who have expertise and who are likable and attractive possess this power, which they can use on subordinates as well as superiors.

Leaders can derive personal power from a number of power sources discussed previously, including expert and referent power. Personal power can also derive from information power—the control over information and its distribution—and association power, which arises when a person has influence with someone else who possesses power. Clearly, because a number of personal factors come into play, power cannot be measured accurately by looking at someone's title.

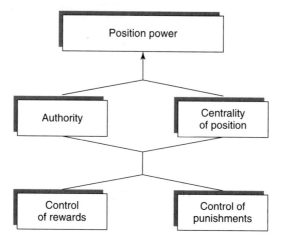

Figure 6–2   Position Power

IMPLICATIONS FOR PRACTICING LEADERSHIP

Which type of power—personal or position—is more effective? Research, says Yukl, comes down clearly on the side of personal power. Of course, leaders use combinations of personal power and position power in most cases.

Rosenbach and Taylor (1993) suggest still another way of viewing power. They break it into

- Power over—the traditional view of domination
- Power to—enhancing other people's power, empowering them (see related sections in this chapter)
- Power from—resisting the power of other people's unwanted demands

Drawing from the sociological perspective, Amitai Etzioni (1993) describes three types of organizational power: coercive, utilitarian, and normative (Figure 6–4).

Coercive power forces with threats or fear. Utilitarian power is achieved by providing rewards. Those with normative power can influence members by urging the "right" thing to do.

Etzioni says there are three kinds of organizations: those with members who are primarily alienative—unhappy, negative, don't want to be in the organization; calculative—assessing the tradeoffs of belonging; and moral—sacrificing to comply with the larger cause.

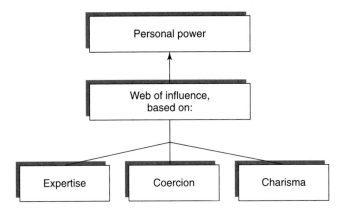

Figure 6–3   Personal Power

Understanding Cultural Values

Practicing leadership in the twenty-first century clearly involves understanding ways in which people differ. To grasp what kind of power is appropriate for such a diverse group requires that leaders have a sense of others' values. In this context, Geert Hofstede conducted extensive research about the ways in which cultural values influence interaction. His work is supplemented by Arvind Phatak's studies, to depict a continuum of values typical of different cultural groups:

1. **Individualism/collectivism reflects different views of the importance of the individual or the group.**
   At one end are typically found cultures that view individualism highly (the United States, Great Britain, and Canada), while at the other end are cultures that view the group and society as more important, such as Japan, Mexico, and Greece.

2. **High-power distance/low-power distance represents the dispersal of power throughout an organization.**

	Type of membership		
	Alienative	Calculative	Moral
Coercive	•		
Utilitarian		•	
Normative			•

Type of power (label at left for the rows Coercive, Utilitarian, Normative)

Figure 6–4   Etzioni's Power Analysis

For instance, such high-power distance cultures as France, Spain, Japan, and Mexico see the leader's ability to make decisions as natural. The followers are ready and willing to comply. By contrast, the low-power distance cultures of the United States, Ireland, and Israel tend to be less willing to subscribe to a power hierarchy. Followers in low-power distance cultures comply with leaders' decisions based on a sense of threat or conviction that the decision is correct.

3. **Uncertainty avoidance marks the culture's willingness to allow or eschew unpredictability.**
   Canada, Australia, and the United States, for instance, are more willing to allow uncertainty, while high uncertainty avoidance cultures include Japan, Israel, and Argentina.

4. **Masculinity/femininity were Hofstede's terms for the continuum of concern for materialism.**
   In this model money and assertiveness are more masculine concerns and concern for personal welfare, that is, personal relationships and quality of life, are more feminine. According to this continuum, Scandinavian cultures would be high on the femininity side and Japan and Italy would rank high on masculinity.

5. **Orientation refers to the culture's tendency to view the long-term (valuing saving, goals for generations in the future) versus short-term perspectives (daily profits, immediate results).**
   Pacific Rim cultures stress the long-term view, while the United States and Canada focus more on the short-term.

6. **Formality/Informality refers to the culture's values regarding tradition, social rules, ceremony, and rank.**
   As you might imagine, the United States and Canada score high on informality, while Great Britain and Latin America tend toward formality.

7. **Time orientation shows the differing values cultures exhibit toward time.**
   Urgent time orientations (the United States) are represented by impatient people who perceive that "time is money," while casual time orientation marks Asian cultures, for example, who exhibit more patience in negotiations and less sense of pressing deadlines.

IMPLICATIONS FOR PRACTICING LEADERSHIP

Even though the continuum reflects only generalizations about cultures, a leader would do well to understand, for instance, that someone from Asia may be less influenced by an immediate personal benefit and more responsive to a longer term advantage for the group. In an organization marked by casual time orientations, scheduling and deadline setting will be less frustrating if the leader takes the prevailing culture into consideration.

The Ethical Perspective: Mother Teresa versus Machiavelli

Now let's use an ethical lens to view various influence tactics. According to Blanchard and Pearl (1980) we should ask ourselves the following questions before proceeding with an influence tactic:

Is it legal?

Is it balanced?

How will it make me feel about myself?

One of the world's most powerful leaders, Mohandas Gandhi, advocated a similar self-questioning:

Whenever you are in doubt, or when the self becomes too much with you, recall the case of the poorest and weakest man who you may have seen, and ask yourself if the step you contemplate is going to be any use to him. Will he gain anything by it? Will it restore him control over his own life and destiny? Will it lead to *swaraj*, that is, self-government for the hungry and spiritually starving millions? Then, you will find your doubts and self melting away. (Nair, 1994)

DuBrin (1995) provides a helpful framework for viewing ethical dimensions. Noting that any of the tactics can be used in a manipulative way, he lists essentially ethical and honest tactics:

- Leading by example
- Using rational persuasion
- Developing a reputation as a subject matter expert
- Exchanging favors and bargaining
- Developing a network of resource persons
- Legitimating a request
- Making an inspirational appeal and showing emotion
- Consulting with others before making a decision
- Forming coalitions
- Being a good team player

Conversely, DuBrin's list of essentially dishonest and unethical tactics include:

- Deliberate Machiavellianism, advocating ruthlessly manipulating others for one's own ends

- "Gentle" manipulation by falsifying statements or using the bandwagon technique to imply that everyone is following the request
- Coercion via threats, criticism, excessive demands
- Debasement, or demeaning one's self to control others
- Upward appeal, going over a person's head to influence his or her actions
- Passive control, by sulking, ignoring, or otherwise giving the person the "silent treatment"
- Ingratiation and charm
- Joking and kidding (can be either ethical or manipulative, depending on tone, tact, and situation)

In a similar approach, McClelland (1975) has studied the ethics of power and explains that power can be used in positive or negative ways. We can all cite negative examples of "power hungry" leaders who seek their own gain. Somewhat less discussed, however, is what McClelland terms *social power,* the positive expression of power unleashed by achieving group goals. McClelland asserts that managers are most successful who combine a high need for social power with a relatively low affiliation need. These leaders, he says, exhibit four characteristics regarding power:

1. They believe in the validity of the authority system, from which they draw their power. They are comfortable with both influencing others and being influenced. They believe in the institution.
2. They enjoy their work and bring to it a sense of order. They value work beyond its income-producing ability.
3. They are altruistic, believing that their own well-being is linked with the corporation. They put the company first.
4. They believe in seeking justice above all else, and that justice should extend to the workplace.

In a final note about ethics, Gregory A. Gull writes in the August, 1995, issue of *Executive Excellence*: "Ethics has to do with that which is common to all of us. Clearly ethics has no meaning in a world of things, for ethics addresses the fundamental issues of life: meaning and self-preservation. . . . The principles upon which our businesses are run are inseparable from the principles upon which we live our lives. . . . In short, business must be practiced on the field of ethics, and not conversely, if the intent is to remain viable."

How Is Power Acquired—and Also Lost?

Obviously, power rarely remains static. The two most commonly accepted theories about how one finds, maintains, and loses power in organization are **vertical dyad linkage** and the **social exchange theory.**

Vertical Dyad Linkage   In some instances, a leader and a few subordinates/followers share a high degree of mutual attraction and influence. These select few people, the in-group, are highly loyal, committed, and trusting of the leader, who most frequently uses referent, expert and reward types of power to influence them.

Conversely, the out-group does not feel the same degree of commitment, loyalty, or trust toward the leader who, in turn, uses reward, legitimate, and coercive power to influence them.

IMPLICATIONS OF THE VDL FOR PRACTICING LEADERSHIP

Effective leaders avoid creating a coterie of insiders and outsiders. Such a dichotomy is divisive and decreases overall group performance. Some leaders find that helping everyone to feel part of the in-group improves group functioning; in fact, charismatic leaders (those with referent power) have an uncanny ability to treat group members as if they all belong to the in-group.

Social Exchange Theory This view posits that leadership is a transaction in which both leaders and followers receive benefits. The benefits may include status, praise, identity, and money or other rewards. In this view, the leader–follower exchange is most effective when the benefits are most nearly equal. Members of a group can acquire power by building up what are termed *idiosyncrasy credits;* that is, stockpiling "points" by showing loyalty, solving key problems, and so on. Leaderless groups may find a leader emerging based on who has the largest amount of these credits.

An application of the social exchange theory has been advanced by George Graen and his associates. This leader–member exchange model suggests that leaders favor some subordinates over others, and thus, the relationships between leader and subordinate are different. Some employees belong to the in-group; others to the outgroup. Graen (1995) found that first impressions were strong predictors of the leader's future relationship with that employee.

Empowering—Why Give Power Away?

Here is the paradox of power: You can find more power by sharing what you already have with others. When your subordinates/followers increase their power, they can perform better, raising the overall productivity of the group. This is **empowerment.** Improved performance means kudos for the leader, too: a win-win situation (see Table 6–2).

Leaders can empower others in many ways, including:

- Rewarding and encouraging followers in visible ways ("worker of the month" appreciation, certificates, membership in special clubs, etc.)
- Creating a positive atmosphere, because confident workers are willing to take on more challenges

TABLE 6–2   Differences in the Empowering Process as a Function of Role: Leaders Compared with Managers

Empowering Process	Leader Activities	Manager Activities
Providing direction for followers/subordinates	Via ideals, vision, a higher purpose, superordinate goals	Via involvement of subordinates in determining paths toward goal accomplishment
Stimulating followers/subordinates	With ideas	With action; things to accomplish
Rewarding followers/subordinates	Informal; personal recognition	Formal; incentive systems
Developing followers/subordinates	By inspiring them to do more than they thought they could do	By involving them in important decision-making activities and providing feedback for potential learning by giving them training
Appealing to follower/subordinate needs	Appeal to needs of followership and dependency	Appeal to needs for autonomy and independence

Source: Burke, W. Warner. "Leadership as Empowering Others," Table 4 p. 73, adapted as submitted. In S. Strivasta and Associates, *Executive Power.* Copyright 1986 by Jossey-Bass, Inc. Publishers.

- Showing confidence—empowering leaders tell their followers verbally and non-verbally that they have confidence in their ability.
- Promoting initiative and increasing responsibility, with appropriate rewards.
- Starting small—taking on massive changes one step at a time.
- Praising initiative, even if results are not all that was hoped for.

Maureen Kempston Darkes is an example of a leader who has practiced the principles of empowerment (see chapter 1).

"This Little Man," an excerpt from a 1947 letter written by Jawaharlal Nehru about Mohandas Gandhi.

This little man has been and is a colossus before whom others, big in their own way and in their own space and time, are small of stature. In this world of hatred and uttermost violence and the atom bomb, this man of peace and goodwill stands out, a contrast and a challenge. In an acquisitive society madly searching for new gadgets and new luxuries, he takes to his loincloth and his mud hut. In man's race for wealth and authority and power, he seems to be a nonstarter, looking the other way; and yet that authority looks out of his gentle but hard eyes, that power seems to fill his slight and emaciated frame, and flows out to others. Wherein does his strength lie, wherein this power and authority?

From a 1968 speech of Indira Gandhi, Nehru's daughter, and herself Prime Minister of India:

In just four weeks in 1919, he changed the outlook of his subcontinent. He transformed the cowed and the weak into a nation that fearlessly asserted its right to be free. He gave his people a new weapon, which ultimately delivered them from colonial rule. This weapon was *satyagraha*, civil disobedience or nonviolent noncooperation. Literally, the word means "insistence on truth." It was a weapon that did not need physical strength. But to be effective it did need the greatest self-discipline.

Three Summarizing Points

1. The most effective leaders are usually those who take advantage of all possible sources of power and select the one or ones to emphasize.
2. The most effective organizations are those in which leaders and followers have high reciprocal influence. No one operates in his or her island, no man—or woman—stands alone.
3. Leaders differ in the amount of power they share.

Barbara Mikulski (1992) said:

I think leadership is creating a state of mind in others. President Kennedy's legislative accomplishments were skimpy, but he created a state of mind in this country that endures long after his death. Churchill created a state of mind in Great Britain and enabled the British to endure the blitz and marshal the resources to help turn the tide of World War II. Martin Luther King Jr. created a state of mind. Florence Nightingale created a state of mind in people about what nursing should be, that it shouldn't be those who were derelicts and ladies of the night, that it was a profession.

As another example, Eisenhower used to tell a story that speaks volumes about power. "On a crucial question during the Civil War, Abraham Lincoln is said to have called for a vote around the cabinet table. Every member voted no. 'The ayes have it,' Lincoln announced."

Now that's power!

MARGARET THATCHER, BRITAIN'S "IRON LADY"

Margaret Thatcher was not only Britain's first woman prime minister, she was the first female prime minister of any European country. She surprised most of the political commentators when she led her Tory party to victory in the country's general election in 1979.

Growing up as the younger daughter of a lay Methodist minister, Margaret learned early on to stand behind her own decisions regardless of other people's opinions. Unbounded determination helped her win a scholarship to Oxford, where she held leadership positions in the Conservative Association.

She continued working for the conservative position, and became the youngest woman candidate in the country when she stood for local election. Despite losing twice in a row, she managed to increase the conservative vote by nearly 50 percent and proved herself a capable, hard-working politician.

She married, had twins, went to law school, and practiced as a barrister specializing in taxation law, but she kept her eye on the goal of being elected to Parliament. After several disappointments, she reached her goal in 1959.

Ms. Thatcher rose to prominence in the conservative Tory party, and in 1961 was appointed secretary to the ministry of pensions and national insurance. From 1964–70, she emerged as an opposition spokesperson to the Labour party, then in power. As the minister of education (after the Conservatives won the 1970 general election), she was dubbed the "most unpopular woman in Britain" for her controversial views on education, including discontinuing free milk for students over seven and increasing school milk charges.

After Conservative Edward Heath lost in the 1974 general election, Margaret announced that she would seek the party's leadership. Although no one took her seriously at first, she emerged the victor after two ballots.

Then, in 1979, she won a narrow victory in a no-confidence vote over James Callaghan, who became the first prime minister to be voted out of office since 1924.

Having campaigned on the promise to "turn the tide against socialism," she introduced legislation to reduce government spending in health care, housing, social security, and education while increasing support for the military and reducing taxation, particularly for the wealthiest people.

She was roundly criticized in Parliament and in the media for what her opposition called "the savage attack on the welfare state." Undaunted, she declared that the country was "sick and needed a dose of strong medicine."

Despite a major victory in quelling the civil war in Rhodesia and helping to hold free elections that resulted in black nationalist leader Robert Mugabe winning, she faced increasingly difficult times at home: massive unemployment, rising numbers of businesses closing, and widespread public uproar over her economic policies. Nevertheless, Ms. Thatcher won three consecutive general elections and held office continuously longer than any British prime minister since Gladstone.

She has been lauded and sneered at for her persistence and her willingness to challenge conventional wisdom. Indeed, even her rise to the top was such a challenge. She was the epitome of an outsider, coming not from the aristocracy of the party, but rather from a provincial town and middle-class parents. Most significantly, she was an outsider in terms of gender.

Writing in the *Atlantic Monthly* (Dec. 1991), Geoffrey Wheatcraft explains:

> She was cut off by the "homosocial" traditions of her party, which thirty years ago were very strong and are scarcely weak even now. It was a chaps' party—chaps who had known each other at school, at university, in the army; chaps who met to talk and drink in the House of Commons smoking room or the clubs of St. James Street. This was a camaraderie from which the lowborn were mostly excluded, and a woman was by definition entirely excluded. And so Margaret Thatcher had to plow her own furrow, make her own friends, and attack the citadel of power from outside.

ROSS PEROT: POPULIST OR PARIAH?

Henry Ross Perot has been called an authentic American folk hero, a hustler, an egomaniac. And it seems like there are plenty of examples to back up each description. The one indisputable fact is his business cunning, even though he insists he's just a common man who's been uncommonly lucky.

In 1957 he joined IBM as a salesman after serving four years in the Navy. Perot's talents in sales can be glimpsed by the fact that one year he made his yearly quota on January 19. But selling for someone else wasn't enough.

He recalls sitting—where else?—in a barbershop when he came across the passage of another Henry, this time Henry David Thoreau: "The mass of men lead lives of quiet desperation."

It may have been the last time he was quiet about anything. He approached IBM about his idea for selling not just hardware, but also software and programming assistance. Not interested, replied Big Blue.

Running from the feared quiet desperation, he convinced his wife to lend him $1,000 and enlisted his mother and sister as the board of directors.

And thus was born Electronic Data Systems, a company that soon put Perot on the list of American industry magnates. When software bounced from 20 percent to 80 percent of the market, he became a billionaire.

Yet in many ways he was very unlike the typical corporate giant America was used to. For example, when he lost more than $500 million in one day (spring 1970), he declared that he would've been a lot more upset if one of his kids had broken a finger.

Perot was born in Texarkana, where he worked from age 7. Today he proudly acknowledges that he holds "Norman Rockwell values," especially the importance of one generation sacrificing for the next. Called by some a high-tech Horatio Alger, Perot still prizes thrift and frugality.

At only 5'6", he takes a lot of public ribbing about his small stature, but he uses his unassuming presence to his advantage. While he was on the board of General Motors, for example, he used to wander through dealerships in sport shirts. No one went up to him; he didn't look like he could buy a Chevy. "Small animals blend in," he says.

A *New York Times* profile (June 28, 1992) describes Perot's combination of largesse (sending a private jet to take the wife of an employee to an eye specialist, for example) with his habit of rescuing others. The rescue aspect, says the article, is a large part of Perot's makeup; he even assumed his dead brother's name to assuage his parents' grief.

Long a supporter of military veterans, and himself a product of the military, Perot brought attention to POWs during the Vietnam era. One year he tried to send 1,420 Christmas dinners to North Vietnam, even though he knew he would be refused landing privileges. Perot then offered money to rebuild schools and hospitals in exchange for prisoners, another offer turned down.

Despite consistently insisting that he did not want to run for president of the United States, his followers mounted campaigns for him in many states' primaries and in the national elections of 1992.

Perot has been hailed both as a man of the people and a haughty, power-hungry shark always looking for the "goods" on his opponents. The mix of personality factors is difficult to pin down. Just as he starts to sound imperious, he gets an impish grin on his face and laughs at himself.

Supporters and detractors alike agree that Perot has incredible focus and determination, as well as a remarkable talent for getting people to do so much more than they thought they ever could.

MILITARY SCIENCE

The military takes a well-defined approach to leadership issues. In this section, we will describe that approach and look at two men with very different leadership styles: General Colin Powell and Mao Zedong.

The military publishes a manual titled *Military Leadership*. The manual serves two purposes: "To provide an overview of army leadership doctrine, including the principles of applying leadership theory at all organizational levels to meet operational requirements and to prescribe the leadership necessary to be effective in peace and war." (*Military Leadership, Field Manual*, No. 22-100, Department of the Army, 1990, p i)

Leadership, the manual says, is the process of influencing others to accomplish the mission by providing purpose, direction, and motivation. Further, the manual details eleven principles of leadership. They are:

1. Know yourself and seek self-improvement.
2. Be technically and tactically proficient.
3. Seek responsibility and take responsibility for your actions.
4. Make sound and timely decisions.
5. Set the example.
6. Know your soldiers and look out for their well-being.

7. Keep your subordinates informed.

8. Develop a sense of responsibility in your subordinate.

9. Ensure the task is understood, supervised, and accomplished.

10. Build the team.

11. Employ your unit in accordance with its capabilities.

Unique contributions to doing leadership: The field guide's breakdown of competencies for practicing leadership into "being, knowing, and doing" (Table 6–3) is helpful to understand the complex factors involved in practicing leadership.

Perhaps one of the best ways to examine the contributions of military science to the study and development of leadership is to present the characteristics that the U.S. Army asserts make an excellent leader. The following traits are addressed within fifteen dimensions of leadership:

1. ORAL COMMUNICATION
    Excellent:

    Conveys ideas and feelings concisely in single transmission

    Uses language and gestures well-suited to audience and situation

    Inspires people's attention, interest, and conviction

    Excellent command of English language

    Not only recognizes when misunderstandings occur and resolves them, but does so in a positive, team-building manner

    Attentive, support listener; makes appropriate notes; can inform others about what was said or done in excellent detail

2. WRITTEN COMMUNICATION
    Excellent:

    Easily understood in single, rapid reading by a broad audience

    Readily legible

    Bottom line is clear, compelling, and up front

    Excellent command of English language

    Uses active voice throughout

    Excellent format, logic, and organization

    Effectively varied style with most writing simple and to the point

    Minimizes the use of acronyms; explains those used or uses common ones

    Clearly, but concisely gets ideas across

    Excellent use of facts or data to support the purpose

    Clearly, completely meets assigned requirements

TABLE 6-3 **Leadership in Action**

As a leader you must	Examples	
Be a person of strong and honorable character	• Determination • Compassion • Self-discipline • Role Modeling	• Initiative • Flexibility • Consistency
Be committed to the professional Army ethic	• Loyalty to the nation, the Army, and the unit • Selfless service	• Integrity • Duty
Be an example of individual values	• Courage • Candor	• Competence • Commitment
Be able to resolve complex ethical dilemmas	• Interpret the situation • Analyze all the factors and forces that apply	• Choose a course that seems best for the nation
Know the four factors of leadership and how they affect each other	• The leader • The situation	• The led • Communications
Know standards	• Sources of Army standards	• How standards relate to warfighting
Know yourself	• Personality and performance • Strengths and weaknesses	• Knowledge, skills and attitudes
Know human nature	• Potential for good and bad behavior	• How depression and sadness contribute to fear and panic, and how fear affects performance
Know your job	• Plan and communicate effectively • Supervise, teach, coach, and counsel • Display technical and tactical competence	• Develop subordinates • Make good decisions that your soldiers accept • Use available systems
Know your unit	• Unit capabilities and unit limitations	
Provide purpose	• Explain the "why" of missions	• Communicate your intent
Provide direction	• Plan • Maintain standards • Set goals • Make decisions and solve problems	• Supervise, evaluate, teach, coach, and counsel • Train soldiers and teams
Provide motivation	• Take care of soldiers • Serve as the ethical standard bearer • Develop cohesive soldier teams • Make soldiering meaningful	• Reward performance that exceeds standards • Correct performance not meeting standards • Punish soldiers who intentionally fail to meet standards or follow orders

3. ORAL PRESENTATION

Excellent:

Very well prepared and well rehearsed

Excellent expertise on the subject at hand; readily answers questions with strong clarity

Enthusiastic, confident, and comfortable with audience

Maintains good eye contact with audience; uses verbal or non-verbal feedback from audience in stride in the presentation; encourages audience interaction

Imaginative, innovative approach

Polished, smooth presentation

Uses inflection to advantage

Clear, concise visual aids

Excellent posture and positioning relative to visual aids

Ensures the presentation site is conducive to the presentation

Wins over the audience

4. INITIATIVE

Excellent:

Provides impetus for getting problems solved, decisions made; makes the team excel

Dynamic self-starter; originates ideas or actions.

Looks for willingness to use new methods

Asks pertinent questions that help clarify instructions or guidance received

Quickly acts in the absence of guidance

Thoroughly seeks out specified and implied tasks

Accurately anticipates requirements/contingencies; attacks problems that impact the mission

Improvises well within commander's intent; excels in a fluid environment

Readily volunteers; makes a difference for the team

Makes excellent use of time available for training, preparation, inspections, rehearsals, etc.

5. SENSITIVITY

Excellent:

Shows genuine care and concern for the safety, well-being, and feelings of others; frequently checks in positive ways

Discreet and tactful when correcting or questioning others

When making corrections, has a plan of action; encourages improved performance

Effective at constructive criticism

Active, supportive listener

Courteous and polite

Has strong, positive impact on team morale; shares hardship

Achieves excellent balance between mission and personal needs

Shares or passes credit to subordinates; shoulders blame

Cheerfully complies with policies and directives

6. INFLUENCE

Excellent:

Inspires confidence and positive attitude in others

Sets excellent example

Clearly wins the proactive support of followers

Makes necessary spot corrections in positive, team-building manner

Takes an active part to influence events beyond the scope of immediate concern; helps the team anticipate and prepare

Excels in a fluid environment

Inspires respect and loyalty from followers when giving orders, conducting training, or supervising

Inspires the initiative of followers; molds results in team effort; gets others to be energetic

7. PLANNING AND ORGANIZING

Excellent:

Plans are well-based or well-focused on desired outcome (uses "reverse planning" or "battle sequence" planning techniques)

Adapts plan from higher HQ to own unit in excellent fashion

Incorporates excellent controls such as time-phasing; uses easily understood culmination points or "trigger points"

Carefully adheres to or enforces the "1/3–2/3 Rule"

Plans well for preparation or rehearsal as required

Determines, prioritizes, and addresses specified and implied tasks very well; supports commander's intent

Makes smart use of available resources

Thoroughly addresses likely contingencies; flexible

Excellent horizontal and vertical coordination

Logical, appropriately simple, readily understood plan; clearly would accomplish the mission

8. DELEGATION

   Excellent:

   > Tailors subordinate chain-of-command for the situation
   >
   > Makes excellent use of subordinate chain-of-command
   >
   > Issues mission-type instructions; ensures expectations are understood; gives subordinates appropriate latitude
   >
   > Delegates authority; retains and fulfills responsibility
   >
   > Makes excellent use of people's strengths and weaknesses; well considers applicable circumstances
   >
   > Delegates work not necessary for the leader (self) to do in a way that facilitates or enhances the team's success
   >
   > Excellent distribution of work; enhances team efficiency
   >
   > Encourages and capitalizes on initiative of subordinates

9. ADMINISTRATIVE CONTROL

   Excellent:

   > Always clear who is supposed to do what
   >
   > Supervises in an encouraging way
   >
   > Correctly evaluates work in progress
   >
   > Ensures standards met
   >
   > Makes smart adjustments in assignments when appropriate
   >
   > Sets priorities/suspenses in an excellent fashion
   >
   > Makes excellent use of time and SOPs (Standard Operating Procedures)
   >
   > Maintains excellent accountability of people and equipment
   >
   > Team effort exceeds expectations ("On time, on target")

10. PROBLEM ANALYSIS

    Excellent:

    > Makes an excellent assessment of the situation
    >
    > Has excellent grasp of actual/potential problems
    >
    > Quickly and accurately determines cause, effect, and contributing factors for each identified problem
    >
    > Works well up the chain when problem must be solved there
    >
    > Thoroughly gathers data relevant to solving the problems
    >
    > Encourages and makes smart use of input from others
    >
    > Maintains excellent perspective
    >
    > Develops more than one feasible course of action; makes excellent analysis of advantages/disadvantages of each course of action; results in a smart choice of one to adopt
    >
    > Poised and composed under pressure

11. JUDGMENT

    Excellent:

    > Makes excellent analysis of advantages/disadvantages of each course of action; makes a smart choice to adopt one
    >
    > Makes excellent use of available, relevant information
    >
    > Encourages and makes smart use of input from others
    >
    > Choices benefit the team (over an individual)
    >
    > Well considers and regards the consequences of decisions
    >
    > Decisions reflect technical and tactical expertise
    >
    > Excellent common sense
    >
    > Chooses to ensure the team is well prepared; makes excellent use of available time for training, inspections, or rehearsals
    >
    > Won't compromise principles
    >
    > Genuinely acts for the benefit of the team

12. DECISIVENESS

    Excellent:

    > Clearly takes charge when in charge
    >
    > Clearly stands firm in decisions and beliefs
    >
    > Balances firm resolve and flexibility; recognizes a better idea and incorporates it into own decisions
    >
    > Recovers quickly after learning a decision was incorrect
    >
    > Clearly thinks and acts quickly, logically, confidently
    >
    > Confidently makes smart, timely decisions as matter of routine
    >
    > Readily accepts responsibility for decisions; passes credit and shoulders blame
    >
    > Makes the "hard, right" decision rather than the "easy, wrong"
    >
    > Drives events

13. TECHNICAL COMPETENCE

    Excellent:

    > Has excellent grasp of small unit tactics, techniques, and procedures
    >
    > Has excellent grasp of squad- and platoon-level drill and ceremony, adequate grasp of company drill and ceremony
    >
    > Thoroughly skilled in preparing operation orders
    >
    > Solid foundation in basic soldiering skills
    >
    > Makes excellent use of reference materials and manuals
    >
    > Pays close attention to detail; wants things done right

Conducts excellent inspections or "Pre-combat" checks

Often sought out by peers for his or her expertise

14. PHYSICAL STAMINA

Excellent:

Mentally and physically durable even in stressful or strenuous situations; sets positive example

Excels in physically demanding endeavors; helps others succeed

Remains poised and effective despite emotional stress and personal fears

"Can do" even when tired, hungry, cold, hot, wet, or muddy

15. FOLLOWERSHIP

Excellent:

Effective team player; contagious positive attitude

Willing to accept, act on tasks, even when on short notice or under pressure

Readily volunteers; makes a difference for the team

Spurs the team to remain positive in confusing or changing situations

Offers supportive suggestions that chain-of-command adopts; facilitates team progress

Adopts unpopular higher HQ decision as his or her own

Regards peers well and is well-regarded by peers

Acts for the good of the team

Cooperative, diligent follower, seemingly without concern whether he or she will get similar help when he or she is in charge

Source: US Army Cadet Command Leader's Guide, 30 December 1995.

GENERAL COLIN L. POWELL: PROBLEM SOLVER

When General Colin Powell's book, *My American Journey*, was published in 1995, he began a book signing tour that drew throngs of people at sites across the nation. What was the attraction?

In part, it may have been the fact that he was the first African American ever to hold such prestigious positions in the U.S. government as Chairman of the Joint Chiefs of Staff and National Security Advisor. His name was being tossed around as a candidate for president and vice president. Powell's hold on the American public, however, was also due to his integrity and to the leadership he showed during conflict.

Born of Jamaican parents, Powell grew up amid a mix of Jews, Poles, Hispanics, Irsh, and Italians in the South Bronx. An indifferent student, he remembered feeling a lack of direction until he entered ROTC (Reserve Officers Training Corps) at City College. There, he says in his autobiography, he felt for the first time a sense of belonging. His admission to the selective Pershing Rifles group deepened his closeness to the military and to other young men with whom he has maintained contact throughout his career.

After accepting a commission as a second lieutenant in the infantry at Fort Benning, Georgia, Powell was sent to a unit in West Germany where he served as platoon leader and executive officer. As he began ascending the military career ladder, he learned that to lead one had to make decisions, often unpopular ones. A quotation he kept on his desk reminded him "Being responsible sometimes means pissing people off."

His years within the military—which he contends is the most democratic institution in the country—were relatively free of discrimination and prejudice. Outside the service, however, he was saddened to see so much hatred and distrust among the races. At the dedication of the memorial for the Buffalo Soldiers, Black soldiers who had fought courageously for the Union during the Civil War but who had received little recognition, Powell noted the injustice these brave soldiers encountered:

> "I know where I came from," I said. "All of us need to know where we came from so our young people will know where they are going. . . . I am deeply mindful of the debt I owe to those who went before me. I climbed on their backs. . . . I challenge every young person here today: don't forget their service and their sacrifice; and don't forget *our* service and sacrifice, and climb on *our* backs. Be eagles!"

Powell learned in his first eight weeks these essential guidelines about the military:

> "Take charge of this post and all government property in view"—the Army's first general order.
> The mission is primary, followed by taking care of your soldiers.
> Don't stand there. Do something!
> Lead by example.
> "No excuse, sir."
> Officers always eat last.
> Never forget, you are an American infantryman, the best.
> And never be without a watch, a pencil and a notepad.

(*My American Journey*, p. 41)

An early assignment, prosecuting three soldiers who had crashed their car, killing several Germans, had shown him that he was skilled in taking a large amount of information, shaping it, and conveying it competently and persuasively. Much of his future accomplishments serving presidents and commanding troops called on and refined this ability.

Powell's take on leadership is straightforward: "Leadership is solving problems. The day soldiers stop bringing you their problems is the day you have stopped leading them. They have either lost confidence that you can help them or concluded you do not care. Either case is a failure of leadership." (p. 52)

His combat service included two tours of Vietnam, where he earned the Purple Heart and the Soldiers Medal for rescuing his colleagues from a helicopter crash.

He completed his masters degree in business administration at George Washgton University and was selected as a White House fellow during the Nixon administration. He chose to serve in the Office of Management and Budget, obtaining invaluable experience about budgetary matters that would help him enormously in his later career.

During his time serving presidents and troops, Powell learned to get along with all types of people. He also learned the importance of acknowledging everyone's effort. In fact, "share the credit" is one of the 13 rules he kept on his desk. He valued teamwork and cherished the existence of a sense of family in the military, of each one looking out for the other.

In many tense situations, including during the Gulf War, Powell resisted others' insistence on quick military reaction. He stressed, instead, the importance of not letting himself be stampeded into an action until he had analyzed it in depth. He vowed to take no action until a clear objective had been established.

Upon Powell's retirement from the Joint Chiefs of Staff, President Clinton had this to say of the General: "He clearly has the warrior spirit and the judgment to know when it should be applied in the nation's benefit. . . . I speak for the families who entrusted you with their sons and daughters . . . you did well by them, as you did well by America."

General Powell counted himself fortunate in many ways: "I had found something to do with my life that was honorable and useful, that I could do well, and that I loved doing. That is rare good fortune in anyone's life. My only regret is that I could not do it all over again."

MAO ZEDONG (MAO TSE TUNG): REVOLUTIONARY AND POET

Born in a rural village 60 miles from the capital of the Hunan Province, Mao endured the privations of poverty as well as the punishments of his harsh father, whom Mao later dubbed "the Ruling Power." Even as a young boy, he hungered for knowledge of China and the outside world. He became an avid reader, sacrificing much to attend school where he was ridiculed for his back country ways. He excelled in debate, however, and learned early that it was possible to defy arbitrary authority.

Mao was 18 before he ever saw a map of the world. Rather than attend school at this age, he stayed in the school library from opening until its closing, taking only enough time to eat his ration of two rice cakes for lunch. He devoured books, reveling in the folk tales and history of his native country, and also in the biographies of world leaders such as Napoleon, Peter the Great, and Americans such as Abraham Lincoln and George Washington. He later compared himself to Washington leading a rebel army against an entrenched power. He also loved to write poetry, often glorying in the delights of the natural world.

As he saturated himself with the proud history of his country, however, he also became by turns saddened and enraged at its domination by foreign powers. He was thrilled by newspaper stories of uprisings against feudal landlords across the country. Stirred by Sun Yat Sen's victory over the Manchu Dynasty, Mao signed up for the revolutionary army, but was later disillusioned when Sun was overtaken by the military and the country broke into warring factions.

Mao tossed about for a future, joining and quitting police, soap-making, and law and business schools. He finally decided on teaching. His remarkable entrance scores earned him free tuition and board for the next four years as he increased his debating skills and continued to rebel against arbitrary authority. He continued reading stories about how sheer willpower could overcome any obstacle, a belief that remained central to his life. He also entered a period of rugged conditioning, eating little and pushing his physical endurance to the limit. His prodigious physical ability would stand him well in the years to come.

After reading about the Bolshevik revolution in Russia in 1917, Mao formed communist study groups in China. He disagreed with the Marxists that the revolution would depend on the working class; instead, Mao stressed the role that the peasants would play in overthrowing the government in China.

While fighting the Nationalist Chinese led by Chiang Kaishek, Mao was captured one day and designated for beheading. He managed to evade his captors and hide, stealing back to his headquarters.

In the newly developing Red Army, Mao had set up a very different organization from traditional armies. Officers (including himself) had no special privileges: they were called *leaders* but wore no outward designation of rank and ate the same food as the others. Mao insisted that the soldiers show kindness and helpfulness to the peasants, helping them in whatever way they could. He told them that they must be servants of the people. This passion for serving the peasants created a love for the Red Army among the villagers, who often helped in significant ways. In addition, Mao sought to enlist women and young people in the great effort of liberating China.

Chiang encircled the Red Army, gradually tightening the stranglehold. After long deliberation, Mao convinced his soldiers that the only way to escape was through the treacherous mountains to the north. This began the Long March, a trek of nearly 7500 miles through rugged territory, often circling back and changing directions to confuse the Nationalists. The journey was exceedingly difficult and resulted in massive deaths. Yet the Reds also took the opportunity to talk about land reform and other issues to the peasants along the way, building strong support for Mao's revolutionary ideas. Out of the 100,000 troops who began the trip, only 20,000 finished it alive. Nevertheless, the amazing feat has often been compared with Hannibal crossing the Alps and helped solidify Mao's growing idolization among the people of China. A personality cult was growing.

Following World War II, an out-and-out battle for control of the leadership of China erupted into civil war. Finally Chiang was defeated, moving his enclave to Formosa (Taiwan) in 1949. Mao announced the founding of the People's Republic of China.

During the next three decades Mao showed himself as an astute strategist, a militarist who enjoyed provoking the major world powers, and a polemicist trying to overturn the cultural practices of Confucianism in China. He instigated the Cultural Revolution, asserting that artists and intellectuals needed to come from their ivory towers to work alongside the peasants. He who had been such a voracious reader now denigrated the need to read anything more than his little blue book, *Quotations from Chairman Mao*. He closed all the universities, turning high school and college students into impassioned members of the Red Guard.

Little else was available to read beyond Mao's works and his likeness loomed everywhere. He delighted in surprising the world, as when he sent a Chinese team to the World Ping Pong championships in Japan and then allowed the U.S. team to play in China. The remarkable meeting between U.S. President Nixon and Mao was another in a long line of unexpected events. It was the first time any U.S. president had set foot on Chinese soil and signaled a thaw in the U.S.–China relationship. During Nixon's visit in 1972, however, Mao was in very poor health, and the country was in suspense about who would take over after his death, which came on September 9, 1977 when Mao was 82.

Summarizing Mao's life, Rebecca Steffof writes in *Mao Zedong:*

> Mao has been viewed as both a hero and a tyrant. His patriotism is undeniable; he fought valiantly to defend China against the Japanese. . . . He was a visionary who dreamed of a new China and had the force of will to reshape the world to fit his dream. Yet sometimes visionaries are dangerous. Sometimes they cannot tolerate the existence of anything or anyone outside their own narrow field of vision. Mao Zedong was an idealist who gave the Chinese people freedoms they had never known. He was also a tyrant, who ruthlessly crushed anyone who dared to dream of freedoms beyond those he offered. He may be both a savior and a villain, but one thing is certain: In shaping the lives of one fifth of the world's population, Mao Zedong had a greater impact on the destiny of the Chinese people than any other single person, except perhaps the emperor who first united China 2,200 years ago.

SUMMARY

This chapter extended the examination of leadership theory to two final perspectives: political science and military science. The major contribution of political science theory to leadership is the study of power. New conceptions of power have included female sensibilities about its use and origin. Five sources of power—expert, referent, legitimate, reward, and coercive—were considered, as were implications for practicing leadership based on personal and organizational factors. The influence of cultural values on interaction among people was addressed. The critical importance of ethics was analyzed. Two commonly accepted theories about acquiring power in organizations were set forth. A brief consideration of empowerment concludes the section.

The contributions of military science were outlined in terms of eleven principles of leadership set forth in the *Military Leadership* field manual.

Currently, the military is considering adding personality differences as an additional trait. How are these traits applied? Profiles of General Colin Powell and Mao Zedong reveal how personality can play a part in leadership.

KEY TERMS

power reward	power
influence	coercive power
influence tactics	position power
politics	personal power
expert power	vertical dyad linkage
referent power	social exchange theory
legitimate power	empowerment

FOR DISCUSSION AND REVIEW

1. What are some common ways of obtaining influence?
2. What are some of the primary issues facing women today in terms of societal expectations of power?
3. What are some of the primary sources of power? Give an example of each.
4. What are some alternatives to a leadership model where there is a well-defined in-group and out-group?
5. What are some ways of empowering others?
6. What role should ethics play in the obtaining and usage of power?

CRITICAL INCIDENT

You are the CEO of an auto manufacturing company that has just settled a one-week strike. Among the demands made by your employees and agreed upon by you was to create a more empowering workplace environment. What are some steps you can take in order to facilitate empowerment in your organization?

EXERCISES FOR CHAPTER 6

Exercise 6–1   Identifying Leadership Traits

DIRECTIONS:

This exercise has two components. In Step One you are asked to identify three individuals you consider to be leaders. Next, using one or two words, describe their most prominent physical characteristics and their dominant personality features (include their attitude toward life), and then briefly note their most important leadership skills.

STEP ONE:
A)   LEADER'S NAME:
      OCCUPATION:
      LEADERSHIP ROLE:

Prominent Physical Characteristics	Dominant Personality Features (inc. attitude)	Important Leadership Skills
1.	1.	1.
2.	2.	2.
3.	3.	3.
4.	4.	4.
5.	5.	5.

Others (?)

B)   LEADER'S NAME:
      OCCUPATION:
      LEADERSHIP ROLE:

Prominent Physical Characteristics	Dominant Personality Features (inc. attitude)	Important Leadership Skills
1.	1.	1.
2.	2.	2.
3.	3.	3.
4.	4.	4.
5.	5.	5.

Others (?)

C)   LEADER'S NAME:
      OCCUPATION:
      LEADERSHIP ROLE:

Prominent Physical Characteristics	Dominant Personality Features (inc. attitude)	Important Leadership Skills
1.	1.	1.
2.	2.	2.
3.	3.	3.
4.	4.	4.
5.	5.	5.

Others (?)

STEP TWO: Please answer the following questions:

A.   Are there commonalities among the three leaders you selected? If so, identify them.

B.   Are the commonalities more prevalent in terms of physical characteristics, personality/attitude, or skills?

C.   In your opinion, are there important leadership traits which were *not* found in the three leaders analyzed? What does that mean?

D.   What does this exercise highlight about the TRAIT Theory approach to the study of leadership?

Modern Leadership Theories

The Leadership Journey:
A map of the terrain
Chapter 7

Words/names to recognize

	Gardner	Blake & Mouton	Multiple linkage theory
Leadership theories	Bennis	Situational leadership	Hersey & Blanchard
of the 70's–90's	Behavioral theories	Path-goal theory	
	The Ohio State studies	Fiedler	

You are here

Industrial Hwy.

Transitional Dr.

Hero's Blvd.

President's Path

Pre-Industrial Rd.

Quality Circle

Covey Circle

Rost Rd.

Post-Industrial Hwy.

Now that we've seen what the related disciplines have contributed to leadership theory, this chapter looks at the various theories that are or have been popular in leadership literature. We'll touch upon trait theory, behavioral management approaches, and situational approaches. It is fitting that our discussion begins with the seminal work of John Gardner, the former U.S. Secretary of Health, Education, and Welfare, and current professor at Stanford University. His book, *On Leadership* (1989), lists ten functions of leadership:

- Envisioning goals
- Affirming and regenerating important group values
- Motivating others toward collective goals
- Managing the processes through which collective goals can be reached
- Achieving unity of effort within a context of pluralism and diversity
- Creating an atmosphere of mutual trust
- Explaining and teaching
- Serving as a symbol of the group's identity
- Representing the group's interests to outside parties
- Renewing and adapting the organization to a changing world

These functions describe an ideal state that can be used as a benchmark to measure the effectiveness of any leader.

This list should be examined in terms of another well-known leadership theorist, Warren Bennis, former president of the University of Cincinnati. Bennis (1985) proposed his own list of competencies for leaders, based on a five-year project that studied ninety effective, successful leaders in corporations and the public sector.

He concluded that there are four major competencies:

1. Management of attention—the ability to attract others, not only through a compelling vision, but also through communicating commitment
2. Management of meaning—to make dreams apparent to others
3. Management of trust—to let others believe in one's constancy and focus
4. Management of self—understanding one's skills and using them well

TRAIT THEORY

Trait theory was very popular as we entered the second part of the twentieth century. Simply stated, this theory suggests that the traits of successful leaders should be studied and emulated. The enormity of the challenge is daunting. How can people who seek to practice leadership gain the needed "traits"?

One answer can be seen in Gardner's fourteen leadership attributes, which he says "seem to be linked with higher probabilities that a leader in one situation could also lead in another." They are:

1. Physical vitality and stamina

2. Intelligence and action-oriented judgment

3. Eagerness to accept responsibility

4. Task competence

5. Understanding of followers and their needs

6. Skill in dealing with people

7. Need for achievement

8. Capacity to motivate people

9. Courage and resolution

10. Trustworthiness

11. Decisiveness

12. Self-confidence

13. Assertiveness

14. Adaptability/flexibility

Rather than merely compiling this list from his own thoughts and experiences, Gardner worked from a five-year field study of organizations and interviews with hundreds of leaders. To what end do leaders employ these traits? Gardner asserts that leaders should focus on building and rebuilding community—on working for the common good. And their primary renewal task, he says, is "the release of human energy and talent."

In studying and questioning great leaders, Gardner and Bennis have returned to the trait theory approach (see Chapter 4). They looked at the person and tried to figure out how he or she practiced leadership. A sports analogy is reviewing video from the game and breaking down the component parts to analyze a power swing, for example.

James M. Kouzes and Barry Z. Posner also made a major contribution to trait theory in their book, *The Leadership Challenge.* In the early 1980s more than 1,500 managers responded to their survey, in which they asked, "What values do you look for in your superiors?" Of the 225 values, characteristics, and attitudes compiled from the answers, the top four listed were being honest, forward looking, inspiring, and competent. They called these four characteristics being *credible*. Please see their essay later in this chapter.

Many others have composed lists of leader characteristics, typically including such traits as energy level, height, general cognitive ability, and, to a lesser extent, particular technical skills and knowledge about a group's task. See Table 7–1 for a summary of effective physical, social, and personal leadership characteristics.

TABLE 7–1   **Personal Characteristics of Leaders**

Physical:	Active
	Energetic
Personality:	Alert
	Creative
	Ethical
Social:	Skilled interpersonally
	Can enlist others in goal
	Sociable
	Cooperative
Intelligence:	Good judgment
	Fluent in speaking
	Knowledgeable
Work related traits:	Task-oriented
	Tactful
	Driven to excel
	Responsible
	Ethical

BILLIE JEAN KING: NET GAINS FOR WOMEN

Billie Jean Moffit King remembers the day she told her mother, "I want to be the best tennis player in the world." It was also the day she bought her first tennis racquet and took her first tennis lesson. Six years later, she surprised the world by winning the women's doubles with Karen Hantze.

Her middle-class family in Long Beach, California, could not afford the kind of travel and tournament schedule that others of her ability could, but Billie Jean King did not let that deter her from her desire. She practiced incessantly, including lessons from tennis great Alice Marble.

She climbed to top ranking in the world, yet was frustrated that even after tennis players were allowed to accept prize winnings, the women received significantly less money than the men. She and husband Larry King decided to start a women's tennis tour. She worked hard to promote the new concept—almost as hard as she had to work to defeat up-and-coming young players like Chris Evert and Yvonne Goolagong. By the end of 1971, she had become the first woman tennis player to earn more than $100,000, as well as the first to win titles on four different types of courts: grass, clay, indoor, and concrete.

In 1973, in a much-promoted match, she defeated 55-year-old Bobby Riggs, a self-proclaimed male chauvinist who jeered that no woman could beat a top male pro. In a nationally televised spectacle, Billie Jean King proved him wrong.

Shortly afterward, she helped form World Team Tennis and the Women's Tennis Association, over which she served as first president. Controversy clouded her life in the early 1980s, as her former secretary brought allegations of a homosexual love affair with King. She weathered the adverse publicity, and the court ruled that she had never made promises of support to her lover.

After numerous knee surgeries and one aborted comeback, King officially retired from tennis in 1981. All told, she won the U.S. singles title four times and set a Wimbledon record with six singles, ten doubles, and four mixed doubles championships.

Despite that remarkable record, she may be remembered more for the changes she helped bring to the sport. Her play and personality forced the sport to alter its country club image, and her courage in fighting for women's rights on the court ensured a bright future for younger female players.

She continues to promote tennis and spends unheralded time giving free lessons to young girls in inner-city neighborhoods so they, too, might come to love the sport.

RIGOBERTA MENCHU: THE GUATEMALAN PEASANT WHO WON THE NOBEL PRIZE

A 37-year-old Mayan Indian woman leveraged the power of language to help rally the world behind the cause of the mistreated indigenous peoples of Guatemala. One of the first Indian activists to learn Spanish, the language of the wealthy landowners and military men running the government, Rigoberta Menchu clearly understood the importance of communicating with the "enemy."

In a similar way, she understood the importance of her fellow Indians keeping their own languages—upwards of twenty Indian dialects are spoken in Guatemala—to preserve their own culture. Once she mastered Spanish, Menchu began defending Indians' rights against a cruel government that all too often viewed Indians as easy prey. In addition, she also learned three of the principal Indian dialects.

Indians make up 60 to 80 percent of Guatemala's 10 million people, but they have repeatedly been subjugated by colonial powers and their descendants since the sixteenth century conquest of Central America by the Spaniards. Menchu believed that part of their vulnerability came from their cultural and linguistic isolation.

Descendants of the advanced Mayan civilization, today's Mayans reside on the mountaintops of Guatemala, living a simple life centered on respect for the land and close community ties. They frequently work on the coffee plantations of wealthy landowners.

Rigoberta Menchu learned to organize from her father, with whom she frequently traveled to villages across the country as a young child. She learned that the source of the government's terror against the Indians came from a concern over owning the land. She taught other villages to master the art of "trapping" government soldiers through a carefully rehearsed plan of hiding and surprising them, making the soldiers think they were armed.

After her father had been killed in an unsuccessful occupation of the Spanish embassy in Guatemala City and her brother and mother were tortured and killed, Menchu vowed to keep organizing the peasants. At a fraction over five feet tall, this powerful leader mobilized peasants, students, and workers in a series of strikes and demonstrations. As death threats escalated, she escaped to Mexico, where she still lives in exile.

Her insistence on nonviolence, despite the government's atrocities that included the deaths of her family members, attracted the attention of the world. Her efforts to bring peace and justice to Guatemala prompted two Nobel laureates, Argentina's Adolfo Perez Esquivel and South Africa's Bishop Desmond Tutu, to nominate her for the Nobel Peace Prize. The nomination itself was controversial, coming as it did amid the celebrations of the 500th anniversary of Columbus' "discovery" of the Americas. She was awarded the Nobel Peace Prize in 1992. She insists that the objective of the movement she heads is not to retaliate against the government's cruelty, but rather, to assure the basic human rights of the people of Guatemala who have no recourse.

She accepted the Nobel prize in 1992 in Oslo. As the chairman of the Norwegian Nobel Committee said, "By maintaining a disarming humanity in a brutal world, Rigoberta Menchu appeals to the best in us. She stands as a uniquely potent symbol of a just struggle."

One of her primary strategies as leader has been to teach other *companeros* to read and write Spanish so that Indians could learn to speak—and understand what the government was really saying—for themselves.

Her award was criticized by the Guatemalan government as well as by some U.S. conservatives in America, who saw her victory as a win for feminist, socialist, and violent causes.

With the $1.2 million award money from the prize, she has established a foundation for human rights of indigenous peoples in Guatemala and throughout the Americas.

BEHAVIORAL THEORIES OF LEADERSHIP

The behavioral approach to studying leadership assumes that leader behaviors rather than personality characteristics are the element exerting the most effect on followers. Significant research on this perspective was conducted at Ohio State University and the University of Michigan.

The Ohio State Studies

The **Ohio State studies** examined the effects of two dimensions of leader behavior: *consideration* and *initiating structure*. Consideration refers to the leader's awareness of and sensitivity to subordinates' interests, feelings, and ideas. Leaders high in consideration are typically friendly, prefer open communications, focus on teamwork, and are concerned with the other person's welfare.

Initiating structure, on the other hand, is a leader behavior marked by attention to task and goals. Leaders who are high in initiating structure typically present instructions and provide detailed, explicit timelines for task completion.

Since the two behaviors are independent of each other, researchers tested the effectiveness of four combinations of leader behaviors: high initiating structure–low consideration (HIS–LC), low initiating structure–high consideration (LIS–HC), high initiating structure–high consideration (HIS–HC), and low initiating structure–low consideration (LIS–LC). The high initiating structure–high consideration style was associated with the best performance and greatest satisfaction. These leaders both met the needs of their subordinates and were effective in accomplishing their task and/or goals.

University of Michigan Studies

Similarly, in the late 1950s, researchers including Rensis Likert looked at the behavior of effective and ineffective supervisors. The **University of Michigan studies** concluded that supervisory behavior could be analyzed in terms of *employee-centered* and *job-centered* behavior. Employee-centered supervisors were found most effective. To these researchers, supervisors exhibited either one or the other of these patterns; there was no middle ground, no combination of centers.

The Leadership Grid

Robert Blake and Jane Mouton developed the concept of the **Leadership Grid** (see Figure 7–1), which graphically depicts the characteristics of leaders based on some of the dimensions examined in the Ohio State and Michigan studies. Questionnaire responses were used to rate managers on a scale from one to nine for two dimensions, concern for people and concern for production. An individual's scores on these two dimensions were then plotted, with a score of (9,9) equaling the ideal leader ("team" style). See chapter 9 for a more detailed discussion of this leadership style.

Based on a person's location on the grid, Blake and Mouton (1964) identified four other distinct management styles. Most managers fall near the (5,5) point on the grid, indicating a "middle of the road style." These managers rate in the middle range on the concern for people scale and in the middle range on the concern for production scale. Those scoring high on concern for people and low on concern for production scales demonstrate a "country club" style. Finally, managers scoring very low on both scales are said to have an "impoverished" style.

While Blake and Mouton concluded that managers perform best when working under a (9,9) "team" style, there is little substantive evidence to support this claim; some question whether a (9,9) is even possible, since often a leader is forced to make a decision that either favors people or production.

LOUELLA THOMPSON, FOUNDER OF "FEED THE HUNGRY"

Since 1987, Louella Thompson has been working on an all-consuming assignment. That year, the Middletown, Ohio, hairdresser says God told her, "Open the door and feed whoever comes. Don't ask any questions."

For the past eight years that's exactly what the 70-year-old has done, fixing hot

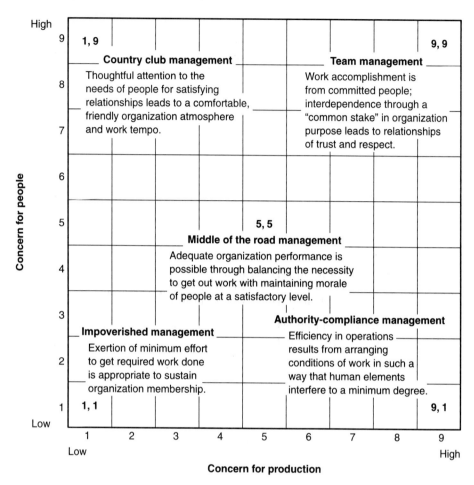

Figure 7–1   The Leadership Grid® Leadership Styles
Source: Leadership Dilemmas—Grid Solutions. pp. 29, by Robert R. Blake, Ph.D. and Anne Adams McCanse. Copyright © 1991, by Robert R. Blake and the Estate of Jane S. Mouton, Austin, Texas. The Grid® designation is property of Scientific Methods, Inc. Gulf Publishing Company, Houston, Texas. Used with permission. All rights reserved.

meals for free carryout or delivery for an average of 600 people a month. (That doesn't count the donuts, juice, and coffee she hands out to a steady stream of children and adults each morning.) She chose the fourth Saturday of the month for the hot meals because by that time, many people's budgets were stretched to the breaking point.

Thompson supervises volunteers from all over the area, and graciously accepts donations of food, money, clothing, and old roasting units (her crowded kitchen now has five electric units in addition to her original stove). There are "five or six" freezers scattered throughout her combination house/office/soup kitchen.

For six years she was a regular presence at county commissioner meetings, promoting the Feed the Hungry project. Her mission of feeding and not asking questions has captured the city's attention, bringing donations and volunteer help from groups and individuals. Community groups, including adults on probation and mentally retarded young people, schedule weekly sessions to help out with bagging food or peeling apples or helping in some other specific way. Thompson welcomes all contributions—of time, service, and money. "I'm not hard to please," she says. "Whatever people want to do to help feed the hungry, that's all right with me."

Her biggest project sits on the lot next to her house: a partially completed two-story community kitchen, which she envisions serving not only the nutritional needs of the community but also its spiritual needs by providing meeting areas for drug and alcohol recovery groups.

The building would have been completed long ago, she acknowledges, if she had accepted government money. "But to do that, I would have to ask the people I feed questions about their work, etc. I won't do that."

As a result, the building has been five long years in the making. Currently the shell is up and the walls are framed, but there is little progress beyond that. She's waiting, patiently, for the electrician who volunteers his time to complete the blueprints so that the city can approve them.

Thompson shies from being called a leader. "God is the leader," she asserts. "I just do what He tells me to." Rev. Martin Luther King Jr. exemplifies leadership for her. "He was humble. People tried to use him, but he kept on doing what he had to do," she says.

For her, that meant visiting the presidents of the local banks—not to ask for money, but to inform them of her plans. "I wouldn't see anyone else but the presidents. I had no fear," she says, smiling at the memory of marching into those executive offices and waiting for an appointment.

Her rewards for leading this effort against hunger? "I just enjoy seeing people happy. It makes me happy to see people eating good food." Her generosity is contagious. Often, people drop off food, saying they were returning the favor of eating there. "They know how it feels to be hungry and get a good meal," she says. "I feel real good to see them giving to someone else."

On a larger scale, her efforts have inspired several other food programs in the community. "I'm glad to see them popping up in other places, because the times are hard. And they're going to get harder before they get better," she says, noting that she meditates each day to find the guidance and energy to persist. Asked how she maintains her vigorous schedule, she admits to getting tired sometimes, especially after staying up the entire night to help prepare the community meal. "I just work it," she says with a shrug.

She maintains a confidence in people's willingness to help. "I just love that I don't have to call people to help. They just do it. That way, I don't feel like I'm making them do it. I feel if I leave it open, they'll do it for themselves, not to please me."

Her advice to younger people: "Search yourself. Let your mind tell you what to do."

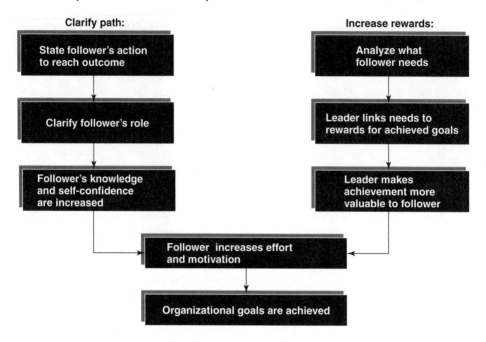

Figure 7–2   **Leader Roles in the Path–Goal Model**

SITUATIONAL APPROACHES TO LEADERSHIP

This section reviews major situational theories about leadership. Situational leadership looks at three elements: the leader; the follower (we prefer the term *collaborator*); and the situation itself. Situational theories, then, look at one behavioral aspect of leadership. The **Path–Goal theory,** for example, centers on motivation and its relationship to the leader, follower and situation (see Figures 7–2 through 7–4).

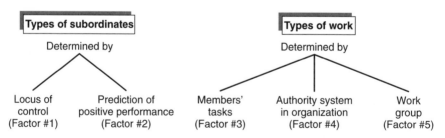

Figure 7–3   **House's Path–Goal Theory: Contingency Factors**

DIRECTIVE	SUPPORTIVE
• Emphasizes management functions such as planning, organizing, and controlling	• Emphasizes concern for well-being of group members
• Gives specific guidelines, rules, and regulations to organization members	• Establishes an emotionally supportive work environment and develops mutually satisfying relationships among group members
• Clearly spells out expectations for group members	• Group members who are unsure of themselves prefer this style
• Typically improves performance when tasks are unclear or organization unstable	• Typically improves performance where tasks are dissatisfying, stressful, or frustrating

ACHIEVEMENT-ORIENTED	PARTICIPATIVE
• Emphasizes setting challenging goals and high expectations for performance	• Emphasizes consultation with group members and takes their suggestions seriously when making decisions
• Continually pushes for work improvement	
• Group members expected to assume significant responsibility	• Typically improves performance of of well-motivated employees who perform nonrepetitive tasks
• Typically improves performance with achievement-oriented team members and with those working on ambiguous and nonrepetitive tasks	

Figure 7–4   House's Path–Goal Theory: Leadership Style In order to use Path–Goal theory effectively, a leader must first assess the revelant factors in the organization (see Figure 7–3 on contingency factors). Second, one must select the leadership style that fits those contingency factors best.

Path–Goal Theory

A leader must motivate followers. Based on expectancy theory, which was discussed in Chapter 4, the Path–Goal approach states that leaders are successful if they can affect five factors:

1. Followers' valences (a valence is one's perspective about what is important). Leaders can help followers identify and pursue an outcome that is under the leader's control.

2. Followers' instrumentalities. Leaders can make sure that high performance means satisfying outcomes.

3. Followers' expectancies. Leaders can reduce followers' frustration by overcoming barriers.

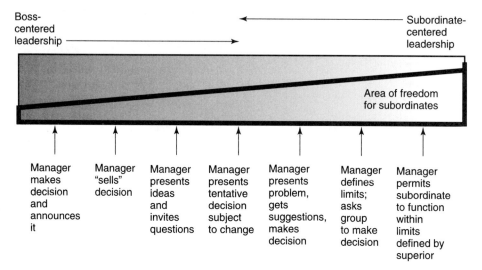

Figure 7–5   Continuum of Leadership Behavior
Source: J. Donnelly, J. Gibson, J. Ivancevich *Fundamentals of Management*, 9th edition 1995. Irwin
Professional Publ. Used with permission.

4.   Equity of rewards. Leaders raise the levels and types of rewards available for
     good performance.

5.   Accuracy of role perceptions. Leaders specify clearly the routes for effective per-
     formance.

A Continuum of Leader Behavior

How do leaders affect the preceding factors? By choosing among four behavioral
styles (Figure 7–4):

Directive: Authoritarian. Collaborators know precisely what is expected and
when, but have no say in decision-making.

Supportive: A directive leader who nonetheless shows concern and interest in
collaborators.

Participative: A leader who enlists and accepts others' ideas, but still makes the
decision.

Achievement-oriented: A leader who establishes challenging but possible goals
for collaborators and fully expects their achievement.

With the five expectancy variables, the four leadership styles, and the knowledge
that situational and follower factors also affect the process, the Path–Goal theory can
become very complicated. As you might expect, wise individuals select a leadership
style based on elements of the task, the situation, or the subordinates. They may fluctuate, too, between leadership styles, depending on which one promises the best results in a given situation.

For example, *participative leadership* produces satisfaction in situations in which the task is not routine and the collaborators are themselves not authoritarian. *Directive leadership* results in high satisfaction and performance only when collaborators have great needs for clarity. *Supportive leadership* produces satisfaction among collaborators only when the task is highly structured, and *achievement-oriented leadership* yields improved performance only when collaborators express commitment to goals.

Chart Summary: Path–Goal Theory

Centers on: expectancy theory, which suggests that people calculate the advantages of different levels of effort (e.g., if I practice the piano for eight hours, how likely is it that I will do well at the recital?); performance (e.g., If I do well at the recital, how likely is it that I will get a record contract?); and values (e.g., how much do I want a performing career?).

Useful for:

Predicting to which tasks people will devote their energy.

Understanding the complexity of the factors involved in practicing leadership.

IMPLICATIONS FOR PRACTICING LEADERSHIP

Effective leaders make sure appropriate rewards are available for followers (the goal) and then help them find the best way to achieve it (the path). Practicing leadership involves helping others see that the more effort and energy they put into a task, the greater the chance of accomplishing it. PLUS, leaders must make sure that achieving the task will have valuable consequences.

Leadership skills needed:

ability to identify and communicate with others

ability to use motivation to encourage activity

ability to accurately assess the situation and the collaborators

flexibility in determining when to use which of the four styles

Most effective when:

Research (Mitchell, Smyser, and Weed, 1975) shows that others' satisfaction with a leader depends not only on the leader's style, but on certain variables of the follower. For example, some studies showed that not everyone was satisfied with participatory leadership approaches. In fact, those who were happiest with participating in decisions were people with internal locus of control—who thought that outcomes were directly related to their behavior. Conversely, those with external locus of control—who felt that the outcomes depended on factors outside their control—were more satisfied with a directive leader.

Another collaborator variable that affects leader style is the collaborators' perception of their own abilities to perform the tasks.

Situational factors:

The task—is it in itself motivating? routine?

The authority system—are there standards for performing the task?

The primary work group—is there an accepted way of performing the task?

The Path–Goal model is very comprehensive (Figure 7–6). It sees leadership within organizations as helping members clarify their goals and identify the best ways to achieve those goals. (See Exercise 7–1)

Normative Decision Model

Vroom and Yetton (1973) and Vroom and Yago (1988) contend that leaders can improve group performance by selecting the most appropriate amount of participation in decision making. Thus, they developed a model designed to assess the amount of input group members should contribute to the decision-making process (Figure 7–7).

Their investigation of decision-making processes in groups led them to propose a continuum of decision processes ranging from autocratic to consultative to group process. Two criteria, they suggest, can be used to evaluate decisions: decision quality and decision acceptance. Quality decisions, for example, would affect profit, cost-saving, or level of service, all measurable objectives. For a decision to be accepted, subordinates/group members would come to consider the decision one they "buy into" and feel comfortable with, not one that they are compelled to obey.

Further, Vroom, Yetton and Yago (1989) proposed a normative decision model. (In this case, *normative* refers to how leaders *ought* to proceed in making decisions— what the norms "should" be.) The decision tree (Figure 7–8) depicts the model, in which a leader states the problem and then asks a series of questions about the problem until an appropriate decision style is determined.

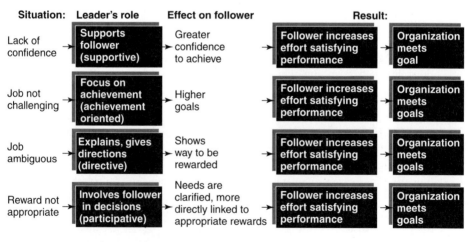

Figure 7–6   Leader Roles in Path–Goal Situations

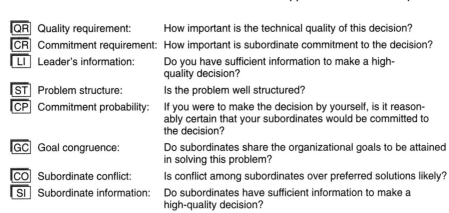

QR	Quality requirement:	How important is the technical quality of this decision?
CR	Commitment requirement:	How important is subordinate commitment to the decision?
LI	Leader's information:	Do you have sufficient information to make a high-quality decision?
ST	Problem structure:	Is the problem well structured?
CP	Commitment probability:	If you were to make the decision by yourself, is it reasonably certain that your subordinates would be committed to the decision?
GC	Goal congruence:	Do subordinates share the organizational goals to be attained in solving this problem?
CO	Subordinate conflict:	Is conflict among subordinates over preferred solutions likely?
SI	Subordinate information:	Do subordinates have sufficient information to make a high-quality decision?

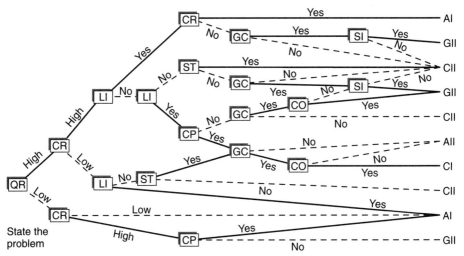

Figure 7–7   The Vroom-Yetton-Yago Model

Source: J. Donnelly, J. Gibson, and J. Ivancevich *Fundamentals of Management*, 9th edition, 1995. Irwin Professional Publishers. Used with permission.

The LPC Model: Least Preferred Coworker

Compared to the Path–Goal Model, which sees the leader as being able to change styles of behavior to suit the situation and the group, the **LPC Model** is very precise and it assumes that leaders possess broad, general orientations that are unlikely to change. Fred Fiedler (1989) suggested that leaders behave with either a task orientation or a relationship orientation. He derived his model from analysis of scores on the LPC checklist shown in Exercise 7–2 at the end of this chapter.

The LPC checklist, while seeming to provide information about coworkers, actually says something about the leader. Categorized as either high or low LPC, leaders are grouped according to their motivation hierarchy.

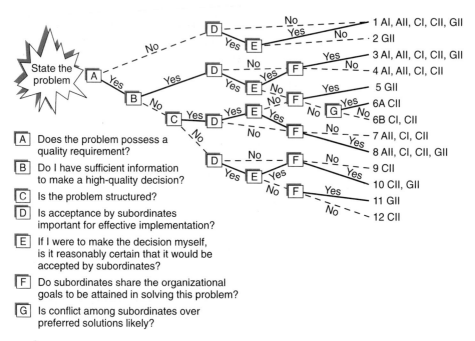

A Does the problem possess a quality requirement?

B Do I have sufficient information to make a high-quality decision?

C Is the problem structured?

D Is acceptance by subordinates important for effective implementation?

E If I were to make the decision myself, is it reasonably certain that it would be accepted by subordinates?

F Do subordinates share the organizational goals to be attained in solving this problem?

G Is conflict among subordinates over preferred solutions likely?

Figure 7–8   Vroom and Yetton's Leadership Decision Tree

Source: Reprinted from *Leadership and Decision-Making,* by Victor H. Vroom and Philip W. Yetton, by permission of the University of Pittsburgh Press, © 1973 by University of Pittsburgh Press.

Fiedler suggested that relationship-oriented leaders are most effective in situations that are moderately favorable and task-oriented leaders are most effective in situations that are either extremely favorable or extremely unfavorable (Figure 7–9).

Hughes, Ginett, and Curphy (1993) draw some helpful corollaries with Maslow's hierarchy of needs. Just as Maslow postulated that lower-level needs must be met first, so high LPC leaders will emphasize task accomplishments after they have established favorable relationships with their followers. Similarly, low LPC leaders will proceed to relationship deepening only after they believe the task is being adequately addressed.

What about those leaders whose scores lie somewhere in the middle? Kennedy (1992) suggests that these people may be able to switch between orientations more easily than those scoring at either extreme.

Situation Favorability

Beyond leader orientation, Fiedler linked situational factors with leadership success. He equated situation favorability with the amount of control a leader held over collaborators. Within situation favorability, he further broke down the elements into the strongest variable, *leader–member relations*; the second most powerful variable, *task structure*; and the weakest element of the three, *position power*. (See Figure 7–10.)

Fiedler's Classification of Situation Favorableness

	Very Favorable			Intermediate		Very Unfavorable		
Leader–Member Relations	Good	Good	Good	Good	Poor	Poor	Poor	Poor
Task Structure	High		Low		High		Low	
Leader Position Power	Strong	Weak	Strong	Weak	Strong	Weak	Strong	Weak
Situations	I	II	III	IV	V	VI	VII	VIII

Figure 7–9   Fiedler's Classification of Situation Favorableness

Source: Fred E. Fiedler, "The Effects of Leadership Training and Experience: A Contingency Model Interpretation," *Administrative Science Quarterly* 17 (1972), 455. Reprinted by permission of *Administrative Science Quarterly.*

He proposed that adding the relative weights of these three elements creates a continuum of situational favorability.

Leader–member relationship is assessed by the degree of cooperation and friendliness or antagonism and difficulty in the leader–collaborator relationship. A high number on this element indicates a generally positive relationship.

Task structure depends on the level of specificity about work products, processes, or objective work evaluations. Here, too, high numbers represent a high level of structure in the task. Position power, according to Fiedler, refers to the title, authority, or rank of the leader.

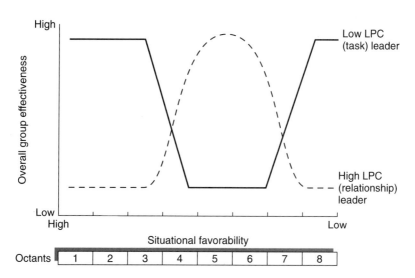

Figure 7–10   Leader Effectiveness Based on the Contingency Between Leader LPC Score and Situation Favorability

Source: From Richard L. Hughes, Robert C. Ginnett, and Gordon J. Curphy. *Leadership: Enhancing the Lessons of Experience,* 1996. Irwin, Inc. Used with permission.

Using this continuum, you can see that the highest degree of situation favorability occurs when leaders and members enjoy a positive relationship, the task is structured, and the leader has legitimate authority. Conversely, the situation is least favorable when the leader and member have a poor relationship, the task is unstructured, and the leader has no position of power.

Fiedler has further refined his theory with research on which type of leader (high or low LPC) is more effective on different levels of situation favorability. As Table 7–2 shows, high LPC (relationship-oriented) leaders do best with moderate situational favorability. Task-oriented, or low LPC, leaders do best at the extremes.

Chart summary: Fiedler's LPC Model

Centers on:

Situational variables that affect group performance (and by extension, leader's effectiveness).

Useful for:

Examining the orientation of the leader

IMPLICATIONS FOR PRACTICING LEADERSHIP

The effectiveness of training in changing leader behavior is questionable in this model, as Fiedler asserted that a leader's task or relationship orientation was the product of years of experiences and not amenable to swift change. He suggests, instead, re-engineering the situations to fit the leader's dominant style. This approach has been called the Leader–Match training program.

TABLE 7–2 **Situational Leadership Applied to Eight Situations**

Situation	Leader-Member Relations	Task Structure	Position Power	Most Effective Leadership	Reason(s) for Effectiveness
1. First-line supervisor at Ford Motor Company	Good	High	Strong	Task oriented	Employees respect task expertise, recognize power, and permit supervisor to lead.
2. Chairperson of college department	Good	High	Weak	Task oriented	Faculty member elected because he possesses group values. Understands what the group needs to do and pushes for task completion.

(continued)

TABLE 7–2   Situational Leadership Applied to Eight Situations *(Continued)*

Situation	Leader-Member Relations	Task Structure	Position Power	Most Effective Leadership	Reason(s) for Effectiveness
3. Sales manager at Procter & Gamble	Good	Low	Strong	Task oriented	Manager has formal authority and power, but salespeople work all over territory. They must have some autonomy because of unstructured nature of job.
4. Committee chairperson	Good	Low	Weak	About equally task and relationship oriented	Chair has little power and must rely on both types of leadership to accomplish job.
5. Middle-level manager at IBM	Poor	High	Strong	Relationship oriented	Manager is not well liked but has power to motivate. Can accomplish more if relationship approach is used.
6. Supervisor at General Mills	Poor	High	Weak	Relationship oriented	Employees know what they're supposed to accomplish. Supervisor is unpopular and has little say-so. More effective to use relationship style instead of creating more hostility.
7. Operating-room nurse supervisor at Massachusetts General Hospital	Poor	Low	Strong	Almost equally task and relationship oriented	Difficult to control unstructured activities through use of power. Because person is unpopular, it is best to use relationship orientation when appropriate and task orientation if necessary.
8. Detective in charge of other detectives working on a case in Washington, D.C.	Poor	Low	Weak	Task oriented	Detective has little power, is not well liked, and case is unstructured. Concentrate on solving the case.

Source: From James H. Donnelly, Jr, James L. Gibson, and John M. Ivancevich *Fundamentals of Management*, 9th edition, 1995. Irwin. Used with permission.

Leadership skills needed:

Ability to analyze situation's favorability

Ability to identify personal leadership orientation

Most effective in:

A complex work setting involving many people

Situational factors:

Analyze the task: how complex or self-rewarding is it?

Analyze the leader's style.

Analyze the sophistication of the work group.

Advantages:

Fiedler's theory prompted an examination of the complexity of leadership factors, and served to introduce the situational approach to leadership.

Despite extensive laboratory and field research using Fiedler's model, the results are equivocal. Nevertheless, as Hughes et al. note, the fact that Fiedler's theories have prompted so much research speaks highly for the initial work. Fiedler has proceeded to answer some of the criticisms of his model, and he has also gone on to develop another situational model, the **Cognitive Resources Theory.**

Cognitive Resources Theory

In this theory, Fiedler and his colleagues (Fiedler, 1986; Fiedler & Garcia, 1987) focus on the impact of the leader's intelligence and experience as these two cognitive traits affect group performance. Naturally, the theory is more complicated than that simple summary. The cognitive traits interact with leader behavior (directive, nondirective) and with elements of the situation (interpersonal stress and the nature of the group's task).

A fairly recent theory, the Cognitive Resources theory has as yet not been the subject of much research to validate its assumptions. Yukl (1995) points out methodological problems and weaknesses in the theory. The Cognitive Resources theory is useful, however, because it focuses on the ability of the leader and collaborator, a component that few other models explore.

According to Cognitive Resources theory, directiveness (giving specific instructions) is most effective when leaders are competent, relaxed, and supported. Because the group is prepared, a directive style is the clearest way to communicate with them. However, when leaders experience stress, experience becomes more important than ability. Low support means the group is less receptive and the leader will have lower effectiveness. A nondirective leader (who does not give specific instructions) with high group support makes group member ability more critical. Weak support, however, gives more power to variables outside the leader or the group members.

Multiple Linkage Theory

Yukl (1995) looked at the interaction of "managerial" behavior and situational factors on the performance of the manager's work group. He recognizes the importance of six intervening variables that are aspects of member motivation and ability.

These intervening variables interact singly or in combination with situational variables comparable to Kerr and Jermier's (1978) "substitutes" and "neutralizers." Yukl offers two major propositions for the **Multiple Linkage theory:**

1. In the short-term, unit effectiveness is greater when the leader acts to correct any deficiencies in the intervening variables.

2. In the longer term, unit effectiveness is greater when the leader acts to make the situation more favorable. After extinguishing fires, in other words, leaders should focus on the situation rather than directly on the intervening variables.

Among the long-term actions he cites are

- Cultivating better relationships with suppliers, finding alternative sources, and reducing dependence on unreliable sources
- Undertaking long-term improvement programs to upgrade personnel, equipment and facilities
- Modifying the work unit's formal structure to solve chronic problems and reduce demands on the leader to perform troubleshooting (Yukl, 1994)

Life Cycle Model

In an interesting turnabout, Paul Hersey and Kenneth Blanchard (1969) envision that the effectiveness of leaders' styles depends largely on their collaborators' maturity, job experience, and emotional maturity. This is the **Life Cycle model.** Maturity is defined as the ability to perform a job independently, the tendency to assume additional responsibility and the desire to achieve success.

Hersey and Blanchard outline four types of leader behaviors:

- Telling (best for group members with low levels of maturity)
- Selling (effective with members at moderately low maturity levels)
- Participating (effective with moderately high levels of maturity)
- Delegating (best with those at the very highest maturity levels)

The model posits two basic decision styles: task orientation and relationship orientation.

As group members become more "ready" (mature), leaders should change their behaviors to reflect this increased maturity. Increased maturity is defined as an increase in collaborator readiness and ability. As collaborators mature, leaders should begin to focus on supportive behavior and less on task behavior until followers reach the highest phase of maturity, a stage Hersey and Blanchard termed *high readiness.*

At this stage, followers have become skilled, confident, and self-sufficient. When followers reach this stage, the task of the leader is to delegate and thus serve as a low-task, low-relationship leader.

Leadership skills needed:

ability to identify followers' maturity for specific tasks

ability to diagnose demands of situations

ability to choose the appropriate decision style to match task and follower requirements.

The model has been received well by leadership practitioners, perhaps in part because it is intuitive and focuses on the followers' feelings of competence as well as on their behaviors.

Leader–Member Exchange (LMX) Model

The **Leader–Member Exchange model,** developed by George Graen (1975), operates on the premise that all subordinates are not treated equally. Because of a combination of time constraints and human nature, the model assumes that leaders tend to spend disproportionate amounts of time with a select group of subordinates who are, thus, the "in-group." Those in the in-group tend to perform at a higher level than subordinates who fall in the out-group.

Graen says that early on in the relationship, a leader determines whether or not another person will be part of the in-group. Precise criteria for making this determination are unclear, but some suggest that the decision is affected by three characteristics of the subordinates/collaborators:

1. Characteristics similar to the leader's

2. A higher degree of competence than members of the out-group

3. Higher levels of extroversion than out-group members

Research on the LMX theory is still preliminary and questions exist about the ways in which leaders make the determinations of in- versus out-groups. What is clear, however, is that leaders invariably devote more time to certain employees and that the selection process is not a random one.

ROSA PARKS: A TIME TO SIT

Rosa McCauley Parks was 42 that afternoon in Montgomery, Alabama. The soft-spoken woman took the bus every day to her job as a seamstress. She fumed with the injustice and indignity of the bus company and its drivers. Once before, bus driver James Blake had tested her spirit: he let her enter the front door to pay, but then insisted she follow the custom in which blacks then got off and re-entered the back door to claim a seat. This time, when she had paid and moved outside to the rear door, he pulled away before she could re-enter. It was an insult that black people faced all the time in Montgomery.

On the next occasion, she was ready for Mr. Blake. He ordered her to leave her seat so a white person could sit, but Parks calmly said no. He insisted, in louder and louder terms. "No," came her reply, just as firmly. It wasn't simply that she was tired. Yes, she was weary from working, but she was more tired of the treatment she and her fellow blacks had to put up with.

What many people don't know is that Rosa Parks was sophisticated about her rights. For twelve years she had been secretary of the local NAACP, watching and learning as the group took on ever more ambitious goals. In addition, shortly before her famous act of resistance, she had participated in a training session at the Highlander School in Tennessee, where blacks and whites met to encourage each other and learn how to organize opposition to injustice. She was much more than a symbol of resistance and protest; but she was an awfully dignified symbol.

Throughout the 11-month bus boycott that Parks's resistance prompted, she and her husband endured hate calls, death threats, and eventually, the loss of both of their jobs before segregation in public transportation was struck down by the U.S. Supreme Court in 1956. The Parks moved to Detroit, where Rosa took care of her ailing mother and husband.

Rosa Parks has continued to be active in civil rights, resisting many people's attempts to see her only as a symbol and not as a woman with definite views and convictions. In addition to winning a seat on the board of the Detroit NAACP, she founded the Institute for Self Development, to encourage young people to work for change and to grow as people.

ARTHUR ASHE JR.: "STEPPING UP"

At age 37, Arthur Ashe Jr. resigned himself to never playing tennis again. The heart disease that eventually necessitated two bypass operations forced him to a premature ending of his successful tennis career. Several years later he contracted AIDS from an inadequately screened blood transfusion. He chose to publicly announce his condition before the story broke in *USA Today.*

Despite these catastrophic incidents, Arthur Ashe didn't stop speaking out about morality and life, particularly as they affected African American youth. From his early days as a player on the professional circuit, Ashe made a point of telling his audiences that professional sports offered a very limited future for the majority of urban youth. He stressed the vital importance of an education and modeled it in his thoughtful speeches and essays.

Having grown up in the segregated schools and segregated society of Richmond, Virginia, Ashe railed against unfair treatment of others, whether in his home town, in the government's actions against refugees from Haiti, or in South Africa's apartheid.

Others at times berated him for being less strident in his political stances. "As for myself," he wrote in his memoir, *Days of Grace* (1993), "I found out a long time ago that I am best when I keep my ego under tight control and try to reason and look ahead, beyond temporary, flashy victories at some other human being's expense, to the future. One consequence of my commitment to reasoning and reconciling would always be to have some people think of me as conservative, or opportunistic, or even a coward. So be it."

Facing his inevitable death, Ashe wasted little time. He established two foundations: Safe Passage, to help poor young people, especially blacks, make the transition from youth to adulthood without a crippling loss of faith in society and in themselves; and the Arthur Ashe Foundation for the Defeat of AIDS, for research and treatment of the disease on a global scale.

Incredibly, he also founded the African American Athletic Association, which he chaired until his death. The AAAA is a mentoring project for African American student athletes.

He explains his determination to fight against AIDS until his death:

> I was bent on telling the story of AIDS so that as many people as possible would be aware of its dangers, its myths and realities. I made up my mind not to withdraw from the world nor even to turn bashfully from the limelight. Unless I fell severely ill and became gaunt and wasted, as many AIDS patients do, I would not become a recluse. 'You come to the realization that time is short,' I told a reporter . . .'These are extraordinary conditions and you have to step up.'

> . . . As I settled deeper into this new stage of my life, I became increasingly conscious of a certain thrill, an exhilaration even, about what I was doing. Yes, I felt pain, physical and psychological; but I also felt something like pleasure in responding purposefully, vigorously, to my illness. I had lost many matches on the tennis court, but I had seldom quit. I was losing, but playing well now; my head was down, eyes riveted on the ball as I stroked it; I had to be careful but I could not be tentative; my follow-through must flow from the shot, fluid and smooth. Experience as an athlete had taught me that in times of danger I had to respond with confidence, authority, and calm. So many looming defeats had turned strangely, sometimes even miraculously, into victories as I applied that lesson to the task before me.

THREE ROLES OF THE LEADER

DR. STEPHEN R. COVEY

The leader of the future, of the next millenium, will be one who creates a culture or a value system centered upon principles. Creating such a culture in a business, government, school, hospital, nonprofit organization, family, or other organization will be a tremendous and exciting challenge in this new era and will only be achieved by leaders, be they emerging or seasoned, who have the vision, courage and humility to constantly learn and grow. Those people and organizations who have a passion for learning—learning through listening, seeing emerging trends, sensing and anticipating needs in the marketplace, evaluating past successes and mistakes, and absorbing the lessons that conscience and principles teach us, to mention just a few ways—will have enduring influence. Such learning leaders will not resist change; they will embrace it.

A White-Water World

The world has changed in a very profound way. This change continues to happen all around us, all the time. It is a white-water world. The consumer revolution has accelerated enormously. People are so much more enlightened and aware. There are so many more dynamic, competitive forces operating. The quality standards have raised to the point, particularly in the global market place, that there is simply no way to fake it. You may be able to survive in a local marketplace without meeting these standards, perhaps even in a regional marketplace, but certainly not in a global marketplace.

In all sectors—business, government, healthcare, social, nonprofit, etc.—the marketplace is demanding that organizations transform themselves. They must be able to produce services and goods and deliver them in a fast, friendly, and flexible way, and on a consistent basis that serves the needs of both internal and external customers. This requires a workforce that is not only allowed, but is enabled, encouraged, and rewarded by giving of its full creativity and talent. Even though tens of thousands of organizations are deeply involved in quality initiatives designed to produce those very results, transformation is still being demanded. The fundamental reason why most quality initiatives do not work is because there is a lack of trust in the culture—in the relationships between people. Just as you cannot fake world-class quality, so also is it impossible to fake high trust. It has to come out of trustworthiness.

I put more faith, however, in what the global economy is doing to drive quality than in any other factor. It is teaching us that principles such as empowerment, trust, and trustworthiness ultimately control the effective results we seek.

The most effective leaders are first *models* of what I call principle-centered leadership. They have come to realize that we're all subject to natural laws or governing principles, which operate regardless of our awareness of them or our obedience to them. Our effectiveness is predicated upon alignment with these inviolate principles—natural laws in the human dimension that are just as real, just as unchanging, as laws such as gravity are in the physical dimension. These principles are woven into the fabric of every civilized society and constitute the roots of every organization that has endured.

To the degree that we recognize and live in harmony with such basic principles as fairness, service, equity, justice, integrity, honesty, and trust, we move toward either survival and stability on the one hand or disintegration and destruction on the other. Principles are self-evident, self-validating natural laws. In fact, the best way to know they are self evident is by trying to imagine a world, or for that matter, *any* effective, enduring society, organization or family based upon its opposite.

Correct principles are like compasses: they are always pointing the way. They don't change or shift, and if we know how to read them, we won't get lost, confused, or fooled by conflicting voices and values. They provide true north direction to our lives as we navigate the "streams" of our environments. Thus we see that a change-less, principle-centered core is the key to having the confidence, security, power, guidance, and wisdom to change the way we address the changing needs and op-portunities around us.

So the first role of the leader is to be a model of principle-centered leadership. Whenever a person or an organization is principle-centered, that person or organi-zation becomes a model—an example—to other people and organizations. It is that kind of modeling, that kind of character, competence, and action that produces the trust among the people, causing them to identify with this modeling and be influ-enced by it. Modeling, then, is a combination of character (who you are as a person) and competence (what you can do). These two qualities represent your potential. But when you actually *do* it—when you put action together with character—you've got modeling.

Three Roles of a Leader

What is it, then, that the principle-centered leader models? I suggest that you can break leadership into three basic functions or activities: pathfinding, aligning, em-powering. Let's explore each one in turn.

Pathfinding   The essence and power of *pathfinding* are found in a compelling vi-sion and mission. Pathfinding deals with the larger sense of the future. It gets the culture imbued and excited about a tremendous, transcendent purpose. But in rela-tion to what?—to meeting the needs of your customers and other stakeholders. Pathfinding, then, ties together your value system and vision with the needs of cus-tomers and other stakeholders through a strategic plan. I call this the strategic pathway.

Aligning   The second activity of a leader is *aligning*. It consists of ensuring that your organizational structure, systems and operational processes all contribute to achieving your mission and vision of meeting the needs of customer and other stake-holders. They don't interfere with it, they don't compete with it, and they don't dom-inate it. They're only there for one purpose—to contribute to it. Far and away the greatest leverage of the principle of alignment comes when your people are in align-ment with your mission, vision and strategy. When your people are filled with true understanding of the needs, when they share a powerful commitment to accom-plishing the vision, when they are invited to create and continually improve the struc-tures and systems that will meet the needs, then you have alignment. Without these human conditions, you cannot have world-class quality; all you have is brittle pro-grams. Ultimately, we must learn that programs and systems are vital, but that *peo-ple* are the programmers.

Empowering   The third activity of a leader is *empowering*. What does that mean? People have enormous talent, ingenuity, intelligence, creativity. Most of it lies dor-mant. When you get true alignment toward a common vision, a common mission, you begin to co-mission with those people. Individual purpose and mission is commingled with the mission of the organization. When these purposes overlap, great synergy is created. A fire is ignited within people that unleashes their latent talent, ingenuity, and creativity to do whatever is necessary and consistent with the principles agreed upon to accomplish their common values, vision and mission in serving customers and other stakeholders. This is what we mean by empowerment.

But then you have to study what happens. What are the results? Are we really meeting the needs of the customers and the other stakeholders? Data and information that indicates whether the needs are truly being met must be fed back to these empowered people and teams inside the culture so that they can use it to make the necessary course corrections and improvements, and continue to do whatever it takes to fulfill the mission and to serve the needs.

A New Paradigm of Leadership

These roles of modeling principle-centered leadership—pathfinding, aligning, and empowering—represent a paradigm that is different in kind from traditional management thinking. There is a very significant difference between management and leadership. Both are vital functions, and because they are, it's critical to understand how they are different so one isn't mistaken for the other. Leadership focuses on doing the right things; management focuses on doing things right. Leadership makes sure the ladders we are climbing are leaning against the right wall; management makes sure we are climbing the ladders in the most efficient ways possible. Most managers and executives operate within existing paradigms or ways of thinking, but leaders have the courage to bring those paradigms to the surface, identify the underlying assumptions and motivations, and challenge them by asking, "Does this still hold water?"

For example:

- In healthcare, new leaders might challenge the assumption that medicine should focus upon the diagnosis and treatment of disease. Some medical schools today don't even teach nutrition, even though one-third of all cancers are nutrition-related and two-thirds of all diseases are tied to lifestyle. Still, the medical community heads down the path of diagnosis and treatment of disease. They claim that they deal with the whole package—the health and welfare of people—but they have a treatment paradigm. Fortunately, new leaders are creating more preventive-medicine alternatives.

- In law, new leaders might challenge the assumption that law is best practiced in courtrooms using confrontational, win-lose litigation. They might move toward the use of synergy and win-win thinking to prevent and settle disputes. Alternative dispute resolution usually results in compromise. New leaders will seek "win-win or no deal" options that lead to synergy. Synergy is more than cooperation; it's creating better solutions. It requires empathetic listening and courage in expressing one's views and opinions in ways that show respect for the other person's view. Out of genuine interaction come synergistic insights.

- In business, new leaders will challenge the assumption that "total customer satisfaction" represents the ultimate service ethic. They will move toward total stakeholder satisfaction, caring for everyone who has a stake in the success of the operation and making decisions that benefit all stakeholders. To bring about this new mindset, leaders must develop a new skill-set of synergy. Synergy comes naturally from the quality of the relationship—the friendship, trust, and love that unites people.

If you can put the new skill-set of synergy together with the new mind-set of interdependence, you have the perfect one-two punch for achieving competitive advantage. When you have the mind-set and the skill-set, you create effective structures, systems, and processes that are aligned with your vision and mission. Every organization is perfectly designed and aligned to get the results it gets. If you want different results, you need a new mind-set and a new skill-set to create synergistic solutions. Because we are so interdependent, it's only enlightened self-interest to keep all stakeholders in mind when making decisions.

Who Is the Leader of the Future?

In many cases, the leader of the future will be the same as the leader of the present. There will be no change in personnel, but rather an internal change: the person becomes the leader of the future by an inside-out transformation. What drives leaders to change, to become more centered on principles?

I think the main source of *personal* change is pain; this pain may come from disappointment, failure, death, troubled or broken relationships with family or friends, violated trust, personal weakness, discouragement, boredom, dissatisfaction, poor health, the consequences of poor decisions, loneliness, mediocrity, fear, financial stress, job insecurity, or life imbalance. If you aren't feeling pain, there is rarely enough motivation or humility to change. Most often there just isn't a felt need. Without personal pain, people tend to be too deeply invested in themselves and their world to rise above their own interests or the politics of running things, both at work and at home. When people are experiencing personal pain, they tend to be more open to a new model of living in which the common elements of humility and personal sacrifice lead to inside-out, principle-centered change.

The primary driving force of organizational change is the global economy. The standard of quality is now so high that unless you have an empowered work force and the spirit of partnership with all stakeholders, you can't compete, whether you work in the private sector, public sector, or social sector. When you're facing competitors who think more ecologically and interdependently, eventually the force of circumstances drives you to be humble. That's what is driving the quest for quality, learning, process re-engineering, and other initiatives. But many of these initiatives don't go far enough. The mindshift is not great enough. The interests of all stakeholders must be dealt with in an orchestrated way.

We either are forced by circumstance to be humble or can choose to be humble out of a recognition that principles ultimately govern. To be humble is good, regardless of the reason. But it's better to be humbled by conscience rather than by circumstance.

The Leader of the Future—A Family Within

The leader of the future has the humility to accept principles and the courage to align with them, which takes great personal sacrifice. Out of this humility, courage, and sacrifice comes the person of integrity. In fact, I like to think of this kind of leader as having an entire family within him or her: humility and courage the parents, and integrity the child.

Humility and Courage the Parents Humility says, "I am not in control; principles ultimately govern and control." It understands that the key to long-term success is learning to align with the "true north" principles. That takes humility because the traditional mind-set is "I am in control; my destiny lies in my hands." This mind-set leads to arrogance—the sort of pride that comes before the fall.

Leaders of the future will have the courage to align with principles and go against the grain of old assumptions or paradigms. It takes tremendous courage and stamina to say, "I'm going to align my personal value system, my lifestyle, my direction, and my habits with timeless principles." Courage is the quality of every principle at its highest testing point. Every virtue is ultimately tested at the highest level. That's where courage comes into play. When you confront an old approach directly, you experience the fear of ripping out an old habit and replacing it with something new.

Integrity the Child Out of the marriage of humility and courage is born the child of integrity. We all want to be known and remembered as men and women of integrity. Having integrity means integrating ourselves with principles. The leaders of the future must be men and women of integrity who internalize these principles. They grow in wisdom and cultivate an abundance mind-set—a sense that there are opportunities for all. If you have integrity, you are not caught up in a constant state of comparison with others. Nor do you feel the need to play political games, because your security comes from within. As soon as you change the source of your security, everything else flows from it. Your security, power, wisdom, and guidance increase, because you constantly draw upon the strength of these principles as you apply them.

A Final Note

We are becoming increasingly and painfully aware of the perilous weakening of our social structure. Drugs, gangs, illiteracy, poverty, crime, violence, breakdown of the familiy, these all continue in a downward spiral. Leaders of the present are beginning to recognize that such social problems put at risk *every* aspect of society. The leaders of the future realize that the solutions to these problems are far beyond the ability of the sectors that have traditionally been expected to deal with them—namely, the government and social sectors. My intent is not to criticize these sectors. In fact, I believe that they would be the first to admit that they are bound to fail without a broader network of helping hands.

The problem is that, on the whole, there has been a marked weakening of the sense of responsibilty that neighborhoods, communities, churches, families and individuals feel toward volunteering. It has become too easy to absolve ourselves from this responsiblity to our communities. I believe that is a family responsibility and that everyone should have a sense of stewardship about the community—every man, every woman, and every child. There should be some real sense of stewardship around service on the part of young people, particularly those who are at the most idealistic age, the late teens and early twenties.

The leader of the future will be a leader in every area of life, especially family life. The enormous needs and opportunities in society call for a greater responsibility toward service. There is no place where this spirit of service can be cultivated like the home. The spirit of the home, and also of the school, is that they prepare young people to go forth and serve. People are supposed to serve. Life is a mission, not a career. The whole spirit of this philosophy should pervade our society. I also think that it is a source of happiness, because you don't get happiness directly. It only comes as a by-product of service. You can get pleasure directly, but it is fleeting.

How, then, do we influence our children toward the spirit of service and meaningful contribution? First, we must look inward and ask,"Am I a *model* of this principle of service myself? Does my family see me dedicating my time and abilitites to serving them and the community?" Second, "Have I taken time to immerse myself and my family in the needs of others in order to create a sense of vision about how our family and each of us as individuals can make unique and meaningful contributions to meet those needs (*pathfinding*)?" Third, "Have I, as a leader in my home, *aligned* the priorities and structures of our life so that this desire to serve is supported, not undermined?" Finally, "Have I created conditions and opportunities in the home that will *empower* my children to serve? Do I encourage and support the development of their minds and talents? Do I organize service opportunities for the entire family and do all I can to create a fun environment around those activities?" Even if the answer to every one of these questions is "No," we all still have the capacity to decide what our lives will be about from today on.

This inherent capacity to choose, to develop a new vision for ourselves, to re-script our life, to begin a new habit or let go of an old one, to forgive someone, to apologize, to make a promise and then keep it, in any area of life, is, always has been, and always will be a moment of truth for every true leader.

THE TEN MOST IMPORTANT LESSONS WE'VE LEARNED ABOUT LEARNING TO LEAD

JAMES M. KOUZES AND BARRY Z. POSNER

1. Challenge Provides the Opportunity for Greatness—in Leading and in Learning to Lead

Draw a line down the middle of a piece of paper. Now think of the leaders you admire. Write the names of leaders you admire in the left-hand column. In the right-hand column, record the events or situations with which you identify these individuals. We predict that you will have associated the leaders from business with corporate turnarounds, entrepreneurial ventures, new product/service development and other business transformations. For those leaders in the military, government, the community, the arts or the church, clubs and student organizations, we predict a similar association with transforming events and times. When we think of leaders, we recall periods of turbulence, conflict, innovation and change.

But we need not investigate well-known leaders to discover that all leadership is associated with pioneering efforts. In our research, we asked thousands of people, both individual contributors and those in management positions, to write "personal best leadership" cases. It struck us that these cases were about significant change. When the participants in our studies—be they college students or senior citizens, from communities or corporations, from the boiler room to the board room—recalled doing their "personal best" as leaders, they automatically associated their best with changing, innovating and overcoming difficulties. These personal best leadership cases illustrate that challenging opportunities provide "ordinary" people the chance to demonstrate extraordinary leadership actions. "The biggest lesson I learned from my personal best [involving his college baseball team]," Karl Thompson explained, "is that you will never know if something will work if you don't try it."

A similar realization came when we asked people how they learned to lead. They responded overwhelmingly: "Trial and Error." Experience, it appears, is indeed the best teacher—but not just any experience. To describe how their "personal best leadership" and learning experience felt, people used the words "exciting," "exhilarating," "rewarding" and "fun." Dull, routine, boring experiences—in the classroom or in the board room—did not provide anyone anywhere with the opportunity to excel or to learn. Only challenge presents the opportunity for greatness. Leaders are pioneers—people who take risks in innovation and experiment to find new and better ways of doing things. Learners are also venturers.

2. Leadership Is in the Eye of the Beholder

Constituents choose leaders. Leaders cannot be appointed or anointed "superiors." Constituents determine whether someone is fit to lead. Power and position may offer the right to exercise authority, but we should never, ever, mistake position and authority for leadership. Only when our constituents believe that we are capable of meeting their expectations will we be able to mobilize their actions.

When we view leadership from this perspective, the relationship is turned upside down. From this vantage, leaders serve their constituents; they do not boss them around. The best leaders are the servants of others' wants and desires, hopes and dreams. And to be able to respond to the needs of others, leaders must first get to know their constituents. By knowing them, listening to them and taking their advice, leaders can stand before others and say with assurance, "Here is what I heard you say that you want for yourselves. Here is how your own needs and interests will be served by enlisting in a common cause."

This notion of leaders as servants flies in the face of the leaders-as-heroes myth perpetuated in comic books, novels, and movies. Yet it is the single most important factor in that dynamic relationship between leader and constituent. Unless we are sensitive to subtle cues, we cannot respond to the aspirations of others. And if we cannot respond to their aspirations, they will not follow.

3. Credibility Is the Foundation of Leadership

We also researched the expectations people have of those whom they would be willing to follow. We asked more than 25,000 people from a range of organizations around the globe to tell us what they admired and looked for in their leaders. According to this data, people want leaders who are honest, forward-looking, inspiring and competent.

While these results aren't surprising, they are extraordinarily significant to all leaders, because three of the four characteristics comprise what communications experts refer to as "source credibility." When determining whether or not we believe someone who is communicating with us—whether that person is a teacher, newscaster, salesperson, manager, parent or colleague—we look for trustworthiness (honesty), expertise (competence),and dynamism (inspiration). Credibility is a leader's single most important asset, and it should be protected and nurtured at all costs. Personal credibility is the foundation on which leaders stand. We call this the *First Law of Leadership*—if you don't believe in the messenger, you won't believe the message. This is precisely what Michael Cole learned as a 16-year-old T-ball coach: "Once the kids [ages 4–8] saw that I wanted what was best for them as well as sharing in their excitement, they became a lot more trusting of me."

4. The Ability to Inspire a Shared Vision Differentiates Leaders from Other Credible Sources

While credibility is the foundation, leaders must envision an uplifting and ennobling future. The one admired leadership quality not a criterion of source credibility is "forward-looking." We expect leaders to take us to places we have never been before—to have clearly in mind an attractive destination that will make the journey worthwhile. "Leadership isn't telling people what to do," says Anthony Bianchi, who organized a ski trip to the Italian Alps for American college students studying in Florence: "It's painting a picture of an exciting possibility of how we can achieve a common goal."

To distinguish ourselves as leaders, we must be concerned with the future of our groups, organizations, and communities. If there is no vision, there is no business. The domain of leaders is the future. The leader's unique legacy is the creation of valued programs and institutions that survive over time.

Equally important, however, is the leader's capacity to enlist others to transform the vision into reality. We found that the ability to inspire others to share the dream—to communicate the vision so that others come to embrace it as their own—was what uplifted constituents and drew them forward. Leaders in any endeavor must demonstrate personal enthusiasm for the dream. Only passion will ignite the flames of our constituents' desires.

5. Without Trust, You Cannot Lead

While we asked people to recount *their* "personal best leadership" experiences, they typically came to realize that it wasn't really "*my* best; it was *our* best. Because it wasn't *me*; it was *us*." Leaders can't do it alone! In fact, no one ever achieved an extraordinary milestone all by themselves—it is a team effort (and notice there is no "i" in the word team).

At the heart of these collaborative efforts is trust. Leaders genuinely desire to make heroes and heroines of others. Without trust, people become self-protective and controlling. Similarly, when there is low trust, people are likely to distort, ignore and disguise facts, ideas, conclusions and feelings. People become suspicious and unreceptive. A trusting relationship between leader and constituents is essential to getting extraordinary things done.

Leaders create a caring climate—a climate of trust. For people to disclose their needs and feelings, to make themselves vulnerable, to expose their weaknesses, to risk failing, they must truly believe they are safe. For example, in learning to parachute jump, people will probably not be eager to jump if they do not trust the instructor or the equipment. Trust must be established before people will risk learning something new.

Another primary task of leadership is to create a climate in which others feel powerful, efficacious and strong. In such a climate, people know they are free to take risks, trusting that when they make mistakes the leader will not ask "Who's to blame?" but, "What did we learn?"

Involvement and participation are essential to create this climate. Giving free choice and listening to others are other important elements of a trusting environment. Leaders focus on fostering collaboration, strengthening others and building trust—on giving their power away—as the most effective strategies for enhancing the power of everyone.

6. Shared Values Make a Critical Difference in the Quality of Life at Home and at Work

Credibility—that single most important leadership asset we mentioned earlier—has at its root the word "credo," meaning a set of beliefs. Every leader must begin by asking, "What do I stand for? What do I believe in? What values do I hold to be true and right?" Through our research, we found that people who reported greater compatibility between personal values and the values of their organizations also reported significantly greater feelings of success in their lives, had greater understandings of the values of their managers and coworkers, were more willing to work longer and harder hours and felt less stress at home and on the job. Shared values are essential for personal and business health.

Shared values provide a sense of alignment, so that, just like a rowing team, everyone is pulling in the same direction. Feeling aligned is empowering, creating a sense of freedom and personal integrity. When people feel that their personal values are in synch with those of their organization, our research indicates they are personally more successful and healthier. They feel liberated and in control of their lives. Shared values enable everyone to experience ownership in the organization.

7. Leaders Are Role Models for Their Constituents

When we asked people to define credibility behaviorally, the most common response was "Do what you say you will do." People believe in actions more than in words, in practices more than in pronouncements. It's simply not sufficient to communicate values and beliefs. We must live them, and leaders are expected to set the example for others.

Mindy Behse, for example, reported that when she was captain of her high school swim team, her teammates watched what she did: "I couldn't ask anybody to do anything I wasn't willing to do. I had to take practices very seriously." Blaine Thomas learned quickly that being captain of his baseball team meant that people not only watched what he did on the field, but off-the-field as well. And, he pointed out, "I couldn't be one kind of a leader, with certain standards on the field, and then be some other kind of person or leader off-the-field with different, especially lower, standards." As the team leader of a group of student painters during the summer, Mike Burciago observed that his willingness to do his share of the "grubby work" made it easier to get others to voluntarily do their share as well.

Credibility is earned—minute by minute, hour by hour—through actions consistent with stated values. Values are often considered the soft side of management, but based on our research, we would say that nothing is more difficult than to be unwaveringly true to one's guiding beliefs.

8. Lasting Change Progresses One Hop at a Time

When we asked Don Bennett, the first amputee to reach the 14,410-feet summit of Mt. Rainier, how he was able to climb to that height, he replied, looking down at his one leg and foot, "One hop at a time." When preparing for the climb, he would imagine himself on top of the mountain 1,000 times a day. But when he started to climb, he'd look down at his foot and say, " 'Anybody can hop from here to there.' So I did."

Big results from small beginnings. "Our goal seemed enormous; so we broke it down into parts and gave one part to each member," is how Richard Cabral accounts for the success of his high school organization in hosting a dinner for more than 300 people, including parents and the city's mayor. Progress is always incremental. The key to lasting improvement is small wins. Choosing to do the easy things first—those that can be accomplished quickly and inexpensively by a team with a local champion—is the only sure way to achieve extraordinary things in organizations. Referring to his own struggles against the seemingly insolvable problem of South Africa's apartheid, Bishop Tutu noted: "You eat an elephant . . . one bite at a time!"

9. Leadership Development Is Self-Development

Leaders take us to places we have never been before. But there are no freeways to the future, no paved highways to unknown, unexplored destinations. There is only wilderness. If we are to step into the unknown, we must begin by exploring the inner territory.

Leadership is an art—a performing art. And in the art of leadership, the instrument is the self. A musician may have a violin, an engineer a work station and an accountant a computer. But a leader has only himself or herself as the medium of expression. Leadership development, then, is essentially a process of self-development.

The self-confidence required to lead comes from learning about ourselves—our skills, prejudices, talents and shortcomings. Self-confidence develops as we build on strengths and overcome weaknesses. As Larry Olin, captain of his college tennis team, learned: "You must be confident in yourself before you can expect others to be confident in you."

People frequently ask, "Are leaders born or made?" We firmly believe that leadership can be learned. Certainly, some people are more predisposed to lead than others. But this is true of anything. Leadership is definitely not a divine-like grace given to a few charismatic men and women. It is a set of learnable practices. We believe it is possible for ordinary people to learn to get extraordinary things done. There is a leader in everyone, and the greatest inhibitor to leadership development is the belief that leadership cannot be learned.

Developing ourselves as leaders requires removing the barriers, whether self-imposed or imposed by the organization, and understanding that development is a continuous improvement process, not an event, a class, a book, or series of programs.

10. Leadership Is Not an Affair of the Head. It Is an Affair of the Heart

Leadership is emotional. Period. To lead others requires passionate commitment to a set of fundamental beliefs and principles, visions and dreams. The climb to the summit is arduous and often frightening. Leaders encourage others to continue the quest by inspiring them with courage and hope.

In our study of leadership, we often asked our interviewees how they would go about developing leaders, whether in school, business, government or volunteer organizations. Major General John Stanford, then Commander of the U.S. Army's Military Traffic Management Command, gave a memorable reply: "When people ask me that question, I tell them I have the secret to success in life. The secret to success is to stay in love." Not the advice we expected from a Major General or from any of the people we interviewed, but the more we thought about it, the more we realized that leadership *is* an affair of the heart. Constituents will not follow unless they are persuaded that their leader passionately believes in his or her view of the future and believes in each of them.

More than ever before, there is a need for people to answer the call for leadership—to seize the opportunities for greatness. Only by looking inside our hearts will we know when we are ready to take that first step along the journey to the future.

James Kouzes and **Barry Posner** are co-authors of two award-winning and best selling books on leadership: *The Leadership Challenge: How to Keep Getting Extraordinary Things Done in Organizations* (San Francisco: Jossey-Bass, 1995) and *Credibility: How Leaders Gain and Lose It, Why People Demand It* (San Francisco; Jossey-Bass, 1993). Kouzes is CEO of The Tom Peters Group/Learning Systems (Palo Alto, Calif.) and Posner is Professor of Organizational Behavior and Managing Partner, Executive Development Center, Santa Clara University (Santa Clara, Calif.).

SUMMARY

This chapter began with a review of trait theories of leadership, featuring the work of such prominent leadership experts as John Gardner, Warren Bennis, James Kouzes, and Barry Posner. Behavioral theories were also addressed, beginning with the Ohio State and Michigan studies. A section on situational approaches included reviews of Path–Goal theory, Continuum of Leader Behavior, Normative Decision model, Least Preferred Coworker theory, Cognitive Resources theory, Leadership Substitutes theory, Multiple Linkage theory, Life Cycle model, and Leader–Member Exchange model.

Three prominent leadership experts—Stephen R. Covey, James M. Kouzes and Barry Z. Posner—shared their thoughts and research about learning to lead.

KEY TERMS

Ohio State studies	achievement-oriented leadership
University of Michigan studies	LPC model
Managerial Grid	Cognitive Resources theory
Path-Goal theory	Leadership Substitutes theory
directive leadership	Multiple Linkage theory
supportive leadership	Life Cycle model
participative leadership	LMX model

FOR DISCUSSION AND REVIEW

1. According to Gardner, what should be the primary aims and tasks of leaders?

2. What are some of the historical assumptions behind the characteristics of "great leaders"?

3. What were the primary similarities and differences between the Michigan studies and the Ohio State studies?

4. Select five leaders. Where would their leadership style fall on the Managerial Grid, and why?

5. In what situations do you feel a directive leadership style would be most appropriate? A supportive style? Participative? Achievement-oriented?

6. In which situations would a relationship-oriented leader be most effective? A task-oriented leader?

7. Of the numerous leadership theories proposed, which speaks to you most, and why?

8. How are the leadership theories in this chapter reflective of American culture? How might other cultures view these approaches?

9. Do you think that there are any universal attributes of leaders, or are leadership traits always culturally and/or situationally bound?

CRITICAL INCIDENT

You work as a computer technician at a large research university in the Midwest. Through the miracles of science and computer technology, a top-secret research project is being conducted, whereby the management department is attempting to create a prototype of the "ideal leader." You have been charged with creating the program from which this prototype will be tested. What types of attributes would be important to "program" into this prototype? How would knowledge of what types of situations this leader would be placed in affect your program?

EXERCISES FOR CHAPTER 7

Exercise 7–1   Using Path–Goal Theory to Select a Leadership Strategy

Directions: Think of a group of which you are or have been a member. This can be a student organization (SGA, activities board, sorority/fraternity, etc.), a team (sports, debate, chess, etc.), an institution (church, Boy/Girl Scouts, college, etc.), or a workplace. Use what you have learned about Path–Goal Theory to select an appropriate leadership style for that particular organization.

Name of group/organization:

Evaluating two sets of contingency factors—types
of subordinates and types of work. Rate each factor
by circling the appropriate indicator below.

Factor #1 - *Locus of Control*:	In this organization, members feel like it is: High..........Medium..........Low
Factor #2 - *Prediction of Positive Performance*:	In this organization, members think that they: Will Be May Be Probably Will Successful......Successful......Not Be Successful
Factor #3 - *Members' Tasks*:	In this organization, they are: Repetitive......Combination......Nonrepetitive
Factor #4 - *Authority Within the Organization*:	In this organization, the authority system is: Authoritarian........Mixed........Democratic
Factor #5 - *Work Group*:	In this organization, there are: High Morale Low Morale and and Satisfying Unsatisfying Relationships..........Mixed..........Relationships

Based on your analysis of the organization's contingency factors, which of House's four leadership styles would be best suited? Circle the most appropriate leadership style.

Directive   Supportive   Participative   Achievement-Oriented

Answer Key

Using the key on page 192, how well did your analysis of the five contingency factors match the selection of the most appropriate leadership style?

Directive Style:	Factor #1 - Low
	Factor #2 - Maybe → Probably Not
	Factor #3 - Ambiguous
	Factor #4 - Authoritarian
	Factor #5 - Low Morale
Supportive Style:	Factor #1 - Low
	Factor #2 - Maybe → Probably Not
	Factor #3 - Combination
	Factor #4 - Nonrepetitive
	Factor #5 - Low Morale
Participative Style:	Factor #1 - Medium → High
	Factor #2 - Will Be Successful
	Factor #3 - Nonrepetitive
	Factor #4 - Mixed → Democratic
	Factor #5 - High Morale
Achievement-Oriented Style:	Factor #1 - High
	Factor #2 - Will Be Successful
	Factor #3 - Nonrepetitive
	Factor #4 - Mixed → Democratic
	Factor #5 - Mixed → High Morale

Exercise 7–2   Using Fiedler's Contingency Theory: Analyzing a Company or Organization

The purpose of this exercise is to utilize Fiedler's contingency theory in order to analyze the match between a particular leader in a specific situation.

Step One: Select a business, company, or organization with which you are familiar:
Name of Organization:

Step Two: Use the Least Preferred Coworker (LPC) scale to measure whether the leader is task-motivated or relationship-motivated. Ask the leader to fill out the LPC assessment as shown on the following page.

The Least Preferred Coworker (LPC) Scale for Measuring Leadership Style

Throughout your life you will have worked in many groups with a wide variety of different people—on your job, in social groups, in church organizations, in volunteer groups, on athletic teams, and in many other situations. Some of your coworkers may have been very easy to work with in attaining the group's goals, while others were less so.

Think of all the people with whom you have ever worked, and then think of the person with whom you could work *least well*. He or she may be someone with whom you work now or with whom you have worked in the past. This does not have to be the person you liked least well, but should be the person with whom you had the most difficulty getting a job done, the *one* individual with whom you could work *least well*.

Describe this person on the scale that follows by placing an "X" in the appropriate space. Look at the words at both ends of the line before you mark your "X." *There are no right or wrong answers.* Work rapidly: your first answer is likely to be the best. Do not omit any items, and mark each item only once.

Now describe the person with whom you can work least well.

										Scoring
Pleasant	8	7	6	5	4	3	2	1	Unpleasant	____
Friendly	8	7	6	5	4	3	2	1	Unfriendly	____
Rejecting	1	2	3	4	5	6	7	8	Accepting	____
Tense	1	2	3	4	5	6	7	8	Relaxed	____
Distant	1	2	3	4	5	6	7	8	Close	____
Cold	1	2	3	4	5	6	7	8	Warm	____
Supportive	8	7	6	5	4	3	2	1	Hostile	____
Boring	1	2	3	4	5	6	7	8	Interesting	____
Quarrelsome	1	2	3	4	5	6	7	8	Harmonious	____
Gloomy	1	2	3	4	5	6	7	8	Cheerful	____
Open	8	7	6	5	4	3	2	1	Guarded	____
Backbiting	1	2	3	4	5	6	7	8	Loyal	____
Untrustworthy	1	2	3	4	5	6	7	8	Trustworthy	____
Cosiderate	8	7	6	5	4	3	2	1	Inconsiderate	____
Nasty	1	2	3	4	5	6	7	8	Nice	____
Agreeable	8	7	6	5	4	3	2	1	Disagreeable	____
Insincere	1	2	3	4	5	6	7	8	Sincere	____
Kind	8	7	6	5	4	3	2	1	Unkind	____
									Total	____

Scoring and Interpretation: To calculate your score, add the numbers in the right column; write the total at the bottom of the page. If you scored 64 or higher, you are a high LPC leader, meaning that you are relations-motivated. If you scored 57 or lower, you are a low LPC leader, meaning that you are task-motivated. A score of 58 to 63 places you in the intermediate range, making you a socioindependent leader.

Source: Adapted from Fred E. Fiedler, Martin M. Chemers, and Linda Mahar, *Improving Leadership Effectiveness*, p. 7. Copyright © 1976. Reprinted by permission of John Wiley & Sons, Inc.

Step Three: Based on what you know about the company or organization (you may need to visit several times to observe or interview members of the organization in order to answer the questions in this step of the analysis accurately), circle the appropriate number next to each question. Once completed, total the scores in each section.

ANALYZING THE SITUATION

A. *Designated Leader-Member Relations*	*Poor*				*Good*
1. There is a friendly atmosphere.	1	2	3	4	5
2. There is a fair amount of good-humored joking between the leader and members.	1	2	3	4	5
3. Conversation between the leader and group members is easy and relaxed.	1	2	3	4	5
4. Members feel as if the leader is interested in them as individuals.	1	2	3	4	5
5. Members feel as if the leader is open and accessible.	1	2	3	4	5
6. The leader believes that they have a good relationship with members.	1	2	3	4	5

B. *Task Structure*	*Low*				*High*
1. There are written company/organization policies.	1	2	3	4	5
2. There are written job descriptions for all positions.	1	2	3	4	5
3. Annual goal-setting is routinely done.	1	2	3	4	5
4. There is a formal evaluation procedure.	1	2	3	4	5
5. Routine functions are performed in a fairly standard manner throughout the organization.	1	2	3	4	5
6. Members are clear about what is expected from them.	1	2	3	4	5

C. *Position Power*	*Weak*				*Strong*
1. The leader has the authority to make hiring decisions.	1	2	3	4	5
2. The leader can promote or significantly affect member promotions.	1	2	3	4	5
3. The leader evaluates member performance.	1	2	3	4	5
4. The leader is expected to discipline problem behaviors.	1	2	3	4	5
5. The leader can fire or significantly affect an employee's termination.	1	2	3	4	5
6. The leader can affect employee salary increases.	1	2	3	4	5

Answer Key

A score of 18 or above in each of the sections (Leader–Member Relations, Task Structure, and Position Power) equates to:

Good leader–member relations
High task structure
Strong position power

The Hero's Journey: A New Leadership Model

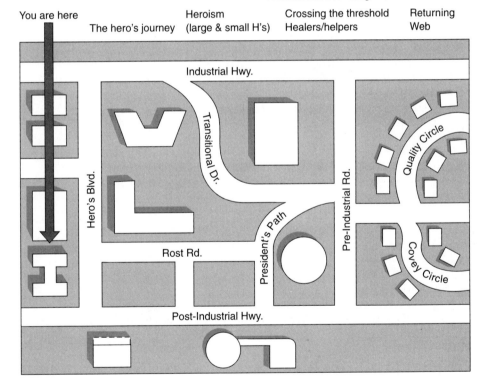

The Leadership Journey:
A map of the terrain
Chapter 8

Words/names to recognize

You are here   Heroism   Crossing the threshold   Returning
       The hero's journey   (large & small H's)   Healers/helpers   Web

Industrial Hwy.

Transitional Dr.

Hero's Blvd.

Rost Rd.

President's Path

Pre-Industrial Rd.

Quality Circle

Covey Circle

Post-Industrial Hwy.

Terri, biting her nails, is pacing in the hallway outside of class.

"What's wrong?" Mike asks.

"I've got to see the dean in a few minutes."

"Uh, oh. Grades? What did you do now?"

"No, I mean, well, I did do something. I asked for the appointment—can you imagine—me, calling up the dean and telling her I had to talk with her?"

"It is kinda hard to see you doing that," Mike says.

"Well, I was so steamed after the student body president's article was censored in the Daily Rag. *I mean, he said the dean just told him abortion was too sensitive to write about. Can you imagine?"*

"Well . . . "

"Anyway, I got so mad, I mean, college is s'pozed to be the place you form your opinions about important things. I don't even care how the guy feels about abortion—it is clearly a violation of freedom of speech. I think the trustees would agree with me, and I've already written a letter to them."

"Hey, you're really into this."

"I know. My parents tried to talk me out of it. They say I'll stir up trouble, the dean won't listen to me, it's really none of my business, and don't I have better things to do—like study—than to get all hopped up about this."

"Hmph," Mike says. "Sounds familiar."

"Well, wait just a minute," Ray says. "I can see your parents' point."

"Oh yeah?"

"Yeah. They're helping you pay for school and you're using a lot of energy on this, it seems. I mean, freedom of speech is okay and all, but why should you take it on? It's not like you're some big wheel on campus."

"Never said I was. I don't know why, either, I just care."

"I think it's pretty neat to call the dean and go in and see her. That must've taken guts," Juanita says.

"Calling wasn't as bad as going to see her. My knees are wobbly I'm so afraid."

"Hey, do you want some support? I'll come with you," Juanita says. "Maybe we could type up a quick petition that we start flying around campus—show her we mean business."

"Really? You'd help me out on this?"

"Sure. I like to stir things up, and it sure beats studying."

*I*f you're saying to yourself, "Who me? I'm no hero!" you're showing a very common reaction. In fact, the way heroism has been portrayed in myths, stories, and the popular media has set it apart from normal human experience. That distancing has meant that we have lost sight of the truth that the heroic journey is really "our story" as human beings.

There is yet another distortion we see in the portrayal of heroes: they are almost always depicted as men. Excluding the feminine perspective limits both men and women, since women have difficulty relating to male-dominated heroism and men are denied access to powerful feminine attributes.

This is heroism with a lowercase *h*, not the capital H associated with mythological figures or those few sterling individuals who perform near superhuman tasks—

say, rescuing a child from a burning building. Nor is a hero someone who regularly accomplishes awe-inspiring feats. There's a big difference between being a hero and living a heroic life.

A scarcity theory seems to operate about heroism: We think we can only have a few heroes because heroism is not for everyone. While I agree it's not for everyone and that it's something not easily earned, I assert that heroism is a challenge open to everyone. Further, there are many more heroes in every walk of life than we credit.

There are probably some people leading heroic lives sitting in this classroom with you. Or in your carpool. Or—get a grip—in your family. Look around.

It may be hard to imagine this scene being about a heroic journey, but it actually contains many of the elements of that classic journey, many elements essential to effective leadership. In fact, this simple scenario demonstrates that what is important is everyday, or "little h," heroism, not the grand event or the grand person.

Consider the following elements, all of which were evident in Terri's scenario and all of which are essential for effective leadership. We face these kinds of challenges frequently, but may not recognize them as leadership challenges, nor understand that our development as leaders depends on how we respond to them. We respond heroically, as Terri did, or we refuse the challenge and miss the opportunity to grow as individuals and leaders.

1. **Being the author.** At the heart of the heroic journey is the challenge to take full responsibility for our lives, to be the author. The alternative is to live the way others want us to live, to "go along to get along." Terri not only knew what was important to her, but matched her actions to her beliefs. She acted with integrity.

2. **Crossing the threshold from the known world into the unknown.** There are many times when living with integrity will require us to leave our comfort zones and venture into territory where there may be a great deal of the unknown. Terri was certainly in that position as she ventured forth into confronting the administration, challenging her parents, and standing out from her peers.

3. **Taking risks.** Risks are an inescapable part of the journey. They may be large or small, they may be worse than we thought or not as bad, but they will certainly be there and we will have to choose whether to continue or not. Terri risked a surprising number of things. She risked aspects of her relationships with her parents and with the school administration. She risked changing how her peers saw her. She risked her own self image ("can you imagine—me, calling up the dean . . ."). She risked failing and feeling foolish or ineffective. She risked losing grade points by being focused on something else. She took a surprising number of risks in that one scenario.

4. **Challenges on the journey can be on many levels (physical, intellectual, emotional, and spiritual).** Different journeys challenge us in different ways, but as we go from journey to journey we will find that we are challenged and that we grow on each of those levels. Terri faced physical challenges in facing the stress of the situation, as well as the competing demands on her energy of school work and citizenship. Intellectually she will be challenged around what

she believes, how she can make her case, and how the experience might change her view of how the world works. Emotional challenges may range from dealing with the battles between hopes and fears or confidence and insecurity to changes in her self-image and the nature of some key relationships. In this case, her spiritual (beyond self) challenge may be in changing how she sees herself in the world.

5. **Heroes don't go alone.** Heroic journeys are almost never successfully completed alone. Heroes have companions on the journey (at least part of the time). We have supporters or mentors or teachers or guides, and we have helpers and healers to deal with the inevitable injuries that occur along the way. Terri began to pick up companions and supporters at the end of the scene. If the challenges ahead of her turn out to be tough ones, she will need more companions and more support if she is to be successful.

6. **Heroes challenge and often disturb others.** Being the author, living with integrity, or leading the changes that need to happen will challenge others to also answer the call to go forth and do what needs doing. Our own heroic journeys, even small ones, challenge others and that can be very disturbing if they aren't ready. Terri clearly disturbed her parents, was about to disturb the dean, and may well disturb other students who see her example and question why they themselves don't act in a similar way. Challenging and disturbing people is not a sure path to popularity.

7. **The three forms of courage required.** Leadership and the heroic journey require three forms of courage that are each more challenging than they at first appear:

   - *The courage to see and speak the truth.* Terri saw censorship and spoke out. Seeing it was disturbing for Terri and led her to take risks in acting. Speaking her truth made her visible to others, some of whom were disapproving.
   - *The courage to create and affirm a vision of the desired state.* Terri was clear that the desired state in this instance was a press free of censorship. The strength of her vision also propelled her to act, made her "knowable" to others, and set her up for significant disappointment if she was unsuccessful in achieving it.
   - *The courage to persevere, to "hold the course."* In this scenario Terri has acted according to her vision. If there is significant resistance, she will be challenged to persevere, perhaps for a long time and through lots of doubts, defeats, mistakes, and with much effort.

WHAT IS THE HEROIC JOURNEY? AN OVERVIEW

The heroic journey is literally the story of the change process in its healthiest form. The classic heroic journey begins with the crossing of a threshold, leaving a known world or comfort zone. A person may "heed a call," be thrown into the journey, be lured in or blunder in.

Moving through the land that lies on the other side of the threshold, we are faced with tests and trials that usually require new or altered ways of perceiving, thinking, and acting. As Alice found, in *Alice in Wonderland*, things often aren't what they seem and what worked before is no longer effective and can, in fact, be counterproductive or dangerous.

Many journeys are failures because we never really leave the known world. We never truly let go and can, therefore, never really discover the new truths, the revelations, and the new life that are possible. The heroic journey is a time of endings and beginnings (of death and birth or rebirth) and of the difficult terrain in between. We may find that our tests are physical, intellectual, emotional, or spiritual and that our changes are, consequently, in one or more of those areas. Different journeys pose different challenges and opportunities.

Some of the tests will be dealing with mistakes and failures; avoiding the seductive lures of taking the easy way out; dealing with uncertainty, doubt, and perhaps despair; and finding sources of energy and renewal along the way.

Few (if any) of the heroes that do truly cross the threshold have to face the trials and tests alone, although the heroic journey is ultimately an individual one. On almost all journeys there are helpers of various sorts who can provide direction, tools, nourishment of various types, encouragement, and coaching in coping in the new environment.

There will also be healers to help overcome the inevitable injuries that happen to us on our journeys. The help and healing, like the tests, might be physical, emotional, intellectual, or spiritual. The nature of the roles of helpers and healers and their importance will vary widely, but they will almost always be present in some form. Whether they are seen and used by us is, of course, one of the challenges.

If alert, we can also often find companions with whom we can travel for parts of our journey. Other characters, such as tricksters, jokers, allies, enemies, opponents, and such can also be encountered.

For those who successfully meet the challenges of the journey, the final phase is some form of return or completion. We "return" with the gifts that we have discovered, whether new knowledge or truths, new abilities, new "ways" or technologies, or new opportunities.

The return may be the most difficult part of all because the impact of a hero's return may imply changes that the rest of the "kingdom" may not look upon with great favor. The hero will be changed and that will require changes in others, for it will change the nature of relationships of various kinds. Those changes can ripple out in many directions and for long distances. The gifts of the hero can easily threaten the status quo.

Sometimes heroes are welcomed and celebrated. Sometimes they are ignored. Sometimes they are even shunned, reviled, or attacked (even crucified). This phenomenon holds true whether the "kingdom" is a family, an organization, a corporation, or a community (regardless of size).

There are major challenges facing us in beginning the journey and crossing the threshold, in traversing the unknown and facing the trials and tests that are found there, and in returning and dealing with the impact of our return.

THE "AW SHUCKS" PLOY

If you've responded, "Aw shucks, I'm no hero," you may not be showing humility as much as avoiding responsibility for answering the call to heroism. Too many people are all too ready to reinforce this "aw shucks" attitude. They're the ones who take delight in shooting down those who dare to apply heroism to themselves.

No doubt about it: the hero's journey requires courage. So does the simple act of identifying the heroic in our lives and in the lives of others, because doing so makes the challenge real, immediate, and personal.

Beware, then, of the "aw shucks" response in yourself and others. Remember that the mythological figures actually represent the challenges and journeys we face as human beings.

THE RATE AND DEPTH OF CHANGE: THE FACTOR REQUIRING HEROISM OF LEADERS

Impermanence has always been an underlying principle of life. Now, however, it is becoming ever more obvious as it manifests in areas ranging from sweeping trends (such as the globalization of the economy and sociopolitical changes) to more immediate changes (such as how organizations are structured and run and how work and jobs are defined). How we are to live together successfully in our communities, from local to global, and who has what responsibility are increasingly important and difficult questions. Media coverage and information capabilities have made impermanence or change a daily focus.

The rate and depth of change have not only become more obvious, they have become more prevalent, more complex, more interdependent in their forms and reach, and more of a central phenomenon in people's lives. Impermanence, for most people, is now reaching into many parts of their lives, from family to organizations to communities. Most people are dealing with multiple changes at the same time and finding fewer and fewer areas of continuity or stability. Impermanence is more of a reality, and we are more aware of it.

Increasingly, prevalent change has profound consequences for people and the organizations and communities of which they are a part. By definition, those in leadership roles are repeatedly challenging themselves and those who choose to follow to embark on heroic journeys to bring about the individual, group, organizational, and community changes required by the world. More is being asked of more people more often and in more varied ways.

WHY HEROISM?

An Individual Perspective

Simply put, heroism is what is really needed, what is being asked of individuals in the midst of the major changes swirling around us. More than that, it's a moral imperative. Framing the challenge in any other way does a disservice to the individual, because it underplays the demands and the effort required.

Calling our role anything else also asks too little of the individual. Heroism dignifies the effort and tells us we can be ennobled in our response to life's challenges. People often find too little of themselves for the simple reason that they don't look far enough: by accepting the conventional messages they blind themselves to possibilities.

The concept of the heroic journey applies to anyone facing or in the midst of a major change. Given the rate, magnitude, and complexity of the changes we are experiencing, anything less will simply be inadequate.

The change may be personal or family in nature, or an organizational or community change (from local to global). The major change may result from normal development of the person or the group, or it may be triggered by specific situations.

In its simplest form the heroic journey involves leaving a known world, traveling a path of tests and trials, letting go of old ways and discovering new ones, and finally, completing the journey or returning in a changed state.

Throughout history, in virtually every culture, heroes have left their known worlds to venture into the unknown, face trials, discover truths and revelations, experience various kinds of deaths and rebirths, and finally "return," bringing something of value. Organizational and community change demands the same venturing forth into the unknown, the same trials and contests, the death of certain things and the birth or rebirth of others, and the return or the arrival at a new state of being.

In our world we face challenges that require of us the same courage and perseverance that have been demanded of heroes who have gone before us. We can take comfort in the fact that others have taken journeys before us and have faced similar challenges. The journey is known even if we have to keep playing it out.

Organizational or Community Perspective

Major changes aren't just managed; they are led. Leading major changes requires heroes, just as effectively and creatively following requires heroes. In some cases, where management is particularly inept, heroes are needed to help the organization simply survive and heal.

Heroism is the level to which we need to go to find sufficient strength, energy, wisdom, and courage to deal successfully with the changes threatening to overwhelm us: changes in technology, demography, the global economy, the environment, and so on. It's time to realize that the health of the economy and the health of our society—from local to world—require significantly different leadership than we have yet witnessed.

Although heroic acts guarantee no specific outcomes or answers, they have traditionally reinvigorated the community and reinfused life with divine energy. As heroes become fully alive, they bring life and possibility to the world. By their actions, heroes also tend to draw people together, a cohesiveness that grows in importance as the forces pulling people apart increase in strength and number.

Are Heroes Always Heroic?

Absolutely not! This is the point of "the journey" concept. Most people go on—or at least, have the opportunity to go on—a number of hero's journeys over their lifetimes. We can also look at an entire life as a journey made up of smaller journeys.

Either way we look at the journey, it is clear that there will be times when the individual (or the group) will be anything but "heroic." Probably there will be times of refusal, withdrawal or retreat, doubt and loss of faith, exhaustion, failure—even cowardice. All are natural responses to the trials we encounter, both externally and within ourselves.

What matters on our journey is how the individual or group deals with these responses. Consider them part of the journey.

WHAT IS THE HERO'S JOURNEY?

Heroes Don't Go Alone: The Required "Web" of Leaders and Followers

Heroes do not go alone. They certainly do not go alone when leading or effectively following in cases of major change. Successful change efforts require effective leadership, but effective leadership is not enough. Successful change also requires effective followership, but effective followership is not enough. What is enough is a web of effective followers and leaders that is aligned and attuned with a vision of the desired state.

Effective Followers: Overlooked and Undervalued

A great deal has been written about leadership and an increasing focus in that body of writing has been on the relationship between leaders and followers. That focus, however, continues to be much too tame, much too limited, much too constrained.

Leaders are still usually portrayed as few in number, significantly different than followers in terms of characteristics and roles, and separated from followers by some gap, across which communications flows mostly from leaders to followers. Lip service is given to the significance of followers, but they are still almost always portrayed as secondary players and only in relationship to the really important person, the leader.

What's Changing?

The emerging wisdom proposes that the basic characteristics and capabilities of effective leaders and effective followers are almost the same and what differentiates them is the role they are playing in a particular situation at a particular time. In some settings a person may be in a leadership role and in others they may be in a followership role.

It is likely that people will play both leadership and followership roles and that it will often be difficult or impossible to differentiate leaders from followers when they are exhibiting effective characteristics. What should be evident, however, is the web that leaders and followers form to manage the change journey.

The change is toward valuing the roles as equal, but different, and in having comparably high expectations of the characteristics of both leaders and followers, characteristics that are strikingly similar.

The Heroic Challenge for Effective Leaders

For those in leadership roles, the challenge is to be worthy of followers: their beliefs, hopes, trust, personal investment and efforts, their sacrifices, and the risks they take regarding job, career, family, and place in the world. That means not only effectively leading others through the heroic journey, but also basing their personal lives on the heroic pattern.

The impact on others of a leader's choices and actions can be profound. Some leaders are acutely conscious of this and others are not. Most of those who have little conscious awareness of this, however, still experience the responsibility unconsciously, although this can leave them with a dull sense of pressure without the awareness to attend effectively to what is really required of them.

Aware or not, those in leadership roles are facing increasingly complex, difficult, and fluid challenges with less certainty on which to rely and less direct control over outcomes. The pressure is significantly greater than even a few years ago, and leaders must reach deeper to find the courage and wisdom necessary to find the way and the strength and flexibility to persevere. They must also rely much more on those who may follow them.

The Heroic Challenge for Effective Followers

Followers can also have a profound impact on others, although this fact is largely overlooked, denied, or underplayed. For followers, the challenge is to take full personal responsibility for their actions and choices, understanding and accepting the impact of their actions and choices on leaders, peers, and those who see them as natural leaders. This is a consequence of being part of the required web of leaders and followers. The responsibility naturally follows the significance of the role.

The personal responsibility involves such tests as accepting and facilitating empowerment, becoming partners with others in the required web of leaders and followers, taking considered risks, making the leap of faith to trust and the commitment to be trustworthy, to exert the extra effort required, to be honest in communicating outward and providing direct feedback, providing support and guidance and care to others, taking care of oneself, sharing in shaping and championing the purpose and the design of organizations and communities, and being willing to wisely sacrifice for the greater good.

The Heroic Challenge for Both Leaders and Followers

For both leaders and followers, then, the challenge is a dual one: conducting their own internal journeys, as well as playing their parts in the journey of the group. "Managing self to lead or effectively follow others" is the challenge.

The importance of the heroic journey for both leaders and followers is that it provides a known path that others have traveled, while leaving room for each person's unique journey. It provides a format for understanding the experience, anticipating, and making choices about actions. It implicitly calls forth the best, is ennobling by its nature, and provides guidance for both the internal and external journeys.

The heroic journey provides those benefits for both the individual's internal journey and the external journey of the group, organization, or community. If leaders and followers cannot manage themselves effectively, they will certainly not be able to effectively fulfill their required roles.

SUMMARY

If you choose to lead or effectively follow, you will be faced with the challenge of the heroic journey. You will be challenged in your own personal journey and in the journey of your group, organization, or community. The challenge is not to be a hero, but to live heroically ("little *h*" heroism).

The importance of your choice to live heroically is important partly for the impact it will have on your ability to effectively lead or follow in a particular setting. It is perhaps more important for the impact it will have over time as you deepen your self-knowledge, become more mature and more whole as a person, and become stronger, more flexible and wiser through being tested on the path.

Remember:

- Classic heroism is required because of the rate and reach of change that we are experiencing.
- At its heart, heroism is about being the author (of your life and of the journeys of your group).
- Risks are inevitable.
- Challenges may be on a physical, intellectual, emotional, or spiritual level.
- Heroes don't go alone. The journey requires others as companions, helpers, and guides.
- Heroes challenge and often disturb others.
- Three forms of courage will be required (to see and speak the truth, to create a vision of the desired future, and to persevere).

AND

- Beware the "aw shucks" phenomenon and the overly masculine portrayal of the journey. Do not be deterred.

FOR DISCUSSION AND REVIEW

1. What are some examples of when you have acted like Terri? What was most challenging about those experiences? What did you learn from those experiences? What skills or capabilities did you draw upon and what skills or capabilities were strengthened or developed?

2. What are some examples of when you wish that you had acted like Terri? What turned you back? What did you learn from those experiences?

3. What are some current or anticipated situations in which you might exhibit this "little *h*" heroism? What might stop you? What might support you?

4. How have you been influenced by the forces that exclude people from living and thinking of themselves heroically (the larger than life and masculine portrayals of heroic journey)?

5. Identify five people who are role models for you in living heroically. What are the characteristics of each that you want to also have? *Note:* A role model is not perfect. They just have some characteristics (maybe only one) that you would also like to have. They may also have characteristics that you don't like.

EXERCISES FOR CHAPTER 8

Exercise 8–1   4 Stages of the Hero's Journey

Using Modern Allegories

Directions: Choose a movie or television show that depicts a hero's journey. Give specific examples from the movie/TV show to illustrate each stage. Remember, a hero's journey can be undertaken by anyone.

STAGE	EXAMPLE
1. Crossing the threshold—leaving the known world.	1.
2. Moving through the land on the other side of the threshold—encountering new ways of thinking, perceiving, and acting.	2.
3. Finding help on the other side— HEALERS/HELPERS who provide direction, tools, nourishment, and coaching.	3.
4. Returning as changed heroes, which demands changes in others. Sometimes returning heroes are welcomed/celebrated, sometimes shunned or reviled.	4.

Exercise 8–2 • Heroes Who Aren't Heroic

Directions: Knowing that those who have embarked upon a hero's journey sometimes act in ways that aren't heroic, give an example that illustrates this point.

Hero:

The heroic journey:

A time/occasion/incident when the person was not heroic:

Did the person resume the hero's journey?

Why or why not?

Leadership in the Twenty-first Century

**The Leadership Journey:
A map of the terrain
Chapter 9**

Leadership in the 21st century

Words/names to recognize

Servant leadership	Post-industrial leadership	Quantum physics & chaos theory
Transformational leadership	Collaborator	Drath & Palus
Rost	Non-coercive persuasion	Old cultures/new cultures

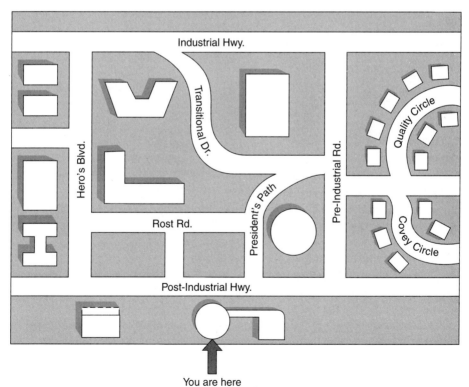

You are here

Mike, Juanita, Terri, and Ray are standing around the professor's desk before class.

"We're, um, having trouble getting our project organized," says Terri, glancing nervously at the others.

"Hmm. I don't know if this will help or not, but a new student is switching to this session from my earlier class. All right with you if he's in your group?" the professor asks.

The group members look at each other. No one speaks.

"Here he is." Lionel, the new student, is introduced.

"Look, I don't want to disrupt your group here. But maybe there's something I can do to help the project," he says.

"Well. . . ."

"How about if I take the notes you've already made and maybe type them up and copy them for everyone. It'll help me catch up with what you've already done."

"Really?" Juanita looks at the group's file folder bulging with assorted-sized pieces of paper, newspaper clippings, and peanut butter cracker wrappers. "That'd be great, but it's kind of a mess."

"No big deal. What else can I do?"

"Well, we're having a few problems getting organized," says Ray.

"Hey, that's always a problem. How can we attack this?" Lionel asks.

They start moving back to their desks. Juanita says, "I've been thinking, we could make two columns, what leadership is and what it is not."

"Yeah," chimes in Mike. "A big chart, with what some important philosophers thought it was and wasn't."

"Maybe add the different disciplines and what they contributed, too," says Terri.

"How about like a cartoon illustrating all the trendy approaches to leadership, you know?" Ray says with excitement.

Lionel looks at them in turn. "This is great! How can we make sure we get all of this done?"

"I'm making an outline, and we'll sign up for the parts we want to do," says Ray.

"And when they'll be done," says Terri.

Lionel smiles. "I really lucked out getting in this group!"

*I*n the midst of the heyday of the industrial approach to leadership, the seeds of a new paradigm of leadership were being planted. Several scholars broke with mainstream thinking about leadership and began to describe it in radically different ways. As we saw in the previous two chapters, the industrial view of leadership:

- Saw leadership as the property of an individual
- Considered leadership primarily in the context of formal groups or organizations
- Equated concepts of management and leadership

However, the reality of leadership as experienced by many did not always fit these circumstances. Leadership occurred outside of formal organizations and was

Portions of this chapter are based on material from J. L. Rogers' "Leadership," in *Student Services: A Handbook for the Profession, Third Edition.* San Francisco: Jossey-Bass, 1996.

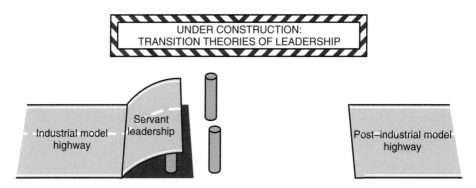

Figure 9–1   Under Construction: Transition Theories of Leadership

sometimes practiced by those other than designated leaders. As Kuhn (1970) taught us, no paradigm can explain all of the facts of a particular phenomenon. Several authors began to explore the aspects of leadership not captured in the old story of leadership. Their ideas served as a bridge from the industrial to the postindustrial perspectives of leaderships (Figure 9–1). We turn now to three of these transition theories to examine their assumptions about leadership.

THE GENESIS OF A NEW PARADIGM: SERVANT LEADERSHIP

In 1970, in his work *The Leader as Servant*, Robert Greenleaf made a radical departure from the industrial paradigm notion of the leader as an all-knowing, all powerful hero. Instead, he proposed that "the great leader is seen as servant first" (p. 2). Greenleaf's conclusion was based on the changes he saw emerging in U.S. society at the time, namely, the questioning of power and authority and the emergence of cooperation and support as more productive ways for people to relate to one another. Greenleaf explains:

> A new moral principle is emerging which holds that the only authority deserving one's allegiance is that which is freely and knowingly granted by the led to the leader in response to, and in proportion to, the clearly evident servant stature of the leader. Those who choose to follow this principle will not casually accept the authority of existing institutions. *Rather, they will freely respond only to individuals who are chosen as leaders because they are proven and trusted as servants.* To the extent that this principle prevails in the future, the only truly viable institutions will be those that are predominantly servant-led. (p. 4)

Greenleaf (1970) fleshed out this notion of **servant leadership** by stressing that the servant leader is servant first. The servant leader takes care to ensure that other people's greatest needs are being met and that those people, while being served by the leader, "become healthier, wiser, freer, more autonomous, more likely themselves to become servants" (p. 7). According to Greenleaf, servant leaders

- Listen first so they may understand a situation
- Develop their intuition and the ability to "foresee the unforeseeable" (p. 14)
- Lead by persuasion, forging change by "convincement rather than coercion" (p. 21)
- Conceptualize the reforms they seek and lift others to see the possibilities also
- Empower by creating opportunities and alternatives for those being served

Servant leaders possess the self-awareness to recognize that their own healing is the motivation for leadership. They also grasp that the connection between the servant leader and the led is "the understanding that the search for wholeness is something they share." And finally, as a change agent, the servant leader recognizes that the first step to changing the world is changing oneself.

The image of servant leader contrasts with the industrial paradigm notions of the leader as a power-wielding authority figure. Here we see the leader as one whose first responsibility is to consider the needs of others and to create conditions where the led can become leaders themselves. To illustrate the idea of the leader as servant, Greenleaf tells the story of John Woolman, an American Quaker who almost single-handedly rid the Society of Friends (Quakers) of slaves. What Greenleaf particularly remarks on is the method that Woolman used to bring about this change— gentle, yet clear and persistent persuasion. Greenleaf elaborates:

> Although John Woolman was not a strong man physically, he accomplished his mission by journeys up and down the East Coast by foot or horseback visiting slaveholders— over a period of many years. The approach was not to censure the slaveholders in a way that drew their animosity. Rather, the burden of his approach was to raise questions: What does the owning of slaves do to you as a moral person? What kind of an institution are you binding over to your children? Man by man, inch by inch, by persistently returning and revisiting and pressing his gentle argument over a period of thirty years, the scourge of slavery was eliminated from this Society, the first religious group in America formally to denounce and forbid slavery among its members. (p. 21)

John Woolman was a man with a personal conviction that led him to seek change in his organization. He achieved his objective through what Greenleaf calls *convincement* rather than coercion. In the process, he made his Quaker brothers and sisters leaders in their own right. This is the essence of servant leadership.

In today's world, a well-known example of servant leadership is Mother Teresa. She has achieved leadership status through serving and advocating for the poor in India and across the world.

MOTHER TERESA: SAINT OF THE GUTTERS

At 85 and after major heart problems, Mother Teresa is still immersed in projects for helping the poor of India and of all the world. Through her service to the ill and destitute, she proclaims her message that the poor must be loved because a loving God created them.

As founder of the Missionaries of Charity, Mother Teresa started rescuing the poor people who were literally dying in the streets of Calcutta. Writer Dominique LaPierre remembers first seeing her washing the wounds of a dying man . . .

So emaciated that he looked like a living skeleton. His flesh seemed to have melted down, leaving only skin over his bones.

Mother Teresa was gently speaking to him in Bengali. I will never forget the eyes of this wretched, dying man. His suffering, staring look progressively changed to an expression of surprise, and then, of peace, the peace of someone who suddenly feels he is loved.

Sensing my presence behind her, the nun turned around. I suddenly felt terribly awkward to have interrupted a dialogue which I could feel was unique. I introduced myself.

Mother Teresa called a young European volunteer who was passing by with a wash-basin in his hands.

"Love him," she told him, "Love him with all your strength."

She . . . invited me to follow her toward the small waiting room that separated the men's and women's wards.

There was a table and a bench, and on the wall a poster which said: "The worst misery is not hunger, not leprosy, but the feeling to be unwanted, rejected, abandoned by everyone."

These words summarize the universality of Mother Teresa's work.

Detractors who accuse her of not providing any real medical treatment to the destitute people who are brought to her homes, and whom she is the only one to rescue, should know that half of them are able to leave her "dying homes" on their feet after a few days, having regained dignity and enough strength, thanks to the loving care received.

Mother Teresa believed that the poor are not just the millions who are starving, but also the millions of excluded, lonely, untouchable, or homeless people. These people most needed the human touch of things like love, justice, hope, and dignity.

She said, "The most terrible disease that can ever strike a human being is to have no one near him to be loved. Without a heart full of love, without generous hands, it is impossible to cure a man suffering of loneliness.

She told reporters in England: "I have walked at night in your streets. I have entered your homes. I have found in them more poverty than in India. I have found the poverty of the soul, the lack of love."

LaPierre said,

Each time I return with my wife to Calcutta to visit the dispensaries and the schools I support with the royalties from my book, 'The City of Joy,' we never fail to attend Mother Teresa's 5:45 A.M. Mass in her convent headquarters, set in the very heart of the teeming megalopolis.

As sole decoration on the walls of the large room that serves as a chapel in the daytime and as a dormitory for the novices at night, there is a simple crucifix with the inscription that says, "I thirst."

. . . What an emotion to rediscover around her all these dark-skinned Indian novices who tomorrow will join their Japanese, European, Australian and American sisters in some 500 orphanages, leprosy homes and rescue centers in more than 100 countries on the five continents.

The order of the Missionaries of Charity cannot accept all the postulants knocking at the door of its novitiates: today it has more than 5,000 sisters, 500 consecrated brothers and more than 4 million lay co-workers.

In 1979, she won the Nobel Peace Prize. Some complain that Mother Teresa could use her charisma and fame to attack the roots of poverty, but she said: "Fortunately there are in this world people who fight for justice and human rights, who struggle to change the structures. The daily contact of our sisters is with people who do not even have a scrap of bread to feed themselves.

"Our mission is to consider the problem on an individual rather than a collective basis. Our concern is for one person, not a multitude. We are looking for the human being with whom Christ identified himself when he said, 'I was hungry and you fed me.'"

LaPierre said,

If this uncommon woman has succeeded in developing so quickly in the whole world the congregation she founded in 1950, it is thanks to an exceptional reunion of gifts and remarkable qualities, among them a faith to lift mountains and a leadership that may sometimes appear tyrannical, an indomitable will to rely for everything only on divine Providence, an exceptional charisma which has conquered the public as well as the media and those who govern the world, an innate gift for organization and a rare capacity to adapt to all situations and face all problems.

For sure, so many qualities represent many handicaps to surmount for the woman who will succeed her. Let's hope the day will come as late as possible and let's quell our fears for the future.

As Mother Teresa has so often said: "The work is not mine but God's. I am only a small pencil in His hand."

From Dominique LaPierre, "Mother Teresa Is Still Offering a Hand at 84," *The Cleveland Plain Dealer*, Dec. 19, 1994.

TRANSFORMATIONAL LEADERSHIP

James MacGregor Burns extended the debate about what comprises leadership by conceptualizing it as occurring in two forms, transactional and transformational. He arrived at this conclusion through analysis of the leadership functions of such political figures as Mahatma Gandhi, Franklin Roosevelt, and Mao Tse-tung. In prefacing his work, Burns noted that the concept of leadership in this century had "dissolved into small and discrete meanings" (p. 2). In seeking to generalize about the

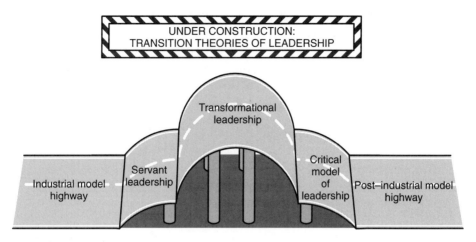

Figure 9–2   Under Construction: Transition Theories of Leadership

leadership process across time and cultures, he wanted to establish a school of leadership where none existed. In addition, Burns also desired to unite the previously unconnected roles of leader and follower. These, then, became the foundational assumptions that underscored his perspectives of leadership (Figure 9–2).

According to Burns, **transactional leadership** is a barter, an exchange of wants between leader and follower. The transactional leader satisfies followers' needs by entering into a relationship of mutual dependence in which the contributions of both sides are recognized and rewarded. The transactional leader helps followers achieve their goals; thus, we follow the transactional leader because it is obvious to us that it is in our own best interests to do so (Kellerman, 1984). The image of leadership as transaction has assumptions in common with the industrial paradigm of leadership.

Transformational leadership, by contrast, goes beyond the notion of exchange. Burns (1978) proposed that transformational leadership includes two essential elements—it is relational, and it deals with producing real change. He explains: "Transformational leadership occurs when one or more persons engage with others in such a way that leaders and followers raise one another to higher levels of motivation and morality" (p. 20). This approach is a commingling of their needs and aspirations and goals in a common enterprise. The purpose of this engagement with followers, Burns tells us, is to bring about change; in fact, in his estimation, the ultimate test of practical leadership is the realization of intended, actual change in people's lives, attitudes, behaviors and in their institutions. Transformational leadership has a moral dimension as well, because those engaged in it "can be lifted into their better selves" (p. 462). This articulation of the moral dimension sharply distinguishes transformational leadership from the views of leadership promoted by management scientists.

Mahatma Gandhi, in particular, epitomized Burns's ideal of the transformational leader. Gandhi's leadership was *causative* in that the nonviolent and egalitarian values he espoused changed people and institutions in India. His leadership was *morally purposeful*, because his objective was to win individual liberty for his countrymen and women by freeing them from the oppression of British rule. His leadership was *elevating* in that he raised his followers to higher moral ground by engaging them in nonviolent activities to achieve social justice. In so doing, Gandhi asked for sacrifices from his followers rather than merely promising them goods and favors.

Burns's seminal work enlightened us to see that leadership is about transformation. It is a relationship between leaders and followers in which both are elevated to more principled levels of judgment. It is about leaders and followers engaged in a change process. It is about power "to" rather than power "over." Burns and Greenleaf's ideas began to transform our notions of leadership.

CLEASTER MIMS: RAISING EXPECTATIONS

Cleaster Mims knew that something major was wrong with the public schools. As a high school English teacher, she felt that the urban system where she taught put students "on a conveyor belt from the school house to the jailhouse."

Her experience with high schoolers and with "boat people" and other immigrants to whom she taught English as a second language showed her that too many students were pigeonholed in terms of their socioeconomic status. Too many students who could achieve were left to languish because not enough was expected of them.

"Kids don't fail," she insists, "teachers fail. And colleges that turn out teachers who cannot teach fail."

The cost of low expectations to the individual is enormous, she said, but the cost to society is even more immense. "We assume someone coming from a certain environment can't achieve, and we end up pushing people to the back of the line who could find a cure for cancer or AIDS."

While listening to a talk by educator Marva Collins, Mims saw the parallels between her experience and the philosophy of Ms. Collins's West Side Preparatory School in Chicago: the pursuit of academic excellence. She determined to start a school in Cincinnati, Ohio, that would demand nothing short of that.

Working with volunteers in the community, she found space in a church basement and made do with cast-offs for supplies and furniture. "We didn't even have books the first year," she says, noting that she eventually bought the school's classical literature at a local Goodwill store.

Now, in the fifth year of the school's operation, what began as a basement program with forty-one students has expanded to more than two hundred, and Mims hopes to convert a recently purchased facility into a boarding component.

Asked about her leadership, Mims deflects credit: "I feel that I'm chosen. When God chooses you, you cannot not do it and find any happiness in life," she says. As the president, CEO, principal, and founder of the school, she says, "The buck stops with me. But I'm not above sweeping the floors."

Although her university teaching career as a professor in oral communications limits her to being at the school only two days per week, she says she has empowered the teachers to carry on without her. "I had a vision about the school and I've been able to pass it on."

She said, "One has not been successful until they have enough to give away."

She attributes much of her success to the hard work and persistence she learned from her upbringing in the South, where she benefited by attending black schools with high-caliber faculty. In those days, she explains, black professionals were severely limited in the types of jobs they could get, so all-black schools profited from their talents. She herself never felt the sting of lowered expectations, and she hopes to help other children avoid it as well.

"We need a metamorphosis of the mind."

A CRITICAL MODEL OF LEADERSHIP

William Foster (1986) and other critical theorists (e.g., Smyth, 1989) honed in on the concept of leadership as transformation by examining the content of the change that the leadership process might produce. They specified that leadership should address social reconstruction: "Leadership is and must be socially critical, it does not reside in an individual but in the relationship between individuals, and it is oriented towards social vision and change, not simply, or only, organizational goals" (p. 46).

Transformational leaders and followers may be mutually pursuing a vision of greatness, but the critical question becomes "whose vision is it?" In the critical perspective, for transformational leadership to actually transform, it must prompt those engaged in the process to question the assumptions upon which their vision is based.

Thus, **critical transformational leadership** requires reflection and analysis: It asks on whose behalf we use our power and makes a place for all voices and arguments to be heard regardless of race, class, and gender (Quantz, Rogers & Dantley, 1991). The critical model of leadership focuses on changing the human condition, and as such, its type of leadership can spring from anywhere. It is not confined to the organizational hierarchy. In this view, leadership is a political and courageous act to empower followers to become leaders themselves.

And finally, Foster (1989) asserts that critical transformational leadership is not "a special or unique occurrence, one that is found only in certain grand moments of human history. Rather, it happens in everyday events, when commonplace leaders exert some effect on their situations" (p. 52).

A good example of leadership from the critical perspective is the work of Brazilian educator Paulo Freire. Rejecting the standard educational pedagogy that helped maintain the social systems oppressing Brazilian peasants, he developed teaching methods he called "liberation education." First Freire taught the peasants to critique the system that kept them in economic slavery and then he taught them about the possibility of reforming that system so their voices would be heard and their needs recognized equally with the wealthier citizens in the society (Freire, 1970). His leadership empowered his followers to initiate change on their own behalf.

Implications

Several common themes emerge from an analysis of this chapter's three perspectives on leadership (servant, transformational, and critical models).

1. **Leadership is a relationship, as opposed to the property of an individual.**

   It is conducted with leaders and followers, and followers are essential parts of the equation. The role of the leader is to serve followers and to empower them to become leaders themselves.

2. **Leadership entails change.**

   Both leaders and followers experience change, originating within themselves and then emanating outward to the community. Leadership requires critical reflection and analysis in order to determine if the vision of change being pursued is inclusive or if it excludes or diminishes some members of the community.

3. **Leadership can be done by anyone, not only those who are designated as leaders.**

These alternative perspectives on leadership gained credence because they more fully captured some aspects of our experience with leadership than did the conventional view. Because the alternative perspectives raised questions that could not be addressed by the industrial paradigm of leadership, they prompted the search for a new paradigm of leadership for the twenty-first century.

THE POSTINDUSTRIAL PARADIGM OF LEADERSHIP

In his 1991 book *Leadership for the Twenty-First Century,* Joseph Rost offered a new definition of leadership that he quite boldly proclaimed as the postindustrial paradigm of leadership. One does not pronounce a new paradigm without substantial evidence of its need. And so it was with Rost. He built a convincing argument for why the industrial paradigm of leadership is no longer adequate to explain both the realities of leadership we experience and the kind of leadership we need in a twenty-first century world.

What are the realities that prompt us to establish a new paradigm of leadership? U.S. culture is in the midst of a major shift in the ways that we make sense of our world. The globalization of the economy, the rapid and continual change resulting from new technologies, the information explosion, and the increasing diversity of our population create a reality that is messy and ambiguous rather than orderly and predictable (Rogers & Ballard, 1995). As a result, we are moving away from a **mechanistic world view** in which objectivity, control, and linear causality are supreme to **a relational approach,** a world view that recognizes the more contextual, complex, and relational aspects of the natural world in which we function (Wheatley, 1992; Kuh, Whitt & Shedd, 1987).

Among the consequences of the shift from a mechanistic world view are the changes in organizational structures and cultures that have been the hallmark of the past fifteen years (Rogers & Ballard, 1995; Peters, 1992). Table 9–1 contrasts the culture of the bureaucratic/mechanistic forms of organization with emerging ad hoc models of organization. The latter are rapidly gaining credibility because they more effectively respond to the kind of environmental turbulence that marks our current reality.

TABLE 9–1   **Organizational Culture Transformations**

Old Culture (disappearing bureaucracy)	New Culture (emerging adhocracy)
hierarchy, specialization	transient units
division of labor	reorganization
slow to change	fast moving
roles sharply defined	roles flexible and temporary
chain of command	fluid, participative roles and structures
self-interested outlook	social responsibility is central to success
stable, predictable environment	accelerating change and need for innovation
vertical power	horizontal power, relationships
communication slow, only as needed	communication fast and lateral
simple problem solving	complex problem solving
staff/line distinctions	team approach
emphasis on efficiency	emphasis on people

Source: Adapted from P. Harris. Innovating with high achievers. *Training & Development Journal,* 34, 10 (1980), 45–50.

Recent research and practice suggest that conventional models of organization are not as suited to understanding events and actions in uncertain, dynamic times; thus, organizations are transforming themselves in order to better respond to change. A key activity of the modern organization is to continuously learn and to master new knowledge in order to innovate, solve problems, and maintain productivity. The quality movement of the 1980s and 1990s is a manifestation of the move away from machine-like forms of organization and management to more team–centered, collaborative approaches.

In a similar vein, Rost (1994) debunks the industrial paradigm of leadership because of its grounding in a mechanistic world view. He argues that the industrial paradigm of leadership is industrial because it takes a bureaucratic view of organizations; it has an individualistic focus because it asserts that only great leaders practice leadership; it is dominated by a goal achievement sense of purpose; it promotes a self-interested outlook on life; it accepts a male model of behavior and power (known as leadership style); it articulates utilitarian and materialistic ethical perspectives; it is grounded in rational, linear, and quantitative assumptions about how the world works, and it asserts a managerial perspective as to what makes organizations tick. Although these characteristics may have been appropriate for a world that was more stable, they are not as relevant in a time of rapid change. In the context of our increasingly complex and ambiguous world, Rost extends the work of Burns, Greenleaf, and Foster and offers a postindustrial paradigm of leadership for our consideration.

Rost's definition—"Leadership is an influence relationship among leaders and their collaborators who intend **real changes** that reflect their mutual purposes" (1994, p. 7)—includes four essential elements of leadership.

1. **The relationship is based on influence rather than positional authority.**
   Noncoercive persuasion is used to influence people in the leadership relationship. The influence is multidirectional, coming from all members, rather than only top down. People are free to agree or disagree and to choose to stay in or leave the relationship.

2. **Leaders and their collaborators practice leadership.**
   The word *collaborators* instead of followers is favored because it more closely fits the values of this perspective. The interactions of leaders and their collaborators comprise the essence of leadership, not the individual behaviors of the leader. In a leadership relationship, collaborators are active rather than passive. Leaders are those who at a particular moment commit more of their resources (i.e., their expertise, their passion, their political savvy) to influence the process.

3. **Collaborators and their leaders intend real change.**
   Rost notes that "*Intend* means that the leaders and their collaborators do not have to produce changes to practice leadership, only intend them and then act on that intention" (p. 7). Thus, the very act of initiating a change movement marks the time when leadership occurs, in contrast to the industrial paradigm view that leadership happens when any goal has been achieved. *Real* connotes that the changes are substantive attempts to transform people's attitudes, behaviors, and values.

4. **The changes that the leaders and their collaborators pursue reflect their mutual purposes.**
   The changes represent what *both* leaders and collaborators desire in a shared enterprise, rather than merely accomplishing the wishes of the leader.

Several important implications are embedded in this definition of leadership. Collaborators choose the leaders with whom they wish to affiliate, and they may or may not be people who hold authority over them. Thus, leadership is not confined to those in power in the organizational hierarchy. Leaders and collaborators often change places in the ebb and flow of the leadership process. A number of leadership relationships may be present in any organization, and the leaders in one relationship may be collaborators in another.

Leadership is episodic, a stream of activities that occur when people intend a specific and real change for their organization or group. One is not a leader all of the time, but rather, when one chooses to exert the most influence on the change process. Rost (1994) elaborates: "Leadership is people bonding together to institute a change in a group, organization, or society. Leadership is a group of activists who want to implement a reformist agenda. Leadership is a band of leaders and collaborators who envision a better future and go after it" (p. 6).

When first introduced to Rost's conceptualization of postindustrial leadership, we may find it difficult to get a fix on just what it entails. Conditioned by our industrial paradigm lenses to view leadership in a particular way, much like the blind men and the elephant in the Indian tale, we have difficulty seeing beyond our own narrow perspective. In particular, we have been so enmeshed in viewing leadership and management as one and the same that untangling these concepts becomes difficult. Similarly, we have problems conceiving of leadership as not grounded in positional authority, hence not naturally accruing to those managers at the top levels of the hierarchy. Yet in order to separate leadership from management, these distinctions are important.

Rost's work challenges us to clearly distinguish between these two concepts. In the industrial paradigm, leadership has been understood as good management, even though it was implied that a manager was somehow less effective than a leader. The industrial paradigm confers much more desirability to being considered a leader than a manager, a perspective captured in the oft-quoted words of Bennis and Nanus (1985): "Managers do things right; leaders do the right thing." While managers are pedestrian, leaders are visionary.

In the postindustrial paradigm, the two concepts are defined as distinct activities. One is not better than the other; they are simply different—and equally important—processes in a postindustrial world. Rost (1991) envisions the two roles playing out in formal organizations in this way:

> Leaders and collaborators are the people involved in a leadership relationship. . . .
> Managers and subordinates are the people involved in managerial relationships. . . .
> The two sets of words are not synonymous. Leaders are not the same as managers. Collaborators are not the same as subordinates. Managers may be leaders but if they are leaders, they are involved in a relationship different from management. Subordinates may be collaborators, but if they are collaborators they are involved in a relationship different than management. Leaders need not be managers to be leaders. Collaborators need not be subordinates to be collaborators. (p. 150)

Rost asserts that the way in which influence is exercised is an important distinction between leadership and management. In his view, leadership is a relationship in which only noncoercive influence behaviors are acceptable, rather than one wherein all legitimate behaviors (including authority and other forms of coercion) are acceptable.

Some Additional Postindustrial Models of Leadership

Just as Rost specifically offered a new definition of leadership and labeled it the postindustrial paradigm, other scholars have also proposed new views of leadership in the face of the dramatic changes occurring in Western culture as we approach the new millennium. For example, Bensimon and Neumann (1993) draw from their own research, their analysis of others' research, and their own experiences in organizations to describe the ideal leader in the future. They conclude that the age of the heroic, solo leader is over. **Collaborative leadership,** they insist, is necessary to respond to the information-rich and complex environment of the twenty-first century. One mind can comprehend only so much; we need the combination of many minds to understand and solve complex problems. As Bensimon and Neumann see it:

> The ideal leader will be someone who knows how to find and bring together diverse minds—minds that reflect variety in their points of view, in their thinking processes and

in their unique capacities as well as unique limitations. . . . Moreover, as the world grows more complex . . . it is likely that we will stop thinking of leadership as the property or quality of just one person. We will begin to think of it in its collective form: leadership as occurring among and through a group of people who think and act together. (p. 12)

In a study of college presidents and their administrative teams, Bensimon and Neumann found that the team builders who encouraged their teams to think in diverse rather than similar ways and to engage in a variety of tasks rather than following a strict division of labor were more likely to be associated with effective leadership. The authors conclude that the ability to build and maintain diverse, "thinking" teams is a critical skill for twenty-first century leadership.

Similarly, Margaret Wheatley (1992) advances the new paradigm of leadership in her work, which compares leadership and the new sciences of quantum and chaos theories. She notes, as have others, that the conventional (industrial) perspectives of organizations and leadership are heavily grounded in the principles of Newtonian physics, specifically, the belief in objectivity, linear causality, and control. These influences produce an emphasis on structure and parts, as well as on "our desire to control a reality that is slippery and evasive" (p. 25). In particular, the belief that we can control nature and thus organizations and people makes the Newtonian frame so seductive, and also so difficult to relinquish. However, Wheatley argues that the new sciences offer a much more realistic perspective on organizational reality and a better foundation for leadership in a new world.

In quantum physics she finds the grounding for participatory leadership: ". . . the quantum realm speaks emphatically to the role of participation, even to its impact on creating reality" (p. 143). She asks, if the universe is participatory, how can we fail to embrace this in our organizations and our leadership practices?

The participatory nature of reality has also focused attention on relationships. In her words, "Nothing exists at the subatomic level, or can be observed, without engagement with another energy source" (p. 14). Thus, in the frame of the new science we move from the separateness and objectivity of the industrial view of leadership to recognizing that leadership is always context-bound and that the context of leadership is established by the relationships we value. The lenses of the new science show us that leadership is a relational act.

Writing from the Center for Creative Leadership, Drath and Palus (1994) offer yet another take on postindustrial leadership. They suggest that leadership is "meaning-making in a community of practice," and they contrast this definition with the conventional view in which leaders use dominance or influence to get followers to do what the individual leader wants. The Drath and Palus view of leadership is grounded in **constructivism,** which asserts that reality is a socially constructed phenomenon known only through our perception of it; that is, we use our own perceptual filters to make sense of what we experience. This meaning-making can be achieved individually or with others (socially). We are driven to make sense of things because meaning-making is an important human activity. It is, in fact, the way we come to understand ourselves and our world.

From this constructivist base, Drath and Palus propose that leadership accrues to those who can frame the experiences of those engaged in a shared activity in such a way that helps the group make sense of its actions. Leadership is the process of providing frameworks by which members of a community make sense of what they are doing, why they are doing it, and what they have learned from it.

> Meaning-making happens through such processes as identifying vision and mission, framing problems, setting goals, arguing and engaging in dialogue, theory building and testing, storytelling, and the making of contracts and agreements. . . . From an individual perspective, it is not so much that a person is first a leader and then creates meaning; it's more that, in making meaning a person comes to be called a leader. . . . It is the process of participating in making meaning in a collective sense that makes leaders out of people. (p. 10–11)

Here again, we see that leadership is a relational process in which everyone in a community is engaged. The question for the leader, then, becomes not how to get individuals to do what needs to be done, but rather, how to create communities in which everyone, even those on the margins, can make important contributions. Bensimon and Neumann (1993) hold strikingly similar views with Drath and Palus about the purpose of leadership as meaning-making. They, too, define leadership as the shared construction of meaning.

> Leadership requires skill in the creation of meaning that is authentic to oneself and to one's community. It also requires the uncovering of meaning that is already embedded in others' minds, helping them to see what they already know, believe and value, and encouraging them to make new meaning. In this way, leadership generates leadership. (p. xv)

Rost, Bensimon and Neumann, Wheatley, and Drath and Palus are among the pioneers in defining new images of leadership. No doubt, as we move into the twenty-first century, the postindustrial paradigm of leadership will continue to be refined, modified, and elaborated upon. Although still in its infant stages, with much work to be done before postindustrial leadership is widely accepted and fully embedded in our theory and practice, this leadership paradigm offers one clear theme: the age of the individual leader-hero is gone. As we look to the new millennium, leadership must be understood as a relationship, a collaborative process, a community of believers pursuing a transformational cause.

RABBI ALEXANDER M. SCHINDLER: TRANSFORMING, REACHING OUT

As a twelve-year-old whose family escaped from the Nazis, Alexander Schindler found himself in a new country surrounded by a strange language. Over the next few years, he mastered English and assumed a leadership role in the U.S. Army, where he earned a Purple Heart for his wounds and a Bronze Star for bravery. He also reached a personal turning point: Alexander decided to become a rabbi.

His experiences as an outsider, a youth traumatized by events around him, may have helped him learn to empathize with others in pain and turmoil. That identification with others has marked his distinguished career in the rabbinate and as president for twenty-three years of the Union of American Hebrew Congregations (UAHC). During his tenure there, Schindler has consistently espoused the cause of the underdog, specifically gay rights and women's rights (especially the ordination of women).

Whereas his predecessor in the UAHC, Rabbi Maurice N. Eisendrath, was known for his controversial stances that sometimes led to angry divisions and opposition within Reform Judaism, Schindler is known for his personal warmth, self-deprecating humor, and his gentle, almost poetic oratory. These traits have done much to diminish rancor within the Reform movement, even though Schindler has not shied from controversy.

Among his accomplishments as UAHC president are the establishment of Reform Jewish day schools, bolstering of youth programs, and his dream, a Torah commentary from a Reform perspective. While Schindler was president of the UAHC, Reform became the largest and fastest growing branch of Judaism.

Schindler also understood the importance of dealing with outreach issues, as shown by his calls for welcoming interfaith marriages and converts. He foresaw the importance of addressing the spiritual needs of millions of Americans he called "religiously unpreferenced."

That he has not shied from difficult positions is evident from the support he gave Menachim Begin, a former terrorist and hard-line right-winger, after his election as prime minister in 1977. Himself a lifelong liberal, Schindler reminded American Jews of the importance of supporting the democratic process in Israel, noting that the people of Israel had duly elected Begin. Schindler flew to Israel to meet with the new prime minister, exerting the force of his leadership to halt an incipient revolt and give the new government a chance. Begin always remembered Schindler's efforts, and although they frequently disagreed over policy matters, the two leaders were good friends until Begin's death in 1992.

SUMMARY

The story of leadership from the postindustrial perspective is quite different from the stories we have told until now. For the greater part of this century we have conceived of the leader as a person apart, whose purpose was to provide us with a vision to follow and with answers for our uncertainties. The postindustrial world does not offer us such simple solutions. In a time of rapid and complex change, it is unrealistic to expect one person to be the expert who solves all our problems. We need a different kind of leadership for a new world.

This chapter has chronicled the evolution of the postindustrial paradigm of leadership. Several models of leadership served as precursors to the new paradigm, specifically servant leadership, transformational leadership, and the critical model of leadership. These models broke with the industrial paradigm view in several major ways: by describing leadership as a relationship versus the property of an individual, by defining leadership as a change process, and by recognizing that leadership is not confined to those who hold positional authority but rather, is something that can be performed by anyone.

These transitional theories influenced the thinking of leadership scholars and led Joseph Rost (1994) to propose a definition of leadership that he labeled the postindustrial paradigm. Rost explained: "Leadership is an influence relationship among leaders and collaborators who intend real change that reflects their mutual purposes" (p. 7). The postindustrial perspectives envision leadership as a process done by both leaders and collaborators; a process of bringing diverse minds together in a collaborative effort to enact some kind of real change; a process through which people make meaning of their experience; and a process separate from management.

KEY TERMS

servant leadership
transactional leadership
transformational leadership
critical transformational leadership
constructivism

relational approach
mechanistic world view
real changes
collaborative leadership

FOR DISCUSSION AND REVIEW

1. What are the characteristics of servant leaders, according to Greenleaf? Why does he believe that servant-led institutions are most successful?

2. What are some of the primary lessons to be gleaned from John Woolman's crusade to eradicate slavery within the Society of Friends? Who are other examples of servant leaders?

3. Contrast transactional leadership with transformational leadership.

4. What are some of the core aspects of the critical model of leadership?

5. What are some of the common themes among servant, transformational, and critical models of leadership?

6. What are some of the societal and historical factors that have triggered movement away from the industrial paradigm and a mechanistic view of leadership?

7. What are Rost's four essential elements of leadership? Do you agree with his assessment? Why or why not?

8. What are some of the distinctions Rost makes between leaders and managers?

9. Think of your own experience doing leadership or your observations of leaders. Which characteristics of postindustrial leadership have you implemented yourself or seen implemented by others? What was the result? From these experiences and observations, what do you think it takes to successfully engage in leadership as a collaborative process?

10. Which elements of postindustrial leadership do you already practice? Which do you think would be most difficult for you to learn and why? Which aspects do you find most useful, and which aspects are the least useful?

11. Do you agree that the age of the individual leader is over? Why or why not?

12. Do you think that it is important to separate leadership and management and describe them as different processes? What do you see as the differences between the two?

CRITICAL INCIDENT

You are the director of Human Resources at a large dairy company. You have received feedback that your recent hires, while well-qualified, have been too traditional in their views on leadership. The company is concerned about being successful in future years and has directed you to hire people who have the potential to be "cutting-edge" leaders. What characteristics in applicants would you most value in conducting this search? What might be some potential negative characteristics in these applicants?

EXERCISES FOR CHAPTER 9

Exercise 9–1   Understanding Transition Theories

In his book *Imaginization*, Gareth Morgan (1993) graphically illustrates that the commonly used team metaphor for leadership is shaded with very different meanings for different individuals. The use of the team metaphor is helpful as we attempt to understand the differences between the industrial model of leadership and the transition theories of Greenleaf and Burns.

Using a sports metaphor, please give an example of a sport (hockey, basketball, football, rowing, soccer, baseball, swimming, lacrosse, golf, bowling, horse racing, etc.) that illustrates leadership as defined in the industrial paradigm, the servant-leader model (Greenleaf), and the transformational leadership of Burns.

SPORTS METAPHORS

INDUSTRIAL MODEL	SERVANT LEADERSHIP	TRANSFORMATIONAL LEADERSHIP
1. Sport:	1. Sport:	1. Sport:
2. This is a good example because:	2. This is a good example because:	2. This is a good example because:
3. In this sport, the leader plays what role?	3. In this sport, the leader plays what role?	3. In this sport, the leader plays what role?

4. Could this leader play this sport so that it would fit into the other two categories?

4. Could this leader play this sport so that it would fit into the other two categories?

4. Could this leader play this sport so that it would fit into the other two categories?

5. How?

5. How?

5. How?

Exercise 9–2   Understanding the Organizational Culture Transformations

Step One: Identify three examples of bureaucratic/mechanistic forms of organizations (old culture) and three examples of the emerging ad hoc models of organizations (new culture). These examples can be drawn from business, industry, politics, government, volunteer, or service organizations.

Bureaucratic/Mechanistic Organizations (Old Cultures)	Ad Hoc Organizations (New Cultures)
1.	1.
2.	2.
3.	3.

Step Two: Answer the following questions about the examples you have given.

1. What are the major differences between the two types of organizations? Be specific.
2. Will the new ad hoc organization be as successful over the next twenty-five years as the older bureaucratic/mechanistic organizations were for the past twenty-five years? Why or why not?
3. Which type of organization would you be most comfortable working in?
4. Which is easier to lead?
5. Do they require the same types of leaders?

Exercise 9–3   Understanding Differences Between the Industrial Model and Rost's Postindustrial Model of Leadership

Directions: Part One: Fill in the chart highlighting the differences between Rost's postindustrial model and the industrial model of Leadership by selecting from the menu of descriptions below. All of the descriptive phrases describe one of the two models.

INDUSTRIAL MODEL	ROST'S POST-INDUSTRIAL MODEL
1.	1.
2.	2.
3.	3.
4.	4.
5.	5.
6.	6.

A. This has a bureaucratic view of organizations.

B. Relationships are based on influence rather than positional authority.

C. Collaborators and leaders intend real change.

D. Model is grounded in rational, linear, and quantitative assumptions.

E. *Leadership* and *management* are often used interchangeably.

F. Leadership is dominated by goal achievement sense of purpose.

G. Leaders and their collaborators DO Leadership.

H. A leader's vision, style, objectives, and personal characteristics determine desired outcomes.

I. This has flexible, multidirectional, ad hoc view of organization.

J. Leadership and management are two distinct and equally important processes.

K. Changes that leaders and their collaborators pursue must reflect their mutual purposes.

L. Model has an individualistic focus—only great leaders do leadership.

Directions: Part Two: Arrange the 6 descriptive phrases for each model in a "point-counterpoint format," so that the descriptive phrase under the Industrial Model is balanced on the Post-Industrial side of the chart with its opposite.

INDUSTRIAL MODEL	ROST'S POST-INDUSTRIAL MODEL
1.	1.
2.	2.
3.	3.
4.	4.
5.	5.
6.	6.

Practicing Leadership: It's Your Turn

The Leadership Journey:
A map of the terrain
Chapter 10
Words/names to recognize

You are here

Yours
Practicing leadership–it is your turn

Industrial Hwy.

Transitional Dr.

Hero's Blvd.

Rost Rd.

President's Path

Pre-Industrial Rd.

Quality Circle

Covey Circle

Post-Industrial Hwy.

"We use journey as a metaphor for how we come to understand leadership over the centuries."

"Leadership is a personal journey."

These quotes from the book's introduction help end it as well. You have effectively ended this portion of your leadership journey by completing this course of study. What does it all mean? What have you really learned? What are the "take-aways"— those ideas that make sense as you attempt to answer the ultimate final exam for this journey: What is Leadership?

We suggest that you attempt to answer that complicated question by completing the exercise that follows. When finished, you should have a personal leadership road sign that briefly details the most important features of your own leadership theory. Remember, as you attempt to describe the various leadership components, this text begins and ends with practicing leadership. Therefore, answer or complete the segments as you intend to practice leadership in the real world.

Table 10–1 provides a road map of where we have been and an atlas of destinations visited, or authors, models and theories studied.

TABLE 10–1 The Leadership Journey

Destinations	Concepts to Remember
Introduction:	"Leadership is one of the most observed and least understood phenomena on Earth."
	The twenty-first century will call for new leadership built on some basic assumptions:
	1. Where we are in our understanding of leadership is a function of where we have been.
	2. This approach is not formula-driven.
	3. Leadership is not differentiated by setting.
	4. Understanding leadership requires multiple perspectives.
	5. Effective leadership must encompass the range of human differences.
	6. Metaphors are useful in studying leadership that is described indirectly through paradigms.
	7. Leadership is a verb. We encourage learning to DO leadership as opposed to studying how to BE a leader.
Ancient Philosophers:	Remnants of the Greek portrait of a leader: decisive; physical prowess; a warrior's guile; and protection of followers are still very widely held even today.
	Plato's notion that leaders possessed inborn traits is echoed by much of the twentieth-century literature.
	Machiavelli argued that a leader's primary task was to subordinate simply being "good" for other more attractive ends (power, order, stability, skill at calculation, manipulation, and seeming to possess virtuous qualities). Successful princes (leaders) did not hesitate to take what they desired by force.

(continued)

TABLE 10–1   The Leadership Journey (*Continued*)

Destinations	Concepts to Remember
Psychology:	Human behavior is motivated by needs, desires, and expectations. (Maslow & ERG Theory)
	Multiple factors affect employee motivation: "Hygiene factors"; Theory X and Theory Y (people like/dislike work; people seek/avoid responsibility; and people need to be controlled, coerced, and closely monitored/people are self-directed and seek to do their best work given the opportunity).
	Equity theory suggests that people seek to equalize the ratios of outcomes (pay, recognition, job status, etc.) to inputs (effort, age, gender, experience, and level of productivity).
Communication:	Communication is used to bring about five outcomes: understanding, pleasure, attitude influence, improve relations, and action.
	An understanding of perceptual filters, communicative stimuli, perception, noise, and formal versus informal communication channels is critical for the effective leader.
Management:	Although the effects of management were felt more than two hundred years ago during the Industrial Revolution as factories developed, it is only in this century that its impact has been systematically studied. Taylor, Fayol, and Weber were the forefathers of the burgeoning classical approach to management.
	Although the words are frequently used interchangeably, management and leadership are not the same thing. A person can be skilled as a leader or manager or both—or neither.
	Management is often described by Mintzberg's ten primary functions or Yukl's fundamental practices.
	Although classical management theory stated that there is only one best way to resolve an issue, today there is widespread agreement with the contingency theory model (House and Fiedler).
Quality Movement:	The quality movement gained widespread popularity in Japan after World War II as the country's businesses tried to rebuild. Ishikawa's major contribution to his new field were cause-and-effect diagrams and the work team concept.
	Deming (perhaps the best known of the "quality gurus") developed control charts, a 14-point quality plan, and the Plan-Do-Check-Act (PDCA) Cycle.
	Juran coined the terms Big Q and Little Q and postulated several important principles: quality defined, the Pareto principle, and the organization's quality demands. In addition, he emphasized his trilogy: quality planning; quality control; and quality improvements.
Trait Theory:	Gardner and Bennis detail the functions, competencies, and attributes of leaders.
Behavioral Theory:	This cluster of theories assumes that leader behaviors, rather than personality characteristics, exert the most influence on followers.
	Although the Ohio State and University of Michigan studies vary, both centered on two aspects of a manager, concern for people and concern for performance. Most individuals seem predisposed to favor one concern over the other.

(*continued*)

TABLE 10–1   The Leadership Journey (*Continued*)

Destinations	Concepts to Remember
The Situational Approach:	Numerous varieties of situational theories exist, but most consider at least three major components: the leader's behavior, the situation, and followers/collaborators.
	Vroom, Yetton, and Yago are names associated with accounting for the amount of participation in decision making. Their investigation of decision-making processes led them to propose a continuum from autocratic to consultative for the group process.
	Fiedler's Contingency Theory attempts to assess additional situational factors like leader–member relations, task structure, and position power.
	Unlike their colleagues, Hersey and Blanchard postulate that the effectiveness of the leaders' styles depends largely on their collaborators' maturity, job experience, and emotional maturity.
	Based on this orientation, Hersey and Blanchard identified four types of leader behaviors (telling, selling, participating, delegating) and two basic decision styles (task orientation and relationship orientation).
The Hero's Journey:	Throughout history and in virtually every culture, heroes have left their known worlds to venture into the unknown, face trials, discover truths and revelations, experience various kinds of deaths and rebirths, and finally 'return,' bringing something of value.
	Heroism is the level to which we need to go to find sufficient strength, energy, wisdom, and courage to deal successfully with the changes threatening to overwhelm us: changes in technology, demography, globization, a fragile environment, and so on.
Transition Theory:	Three important transition theories help bridge the gap between what we have learned thus far about leadership and the radically different kind of leadership that will be needed in the next century.
	Servant leadership, transformational leadership, and the critical model of leadership provide a departure from leadership as previously understood.
The 21st Century:	James Rost has constructed what he terms the postindustrial model of leadership—the kind of leadership, he asserts, that will be absolutely necessary in the twenty-first century.
	There are four essential elements of Practicing Leadership as envisioned by Rost. They are:
	1. The leader-collaborator relationship is based on influence rather than positional authority.
	2. Leaders and their collaborators practice leadership together.
	3. Collaborators and their leaders intend real change.
	4. The changes that leaders and their collaborators pursue reflect their mutual purposes.

Figures 10–1 and 10–2, in conjunction with Exercise 10–1, ask that you describe where and how you intend to practice leadership in your own life.

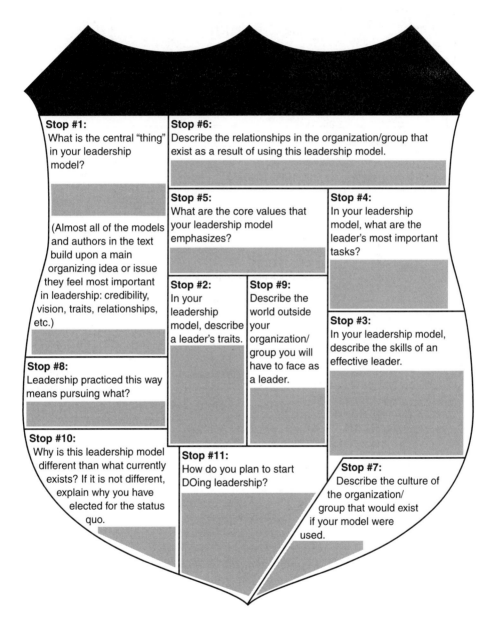

Stop #1:
What is the central "thing" in your leadership model?

(Almost all of the models and authors in the text build upon a main organizing idea or issue they feel most important in leadership: credibility, vision, traits, relationships, etc.)

Stop #6:
Describe the relationships in the organization/group that exist as a result of using this leadership model.

Stop #5:
What are the core values that your leadership model emphasizes?

Stop #4:
In your leadership model, what are the leader's most important tasks?

Stop #2:
In your leadership model, describe a leader's traits.

Stop #9:
Describe the world outside your organization/group you will have to face as a leader.

Stop #3:
In your leadership model, describe the skills of an effective leader.

Stop #8:
Leadership practiced this way means pursuing what?

Stop #10:
Why is this leadership model different than what currently exists? If it is not different, explain why you have elected for the status quo.

Stop #11:
How do you plan to start DOing leadership?

Stop #7:
Describe the culture of the organization/group that would exist if your model were used.

Figure 10–1 What is leadership and how do I intend to practice it in a business/professional/organizational setting?

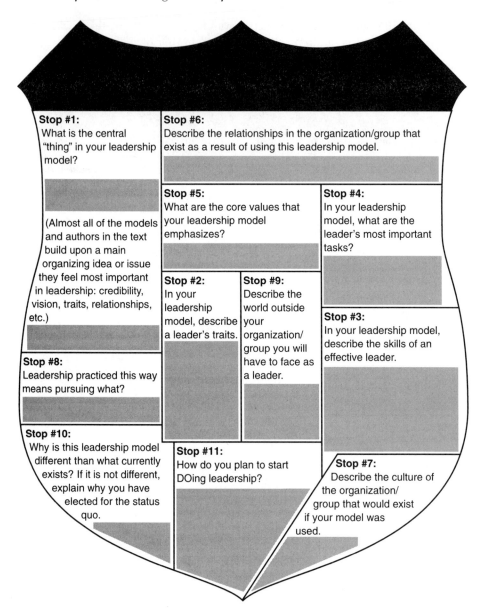

Stop #1:
What is the central "thing" in your leadership model?

(Almost all of the models and authors in the text build upon a main organizing idea or issue they feel most important in leadership: credibility, vision, traits, relationships, etc.)

Stop #8:
Leadership practiced this way means pursuing what?

Stop #10:
Why is this leadership model different than what currently exists? If it is not different, explain why you have elected for the status quo.

Stop #6:
Describe the relationships in the organization/group that exist as a result of using this leadership model.

Stop #5:
What are the core values that your leadership model emphasizes?

Stop #2:
In your leadership model, describe a leader's traits.

Stop #9:
Describe the world outside your organization/ group you will have to face as a leader.

Stop #11:
How do you plan to start DOing leadership?

Stop #4:
In your leadership model, what are the leader's most important tasks?

Stop #3:
In your leadership model, describe the skills of an effective leader.

Stop #7:
Describe the culture of the organization/ group that would exist if your model was used.

Figure 10–2 **What is leadership and how do I intend to practice it in my personal/social life?**

EXERCISE FOR CHAPTER 10

Exercise 10–1   What Is Leadership: Key for Figure 10–1

What is leadership, and how do I intend to practice it in a business/professional/organizational setting?

Stop #1: What is the central *thing* in your leadership model? (Almost all the models and authors studied in the text build upon a main organizing idea or issue they feel most important in leadership credibility, vision, traits, relationships, etc.)

Stop #2: In your leadership model, describe a leader's traits.

Stop #3: Using your leadership model, describe the skills of an effective leader.

Stop #4: In your leadership model, what are a leader's most important tasks?

Stop #5: What are the *core values* that your leadership model emphasizes?

Stop #6: Describe the relationships in the organizational group that exist as a result of using this leadership model.

Stop #7: Describe the *culture* of the organization/group that would exist if your model were used.

Stop #8: Leadership practiced this way means pursuing what?

Stop #9: Describe the world outside your organization/group that you will have to face as a leader.

Stop #10: Why is this leadership model different than what currently exists? If it is not different, explain why you have elected for the status quo.

Stop #11: How do you plan to start practicing leadership?

Bibliography

Aguayo, R., *Dr. Deming: The American Who Taught the Japanese about Quality.* New York: Simon & Schuster, 1990.

Albanese, R., and D. D. Van Fleet, *Organizational Behavior: A Managerial Viewpoint.* Hinsdale, Ill.: The Dryden Press, 1983.

Archer, J. *Mao Tse-Tung.* New York: Hawthorn Books, 1972.

Ashe, A., *Days of Grace.* New York: Alfred A. Knopf, Inc., 1993.

Aquinas, T., *On Kingship.* Toronto: Pontifical Institute of Medieval Studies, 1982.

Bandura, A.,"Self-Efficacy: Toward a Unifying Theory of Behavioral Change." *Psychological Review* 84 (1977), 191–215.

Bass, B. M., *Stogdill's Handbook of Leadership,* rev. ed. New York: Free Press, 1981.

Batten, J. D., *Tough-Minded Leadership.* New York: American Management Association,1989.

Belansky, M. F., Clinchy, B. M., Goldberger, N. R., and J. M. Tarule, *Women's Ways of Knowing.* New York: Basic Books, 1989.

Belasco, J. A. and R. C. Stayer, *Flight of the Buffalo: Soaring to Excellence. Learning to Let Employees Lead.* New York: Warner Books, 1993.

Belasco, J., *Teaching the Elephant to Dance: The Manager's Guide to Empowering Change.* New York: Plume, 1990.

Bellman, G. M., *Getting Things Done When You Are Not in Charge: How to Succeed from a Support Position.* San Francisco: Berrett-Koehler Publishers, 1992.

Bennis, W. G., & Nanus, B., *Leaders: The Strategies for Taking Charge.* New York: Harper & Row, 1985.

Bennis, W. G., *On Becoming a Leader.* Reading, Mass.: Addison-Wesley, 1989.

Bensimon, E. M., & A. Neumann, *Redesigning Collegiate Leadership.* Baltimore: The Johns Hopkins University Press, 1993.

Bienen, H., ed., *Voices of Power: World Leaders Speak.* Hopewell, N.J.: Ecco Press, 1995.

Blake, R. R., and A. A. McCanse, *Leadership Dilemmas-Grid Solutions.* Houston: Gulf Publishing Co., 1991.

Blake, R. R., and J. S. Mouton, *The Managerial Grid.* Houston: Gulf Publishers, 1964.

Blanchard, K. and S. Johnson, *The One Minute Manager.* La Jolla, Calif.: Blanchard-Johnson, 1981.

235

Blanchard, K., and N. Pearle, *The Power of Ethical Management.* New York: Fawcett Crest, 1988.

Block, P., *Stewardship.* San Francisco: Berrett-Koehler, 1993.

Bolman, L. G., and T. E. Deal, *Reframing Organizations: Artistry, Choice and Leadership.* San Francisco: Jossey-Bass, 1991.

Burke, W. W., "Leadership as Empowering Others," in *Srivastra and Associates, Executive Power.* San Francisco: Jossey-Bass, 1986.

Burns, J. M., *Leadership.* New York: Harper & Row, 1979.

Business Horizons, "Different Forms of Political Manipulation," March–April 1987.

Cantor, D. W., and T. Bernay, *Women in Power: The Secrets of Leadership.* New York: Houghton Mifflin, 1992.

Conger, J.A., *The Charismatic Leader.* New York: Jossey-Bass, 1988.

Chandler, A. D. Jr., *The Visible Hand: The Managerial Revolution in American Business.* Cambridge, Mass.: Harvard University Press, 1977.

Daft, R. L., *Management* (3rd ed.). Fort Worth, Tex.: Dryden Press, 1994.

Deming, W. E., *Out of the Crisis.* Cambridge, Mass.: Massachusetts Institute of Technology Center for Advanced Engineering Study, 1986.

DePree, M., *Leadership Is an Art.* New York: Dell, 1989.

DePree, M., *Leadership Jazz.* New York: Dell, 1992.

Drath, W. H. and C. J. Paulus, *Making Common Sense: Leadership as Meaning-Making in a Community of Practice.* Greensboro, N.C.: Center for Creative Leadership, 1994.

Drucker, P. F., *The Practice of Management.* New York: Harper & Row, 1954.

DuBrin, A., *Leadership: Research Findings, Practice and Skills.* Boston, Mass.: Houghton Mifflin, 1995.

Eisenhower, D. D., *The White House Years: Mandate for Change, 1953–1956.* Garden City, New York: Doubleday, 1963.

Etzioni, A. *The Spirit of Community.* New York: Crown, 1993.

Evans, M. G., "The Effects of Supervisory Behavior on the Path-Goal Relationship." *Organizational Behavior and Human Performance* 5 (1970), 277–98.

Evans, J. R., and W. M. Lindsay, *The Management and Control of Quality* (2nd ed.). St. Paul, Minn.: West Publishing Co., 1993.

Fayol H., *General and Industrial Administration.* New York: Pitman, 1949.

Fiedler, F. E., "The Effects of Leadership Training and Experience: A Contingency Model Interpretation," *Administrative Science Quarterly,* 17, 1972, 455.

Fiedler, F. E., Chemers, M. M., and L. Mahar, *Improving Leadership Effectiveness.* New York: Wiley, 1976.

Fiedler, F. E., and J. E. Garcia, *New Approaches to Leadership: Cognitive Resources and Organizational Performance.* New York: Wiley, 1987.

Foster, W., *Paradigms and Promises.* Buffalo, N.Y.: Prometheus Books, 1986.

Foster, W. "Toward a Critical Practice of Leadership," in J. Smyth (ed.), *Critical Perspectives on Educational Leadership.* London: Falmer, 1989.

Freire, P., *Pedagogy of the Oppressed.* New York: Continuum, 1970.

French, J., and B. Raven, "The Bases of Power ," in D. Cartwright, ed. *Group Dynamics: Research and Theory.* Evanston, Ill.: Row, Peterson, 1962.

Gardner, J., *On Leadership.* New York: Free Press, 1990.

Gibbs, R., *In Profile: Women Prime Ministers.* Morristown, N.J.: Silver Burdett Company, 1981.

Gilligan, C., *In a Different Voice.* Cambridge, Mass.: Harvard University Press, 1982.

Goldberg, J., *Rachel Carson: Biologist and Author.* New York: Chelsea House Publishers, 1992

Goodwin, D., *Caesar Chavez: Hope for the People.* New York: Fawcett Columbine, 1991.

Graen, G. B., and M. Uhl-Bien, "Relationship Based Approach to Leadership." *Leadership Quarterly* 6 (2), 219–249, 1995.

Graen, G. B., and J. F. Cashman, "A Role Making Model of Leadership in Formal Organizations: A Developmental Approach," in *Leadership Frontiers*, ed. J. G. Hunt and L. L. Larson. Kent, Oh.: Kent State University Press, 1975.

Greenleaf, R. K., *The Servant as Leader*. Newton Center, Mass.: The Robert K. Greenleaf Center, 1970.

Gull, G. A., "Being Ethical," *Executive Excellence*, 12 (8), Aug. 1995, 20.

Harris, P., "Innovating with High Achievers," *Training & Development Journal*, 34 (10), 45–50.

Helgesen, S., *The Female Advantage: Women's Ways of Leadership*. New York: Currency Doubleday, 1990.

Hersey, P. and K. H. Blanchard, *The Management of Organizational Behavior* (3rd ed.). Englewood Cliffs, N.J.: Prentice Hall, 1977.

Hersey, P., and K. H. Blanchard, "Life Cycle Theory of Leadership." *Training and Development Journal* 23 (1969), 26–34.

Herzberg, F., *Work and the Nature of Man*. Cleveland, Oh.: World Publishing, 1966.

Hess, P., and Siciliano, J., *Management: Responsibility for Performance*. New York: McGraw-Hill, 1996.

Hobbes, T., *Leviathan*. London: Oxford University Press, 1947.

Hofstede, G., *Culture's Consequences: International Differences in Work Related Values*. Beverly Hills, Calif.: Sage, 1980.

House, R. J., and T. R. Mitchell, "Path–Goal Theory of Leadership." *Journal of Contemporary Business*, 1974 (3), 81–97.

Hughes, R. L., R. C. Ginnett and G. J. Curphy, *Leadership: Enhancing the Lessons of Experience*. (2nd ed.) Chicago: Irwin, 1996.

Hunsaker, P. L., and A. J. Alessandra, *The Art of Managing People*. New York: Simon & Schuster, 1980.

Hunsaker, P. L., and C. W. Cooke, *Managing Organizational Behavior*. Reading, Mass.: Addison Wesley, 1986.

Ishikawa, K., *What Is Total Quality Control? The Japanese Way*. Englewood Cliffs, N.J.: Prentice Hall, 1985.

Jaeger, W., *Paideia: Ideals of Greek Culture*. New York: Oxford University Press, 1965.

Jago, A. G., "Leadership: Perspectives in Theory and Research." *Management Science*, March 1992, 315-318.

Juran, J. M., *Juran's Quality Control Handbook* (4th ed.). New York: McGraw-Hill, 1988.

Juran, J. M., *Managerial Breakthrough* (2nd ed.). New York: McGraw-Hill, 1994.

Kotter, J. P., *A Force for Change: How Leadership Differs from Management*. New York: Free Press, 1990.

Kotter, J. P., "What Leaders Really Do" in Rosenbach, W.E. and R. L. Taylor, eds. *Contemporary Issues in Leadership*. Boulder, Colo.: Westview Press, 1993.

Kouzes, J. M. and B. Z. Posner, *Credibility*. San Francisco: Jossey-Bass, 1993.

Kuh, G. D., Whitt, E. J., and J. D. Shedd, *Student Affairs Work, 2001: A Paradigmatic Odyssey*. Alexandria, Va.: American College Personnel Association, 1987.

Kuhn, T. S., *The Structure of Scientific Revolutions* (2nd ed.). Chicago, Ill.: University of Chicago Press, 1970.

Lander, H. H., and I. W. Porter, "The Effect of Performance on Job Satisfaction," *Industrial Relations*, Oct. 1967, 23.

LaPierre, D. "Mother Teresa Is Still Offering a Hand at 84," *The Cleveland Plain Dealer*, Dec. 19, 1994.

Lawler, III, E. E., and L. W. Porter, "The Effect of Performance on Job Satisfaction," *Industrial Relations*, Oct. 1967.

Lazo, C., *Rigoberta Menchu*. New York: Dillon Press, 1993.

Levine, S. R. and M. A. Crom, *The Leader in You: How to Win Friends, Influence People, and Succeed in a Changing World*. New York: Simon & Schuster, 1993.

Lewis, P. V., *Occupational Communication: The Essence of Effective Management*. 3rd ed. New York: Wiley, 1987.

Locke, J., *The Second Treatise of Government*. Indianapolis: Bobbs-Merrill, 1977.

Machiavelli, N., *The Prince*. New York: Signet, 1952.

Magolda, B., *Knowing and Reasoning in College*. San Francisco: Jossey-Bass, 1992.

Mandela, N., *Long Walk to Freedom*. Boston: Little, Brown & Co., 1994.

Manz, C. C. and H. P. Sims, Jr., *Superleadership: Leading Others to Lead Themselves*. New York: Prentice-Hall, 1989.

Maslow, A. H., *Motivation and Personality*. New York: Harper & Row, 1954.

Mayo, E., *Human Problems in an Industrialized World*. New York: Macmillan, 1953.

McClelland, D. E., *Power: The Inner Experience*. NY: Irvington, 1975.

Mikulski, B., "Power and the Ability to Lead," in Cantor, D. W., and T. Bernay, *Women in Power: The Secrets of Leadership*. New York: Houghton Mifflin, 1992.

Miller, D. S., Catt, S. E., and J. R. Carlson, *Fundamentals of Management. A Framework for Excellence*. St. Paul, Minn.: West Publishing Co., 1996.

Miller, J. B., *Toward a New Psychology of Women*. Boston: Beacon Press, 1976.

Miller, J. B., in *Women in Power: The Secrets of Leadership* by D. W. Cantor and T. Bernay, New York: Houghton Mifflin, 1992.

Mintzberg, H., *The Nature of Managerial Work*. Englewood Cliffs, N.J.: Prentice Hall, 1979.

Mitchell, R. R., Smyser, C. M., and S. E. Weed, "Locus of Control: Supervision and Work Satisfaction." *Academy of Management Journal*, 18, (1975), 623–30.

Nair, K., *A Higher Standard of Leadership: Lessons from the Life of Gandhi*. San Francisco: Berrett-Koehler Publishers, 1994.

Nanus, B., *Visionary Leadership*. San Francisco: Jossey-Bass, 1992.

Nehru, J., "Nehru: The First Sixty Years. 1947 Correspondence Referring to Gandhi," in *Voices of Power: World Leaders Speak* by H. Bienen (ed.). Hopewell, N. J.: Ecco Press, 1995.

Nelson, D. L. and J. C. Quick, *Organizational Behavior*. St. Paul, Minn.: West Publishing, 1996.

Otfinoski, S., *Marian Wright Edelman, Defender of Children's Rights*. New York: Blackbirch Press, 1991.

Ouchi, W. G., *Theory Z: How American Business Can Meet the Japanese Challenge*. Reading, Mass.: Addison-Wesley, 1981.

Palmer, P., "Community, Conflict and Ways of Knowing," *Change Magazine*, Sept.–Oct., 1987.

Peters, T., *Liberation Management*. New York: Alfred A. Knopf, 1992.

Phatak, A., *International Dimensions of Management*. Boston: Kent, 1983.

Powell, C.L., *My American Journey*. New York: Random House, 1995.

Quantz, R. A., Rogers, J. L., and M. Dantley, "Rethinking Transformational Leadership: Towards the Democratic Reform of Schools," *Journal of Education* 173 (3), 96–118.

Robbins, S. P., *Organizational Behavior Concepts, Controversies and Applications* (6th edition). Englewood Cliffs N.J.: Prentice-Hall, 1993.

Rogers, J. L. and S.C. Ballard, "Aspirational management: Building effective organizations through shared values," *NASPA Journal*, 32 (3), 1995.

Rosenbach, W. E. and R. L. Taylor (eds.), *Contemporary Issues in Leadership*. Boulder, Colo.: Westview Press, 1993.

Rost, J. C., *Leadership for the Twenty-first Century*. New York: Praeger, 1994.

Senge, P., *The Fifth Discipline: The Art and Practice of the Learning Organization.* New York: Doubleday, 1990.

Sims, H. P. Jr. and P. Lorenzi, *The New Leadership Paradigm: Social Learning and Cognition in Organizations.* Newbury Park, Calif.: Sage, 1992.

Smyth, J. *Critical Perspectives on Educational Leadership.* London: Falmer Press, 1989.

Steffof, R. *Mao Zedong: Founder of the People's Republic of China.* Brookfield, Conn.: Millbrook Press, 1996.

Swift, J. A., *Introduction to Modern Statistical Quality Control and Management.* Delray Beach, Fla.: St. Lucie Press, 1995.

Tubbs, S. L. and S. Moss, *Interpersonal Communication.* New York: Random House, 1981.

Tjosvold, D. and M., *Psychology for Leaders: Using Motivation, Conflict and Power to Manage More Effectively.* New York: Wiley, 1995.

U.S. Army Cadet Command, *Leader's Guide.* Fort Monroe, Va.: Dec. 30, 1995.

Vaill, P. B. *Managing as a Performing Art.* San Francisco: Jossey-Bass, 1989.

Vroom, V. H., and A. G. Yago, *The New Theory of Leadership: Managing Participation in Organizations.* Englewood Cliffs, N.J.: Prentice Hall, 1988.

Vroom, V. H., and P. W. Yetton, *Leadership and Decision Making.* Pittsburgh: University of Pittsburgh Press, 1973.

Walton, M., *The Deming Management Method.* New York: Putnam, 1986.

Wheatley, M. J., *Leadership and the New Science: Learning about Organizations from an Orderly Universe.* San Francisco: Berett-Koehler, 1992

Wood, J. T., *The Little Blue Book on Power.* Winslow, Wash.: Zen'n'Ink Publishers, no date.

Yukl, G., *Leadership in Organizations* (3rd ed.). Englewood Cliffs, N.J.: Prentice Hall, 1995.

Yukl, G., *Skills for Managers and Leaders: Test Cases and Exercises.* Englewood Cliffs, NJ: Prentice Hall, 1990.

INDEX